MANHUNTERS

MANHUNTERS

HOW WE TOOK DOWN PABLO ESCOBAR

STEVE MURPHY
AND
JAVIER F. PEÑA

HEADLINE

First published in the United States in 2019 by St. Martin's Press, an imprint
of St. Martin's Publishing Group

First published in the UK in 2019 by
HEADLINE PUBLISHING GROUP

1

Cataloguing in Publication Data is available from the British Library

Hardback ISBN 978 14722 6834 1

Trade paperback ISBN 978 14722 6836 5

Offset in 13.08/18.80 pt Adobe Caslon Pro by Jouve (UK), Milton Keynes

Printed and bound in Great Britain by Clays Ltd, Elcograf S.p.A.

Designed by Steven Seighman

Headline's policy is to use papers that are natural, renewable and recyclable
products and made from wood grown in well-managed forests and other
controlled sources. The logging and manufacturing processes are expected
to conform to the environmental regulations of the country of origin.

HEADLINE PUBLISHING GROUP
An Hachette UK Company
Carmelite House
50 Victoria Embankment
London EC4Y 0DZ

www.headline.co.uk
www.hachette.co.uk

"Blessed are the peacemakers, for they will be called Children of God."   *—Matthew 5:9*

For Connie, for her never-ending love and support.
         —Steve Murphy

For the real heroes: the Colombian National Police and our fellow DEA agents. And in memory of all the innocent people killed by Pablo Escobar.   *—Javier F. Peña*

INTRODUCTION

JAVIER

I knew something was very wrong when I picked up the phone at my new apartment in Bogotá.

"Javier?"

I recognized the voice of my group supervisor, Bruce Stock, on the other end, but there was a slight tremor, a hint of uncertainty in the way he pronounced my name.

Bruce was in his early fifties and had worked as a Drug Enforcement Administration agent around the world for most of his career. He was a big man, about six foot four, and just about one of the nicest people I had ever met—a gentle giant. He was also unflappable. He had to be; he was heading up one of the most dangerous missions in the history of the DEA. Bruce's priority was capturing Pablo Escobar, the billionaire Medellín Cartel chief who was responsible for the myriad car bombs that were going off around Colombia, not to mention smuggling tons of cocaine to North America and Europe. Escobar and his brutal *sicarios*—most of them teenage assassins plucked from the shantytowns that surround the city of Medellín—were killing anyone who stood in their way. They had already gunned down Colombia's minister of justice, massacred most of the country's Supreme Court judges, and killed a prominent newspaper editor who dared denounce the power of the cartel. All these assassinations took place before I arrived in Colombia, but you could feel the tension everywhere. There were tanks at the airport and fierce-looking soldiers armed with machine guns on the streets.

At the beginning of 1989 when Bruce called me at home, I had already been in Colombia for eight months, and, like everyone else at DEA headquarters in the U.S. embassy, I was totally obsessed with my new assignment—getting Escobar. It was my job to help capture and put him on a plane to the United States, where he would stand trial for all his crimes. It was the threat of extradition that led to Escobar's war—his reign of terror—against the Colombian government and us American law enforcement agents.

I arrived in Bogotá from my first DEA posting in Austin, Texas, where I focused on small-time Mexican meth and coke dealers. I knew Colombia would be the biggest challenge of my career, and I thought I was ready. I had already inserted myself into the Bloque de Búsqueda—the so-called Search Bloc made up of elite Colombian cops and intelligence agents who had six hundred men searching for Escobar pretty much twenty-four hours a day. The Search Bloc worked from a police garrison in Medellín, and I spent a good part of every week there, with the Colombian National Police as they hunted for the murderous drug kingpin in his hometown. I had been told that some members of the force were corrupt and on Escobar's payroll, so I was pretty cautious about who I hung out with, who I spoke to.

On weekends, if I wasn't working, I sat for hours in my Bogotá pad. I loved my sprawling four-thousand-square-foot home on a busy intersection in the center of town. I had breathtaking views of the city below and the towering Andes on one side. From my living room window, which was about forty feet wide, I felt I could reach out and touch those majestic mountains. For the truth is, I felt on top of the world in that four-bedroom palace with its separate maids' quarters in the heart of Bogotá nightlife. It was all too big and too grand for a bachelor from Texas, but it was a great place to bring my dates. They were always stunned by the view, which frankly made seduction all that much easier. It was a far cry from my boxy one-bedroom in Austin, which impressed no one—least of all me.

Little did I know that my life of luxury was about to end that Saturday afternoon when I heard Bruce's tremulous voice on the phone.

He didn't say much, and I could tell from his breathing that he was trying to steady his voice, to remain as calm as possible. At that moment, I knew my life was in grave danger.

"Javier, listen to me: Go get your gun, leave everything else behind, and get the hell out of there," he said. "Sorry, but there's no time to explain. It's Escobar. He knows where you are."

It's Escobar. He knows where you are.

I searched for my weapon—a 9 mm semiautomatic pistol—and headed to the elevator, scanning the hallways like a frightened fugitive, watching to see if anyone was lurking in the corners or behind a door. My hands shook as I pressed the elevator button, and every few seconds, I felt for my waist holster to make sure that my gun was in place. Somehow, it was reassuring to graze the cold metal with my fingertips.

Calma, calma, Javier! Tranquilo, hombre.

I heard the voice of my *abuela*, the toughest person I knew. She'd once stood up to would-be burglars in our home in Laredo and also got me out of countless difficult situations.

Tranquilo, tranquilo!

I rushed through the garage, furtively looking around to make sure no one was following me. I felt for my gun and unlocked the door of my OGV—official government vehicle—which in my case was a bulletproof Ford Bronco. As I started the engine with a roar, I immediately realized that I hadn't bothered to check under the chassis for explosives. Thankfully, the truck didn't blow up, and I screeched out of the underground garage and gunned it to the U.S. embassy, which was only a few miles away.

I thought of my grandmother and willed myself to breathe deeply as I sat in what seemed like endless Bogotá traffic. I chose to go through the most congested route to the embassy because I figured that I could easily blend into a traffic jam and become anonymous. I breathed a long sigh of relief when I saw the steel gates of the embassy, which was built like a fortress. Bruce met me at the DEA offices, which were next to the embassy garage, when I arrived.

I never found out if Escobar had planned to kill me or just kidnap me—an important American pawn in his battle against extradition. Our intel was that he had ordered his *sicarios* to find "the Mexican" DEA guy, which could only be me, since I was the only American of Mexican origin on staff. Escobar's men didn't have the exact address, but they knew that I lived at the corner of Seventh and Seventy-second, and it would be a matter of a few days or even a few hours before they traced me to my building, where I was one of the only gringos in residence. Between the CNP and the DEA intelligence experts, we tried our best to get to the bottom of the threat but couldn't find anything.

That night, I moved into a safe house that the embassy had set aside for emergencies like mine. After a few weeks passed with no new threats from Escobar's people, Bruce found me an apartment in Los Rosales, close to where the

U.S. ambassador lived. It was a much fancier part of the city, cut with manicured hedges, lavish mansions, and beefy private security dressed in black, heavily armed, and carrying walkie-talkies. I missed my downtown aerie.

But I didn't miss it that much. Knowing that the world's biggest drug dealer is actively looking for you is unnerving, to say the least. For weeks after the threat and my flight from my beloved apartment, I couldn't relax. Sleep was elusive.

But if you want to know the truth, my biggest fear was that the DEA was going to send me home. For my own protection.

So I downplayed the threat, brushed it off whenever I went out for drinks with my fellow agents. But I repeatedly checked our intel to find out if the cartel was still looking for me. I pretended I was okay with everything. I can admit it now: I was scared to death.

But you know what? I was damned if I was going to let Escobar win. And I was damned if I was going to go back home when I was working on the case of a lifetime.

I thought again of my *abuelita* and forged ahead.

STEVE

The blue Renault cut in front of us, forcing us off the road, ushering Connie and me into our worst nightmare.

I was driving one of the older-model embassy-issued

g-cars. It was a large SUV with huge, West Coast–style mirrors sticking out from the sides. If we were in California, it might look like we were surfers on our way to a deserted beach. But this was Colombia, and the SUV was outfitted like a tank for a reason. I joked to Connie that it could survive a shoot-out and even the apocalypse. Still, its ballast made me feel safe. There were steel plates in all the doors, under the vehicle, and built into the roof. All the windows were bulletproof with extremely thick glass that made them impossible to open. The front and rear were equipped with chrome-plated steel bars known as cattle guards. With all these security devices built in, it weighed about twice as much as a normal vehicle.

Connie and I were headed home from the embassy and had decided to take some of the back roads, next to a military base, to avoid the snarling traffic and to stop by our favorite restaurant for some take-out roast chicken for dinner. We had both put in a long day and were looking forward to unwinding in front of the TV with spicy chicken, roasted potatoes, and a glass of merlot. With me in Medellín most weeks, we rarely had a night to ourselves, and we were really looking forward to being together in our apartment in the northern part of the city.

When the Renault suddenly cut in front of me, I pumped the brake and pushed in the clutch, trying to stop before I hit the tiny car. With all the weight of the SUV, it wasn't very difficult to lose control, and I knew if I hit the Renault, there would be serious injury to the passengers.

Maybe even death. I managed to slide the vehicle to a stop just a few inches from the smaller car.

After checking to see if Connie was okay, I was furious and prepared to get out of the car and give them a piece of my mind. Except when I looked up, I saw that the three occupants of the car were walking menacingly toward us. They were dressed in light jackets and jeans, and as they drew closer, I could see that each of them had a pistol tucked into the waistband of his pants.

After arriving in Colombia to work on the Pablo Escobar case more than a year earlier, I had a lot of enemies. The world's most wanted criminal knew my name and the name of my partner, Javier Peña. We knew this because Colombian intelligence had intercepted the drug lord speaking on the phone to one of his thugs and talking about the "two gringos" at the Carlos Holguín base in Medellín. During one conversation, he even referred to "Peña and Murphy."

So when the three men approached the driver's-side door of our vehicle and began yelling in Spanish for us to get out of the car, I worried this was no ordinary case of road rage. This was a trap, and we were outnumbered. Besides that, I had the person I loved most in the world sitting right next to me. I needed to protect Connie no matter what happened to me.

At first, I refused to open the door, and I flashed them my Colombian police identification badge, hoping it would scare them off. But they refused to budge, which is when I frantically tried to radio for backup from the embassy. Each embassy car was equipped with portable emergency radios so that we could call the Marines if we got into any trouble. I was hoping the Marines would simply dispatch a roving patrol and scare off the jokers who were holding us hostage inside the car.

But I called once. I called twice. I called three times. No one answered.

By this time, the three men were kicking at the tires and trying to open the doors. I looked over at Connie, who was trying to remain calm, but I could tell she was really scared. The truth is, so was I.

Shortly after trying to contact the embassy, the wife of a DEA agent called us from her portable radio to make sure we were all right. I told her where we were and asked her to radio for help immediately. A few minutes later, our DEA supervisor was on the radio. I told him to hurry and to bring the "margarita" with him—our code name for the mini Uzi that we kept in the office for just such occasions.

While we waited, helpless as the men continued to taunt us and kick in the doors of the car, my darling wife surprised me as she always did when we faced what seemed like impossible odds.

"They're not that big," she said, pointing to the men. "I can take that one out if you handle the other two."

I might have said yes except that they were all armed,

and if I opened the door of the car, I would be exposing Connie to being shot or worse.

Once the DEA supervisor was in place with the margarita behind us, I prepared to walk out of the car and confront the three men. We were both good marksmen, and if they tried anything funny, I knew we could easily kill them. But none of us wanted to kill anyone. We just wanted to get home and have our chicken!

Just as I was opening my door, a Colombian National Police motorcycle patrol approached. I saw they were looking at us but showed no indication of stopping. I began blowing my horn to get their attention, which caused the patrol to turn around to investigate. Out of the corner of my eye, I saw our supervisor, holding tight to the margarita.

Clutching my pistol and then tucking it into my waistband, I walked over to the police and showed them my badge and told them who I was: I was DEA and working on capturing Colombia's most wanted criminal. I told them we had been cut off by the three men in the Renault, and I was worried that they could be *sicarios* working for Escobar. After all, it was only a few years before that fellow DEA special agent Enrique "Kiki" Camarena Salazar was kidnapped by corrupt police officers in Mexico and tortured and killed on the orders of drug lord Miguel Ángel Félix Gallardo. All DEA agents working in Latin America after Kiki's death worried that the same thing could happen to them.

I told the cops the men in the blue Renault were all armed.

At the mention of handguns, the police surrounded the men and pointed their weapons at them.

It took a while to sink in, but when the cops realized who I was and that I had contacts at the highest levels of the Colombian police, they began to apologize to Connie and me. As for the three men who had nearly caused an ugly accident, they were low-ranking members of the Colombian military on a joyride. It turned out to be nothing more than a case of road rage and the three young men wanting to intimidate us. They still don't know how close they came to death that night.

I cursed them out in my best street Spanish and threatened to call their commanding officer. They all became very apologetic and begged me not to call anyone. I believe they knew they would end up in the stockade for their actions, and all they wanted was to get away from us as quickly as possible.

After thanking the police, Connie and I drove home, rattled by the whole experience. As we sat in our living room with our Styrofoam boxes of chicken and potatoes, and Connie poured us each a glass of wine, I worried about the next close call.

And this time, I knew that an armored embassy vehicle wouldn't be able to protect me. Not against the apocalypse, and certainly not against Pablo Escobar.

PART ONE

STEVE

As a little boy, I was obsessed with the police. I envied their starched military-style uniforms and their speeding cruisers with their flashing lights and blaring sirens.

I dreamed of being a cop, of catching the bad guys, especially if they were taking advantage of innocent people. For me, police officers were superheroes. I knew law enforcement was my calling, even as a very young boy growing up in Tennessee.

I was born in Memphis, but by the time I was three, we—my parents, my older sister, and I—moved to Murfreesboro, a small municipality of wide lawns and fading antebellum plantations just south of Nashville in the deep, humid middle of the state. Nothing much had happened there since the Civil War. In school, we learned about the Battle of Stones River, which took place in Murfreesboro over three days at the end of 1862 and the beginning of 1863—one of the war's bloodiest clashes, resulting in more than twenty-three thousand casualties on both the Confederate and Union sides.

When I was eleven years old, I had my own historic battle in a suburban backyard. Looking back, it wasn't so much a battle as the defining moment of my young life. That's when I found myself caught red-handed, squinting in the glare of police spotlights—my first encounter with the law.

In the summers, my friends and I would camp out in one another's backyards, lying with our sleeping bags on freshly mown grass, gazing up at the stars, or huddled together in a pup tent, scaring one another other with our made-up stories of ghosts, zombies, and grisly murders, falling asleep to the sounds of crickets and bullfrogs. Summers in Tennessee were hot, and the evenings didn't cool down much, so most nights, we'd take our sleeping bags outside the tents, waking up in the morning covered with dew.

One summer night, it was so hot and sticky none of us could sleep, which was why a group of us decided to sneak into one of our fellow camper's house. I'm not sure why we did this, although I seem to recall that we wanted to retrieve something that we thought was important at the time. As we argued with one another in loud whispers, trying to pry open a bedroom window, we suddenly heard the wheels of a cruiser approaching us in the dark and knew we were in trouble. It was a police car. Someone must have called the cops when they heard us making a ruckus. We froze, too frightened to even turn around. I could barely make out the two officers who emerged from their squad car, as I was blinded by the headlights. They told us to stand still, although they needn't have said anything at all because we were all too frightened to move. Beads of sweat poured down my cheeks as I held my hands up. As my eyes adjusted to the glare, I could see that the cops were tall and muscled. They seemed to me larger than life in their neatly pressed black uniforms and polished black boots. When they asked us if we wanted to be taken to the Rutherford County Sheriff's Office and put in jail, or go to our parents, we all answered at the same time. We all knew what would happen if our parents got involved, so we unanimously opted to go to jail. That sent the officers into fits of laughter. We were mortified and all stood uncomfortably at attention as they wrote down our names and addresses and escorted us back to our homes, where they woke up our moms and dads. Somehow, we all survived that terrible night, but we lost our taste for camping. At least during that summer.

Over the years, I have often thought back to that first encounter with the law and how much I admired those officers for using common sense with a group of mischievous kids.

More than anything, I wanted to be a police officer, but it was years later that I discovered that my parents had different plans for me.

I grew up in a strict Baptist household, the youngest of three children. Or I should say, the youngest of two. An older brother died when he was just three, before I was born. My sister was eight years older than I was, and we spent much of our childhood locked in battle.

My father stood six foot four, and he was the strongest and smartest person I ever knew. My uncles liked to tell me that when my father was a young man, he loved to fight and he never lost a bout. He wasn't afraid of anything or anyone, and he was once asked to try out for the Washington Redskins—an opportunity he politely turned down because he didn't see professional football as a solid career path.

When my dad was old enough, he volunteered for the U.S. Army, although he had to cheat on his physical exam to get in. My dad had poor vision in his left eye. When he took the exam, the doctor told him to cover his left eye with his left hand and read the chart. No problem. When they asked him to do the reverse on his right eye, he simply used his right hand to cover the left eye and passed the vision test!

My dad started off in the infantry and was sent to Europe after the attack on Pearl Harbor plunged the United States into World War II in 1941. Because of his size and strength, he worked with the medical corpsmen in France and Belgium, carrying wounded soldiers to safety and holding them down for medical procedures when needed.

When he returned from Europe, my father decided to enroll at Bob Jones University in Greenville, South Carolina, to become a minister. He was the first in his family to attend college, and after he graduated, he moved with my mother and sister to his first church in Memphis, where I was born. Later, in Murfreesboro, he rotated through several small churches and worked odd jobs to make extra money. I remember him going door-to-door selling vacuum cleaners. He was very good at it and frequently said that God directed him, telling him where to go and what to say to do his job.

Eventually, God directed my father out of the ministry and into broadloom. After he got a job at a flooring store in Nashville, he urged his youngest brother, who had retired from the air force, to go into business with him. They did well with their fledgling carpet store in Nashville, but there was too much competition in that city to expand on a grand scale, and they decided to look elsewhere.

Two years after my encounter with the police, we left Tennessee and moved north to my parents' home state of West Virginia, where my father and uncle were poised to create a broadloom empire. We settled in Princeton, a quiet railroad town of some six thousand people surrounded by coalfields and nestled in the Appalachian Mountains. We had solid family roots in the state, where my maternal grandparents had settled after they emigrated from England. My grandfather had worked in the coalfields his entire adult life.

I wasn't happy with the move. As a teenager, I was upset about leaving my friends behind in a place where I was one of the popular kids. When school started in Princeton, I went to the local junior high school, but I don't recall it as a very pleasant experience. Kids made fun of my Tennessee accent, which pegged me as being from the really Deep South. I tried every which way to blend in and eventually learned to stifle my accent to match the way the Princeton kids talked. Outside of sports and church, my new town seemed to have little to offer kids, although town leaders eventually did open up a youth center in an old bowling alley and installed Ping-Pong tables, a snack bar, and a dance floor, where I had my first dance with a girl.

In Princeton, my father and uncle set about turning their store into a successful family business, and we were all dispatched to help them. My mother was the bookkeeper and worked with walk-in customers, scheduled installation jobs, and ordered supplies for the store while my father and uncle hawked linoleum and carpeting to their clients. Truth be told, my mother was really the heart and soul of the business, which might have failed if not for her enthusiasm and hard work. My sister also worked part-time at the store. By the time I was fourteen, I began working there, too. It was my father's hope that I would take over the business, and he believed that I needed to start at the bottom. My first duties included sweeping, mopping, cleaning the bathrooms, and taking out the trash. Eventually, I graduated to meeting customers and guiding them through hundreds of carpet and linoleum samples.

To this day, broadloom makes me claustrophobic.

In the late '60s and early '70s, while other teenagers were growing their hair long, smoking weed, protesting the war in Vietnam, and mourning the breakup of the Beatles, I was leading a pretty sheltered life in a conservative Appalachian town. And even though he had long left the ministry, my father remained a strict disciplinarian. I wasn't allowed to go to the cinema until I was eighteen, and we weren't allowed to play card games—not even Old Maid—in our home. My parents forbade my sister from wearing pants or shorts, and dresses had to be worn well below the knee. My father spanked us with a belt when we were caught doing something wrong. To some people, this probably sounds rather harsh, and in today's permissive society, our parents would probably be accused of child abuse. But that's how we grew up—with very strict boundaries. We knew what we could and could not do and what was expected of us.

As we did in Tennessee, our family attended the First Baptist Church in Princeton. I wasn't interested in much of anything to do with religion or church socials at the time, not until I attended a performance of the church kids' choir. The choir was called the Sounds of Conviction, known as the Sounds for short. And after that first performance, I was so impressed by the professional staging, the lighting, and the singing that I joined the group and didn't leave until after my senior year of high school. I wasn't the greatest singer, but I loved the mix of kids and being part of a team. We traveled throughout West Virginia and Virginia, appearing at schools and churches. The show was so popular that the choir grew from about forty kids when I joined them to more than four hundred by the time I left.

After high school, I left for West Virginia University in Morgantown, excited to be on my own and living in a dorm with other kids my age. At my parents' direction, I majored in business administration, but I had no interest in learning about economics and finance. In hindsight, I feel like I spent my first semester at one long party. When my grades came out, my parents decided that they were not going to throw their money at a lost cause. Who could blame them? At Christmas break, I reluctantly packed my things, withdrew from WVU, and returned home.

Carpet samples became my future.

Still, eager to pursue law enforcement, I enrolled at Bluefield State College. I signed up for the school's newly created criminal justice administration program without my parents' knowledge. And, boy, did I love it! During the spring semester in 1975, I volunteered to be the first BSC student in a new summer internship program at the Mercer County Sheriff's Office and the Bluefield Police Department (BPD). I met deputies and officers from both agencies who encouraged me to take the civil service exam to qualify to become a cop. I studied in secret and took the test without my parents ever finding out. When the results were announced, I got the highest score, and my name was placed at the top of a potential hiring list for both the sheriff's office and police department.

The BPD was the first agency to call me and offer me a job interview. That's when I had to confess to my parents about my college major and that I'd secretly taken the police entrance exam. My parents were much smarter than I'd given them credit for and had already figured out what I was up to. After I passed the physical exam and background investigation, I was sworn in as a patrolman with the BPD in November 1975. I was all of nineteen years old.

On the day I went to try on my new uniform, I was ecstatic, although I was told that I was too young to purchase a weapon. The minimum age to buy a gun in the state was twenty-one, which meant that I would have to persuade one of the older cops to go out and get me my first handgun—a blue-steel four-inch Colt Python .357-caliber revolver.

I didn't expect my father to be pleased with my success, but on some level, he was proud of me, because he went out and bought the ammo.

As a rookie officer, I patrolled a section of the town and did my share of desk duty, but I was drawn to drug traffickers. It was 1976, and it seemed to me that illegal drugs were everywhere. Even back then, I saw how harmful drugs were to society and how dealing drugs and addiction were messing up young lives. In the mid-1970s, cocaine was going through a resurgence, becoming the recreational drug of choice of the glitterati at discos and swanky parties around the country, especially New York's Studio 54. Elsewhere, freebasing, or inhaling the vapors of cocaine at its melting point, was giving junkies incredible highs. Underground chemists were experimenting with rock cocaine, mixing baking soda and other substances to produce crack, which would have devastating consequences in American inner cities by the 1980s. And with the end of the Vietnam War in 1975, hundreds of soldiers were returning home impossibly hooked on heroin.

But marijuana was enough of a scourge for me as a young cop, and in my free time, I found myself pursuing drug pushers. In 1976, I got to know a snitch who told me about a trafficker who was selling multi-pound quantities of grass. At that time, a pound of marijuana fetched more than $1,300. I called Jack Walters, another rookie cop who was my closest friend on the force, and we set up a plan to bust the bad guy on our day off. Working with our informant, we asked him to call the target.

That evening, the snitch called the target to inquire about the price of one pound of weed. Less than twenty minutes later, we arranged to meet him at a local gas station to make the purchase. Jack and I hid in the back of the gas station while the snitch led the target through the transaction.

As soon as we spied the target removing a small bag from his car, we swooped in for the arrest. The culprit turned out to be a seventeen-year-old high school senior from an upper-middle-class home. He didn't need the money, but had watched too many bad-guy movies and thought he could get away with this little criminal enterprise in a small town where he thought the cops knew nothing.

Jack and I handcuffed the frightened teenager and called for a detective to come to the scene. The detective was astonished that two rookie cops were involved in a successful drug bust on their day off.

The seventeen-year-old was charged and eventually released to his parents. Fortunately for him, an agreement was reached in the courts, and he was placed on probation. Because he was a juvenile, his criminal record was expunged when he became an adult and finished his probation.

Despite my success, I felt my dad wasn't so happy about my chosen field, clearly disappointed that I hadn't followed in his footsteps in the family business. After I had been in the police department for eighteen months, my guilt got the better of me, and in 1977, I took a ninety-day leave of absence to return to my father's store to give flooring another try. But I lasted less than two months among the broadloom and linoleum samples. I was clearly miserable, and I returned to the police department before my leave was up.

It was only after I'd been a cop for five years that my

dad finally told me how proud he was. That made all the difference, and it gave me the strength to go forward.

I never looked back.

JAVIER

I cried all the way on the five-hour drive from Hebbronville to Huntsville—what was supposed to be the first major step in my career in law enforcement.

I was a sociology major at Texas A&I in Kingsville and had scored a three-month internship with the state's department of corrections. I would get college credit and a small salary for working at the prison where the state housed its most notorious prisoners, who were all on death row.

I was thrilled.

But my parents worried for my safety and tried to convince me not to go. To be sure, there were other things holding me back in my southern Texas town. My family was going through a rough time because my mother, Alicia, had just been diagnosed with breast cancer. It was a cruel fate for a God-fearing, clean-living woman who never had a drink or smoked a cigarette in her life. She went to church every Sunday and always managed to have a meal ready for my older brother, Jorge, my dad, and me. It was hard to make ends meet in Hebbronville. We owned a small family ranch that didn't yield much money, and my brother and I helped my dad mending fences and working the cattle every summer. Through the leanest years, my mother remained a great optimist, even as she eventually lost both her breasts to the cancer. She loved going to bingo at the church on Friday nights. She always came back saying that she was one number away from hitting the jackpot, even though she never won a penny.

Choking back sobs, she begged me to stay. My father, whose name was Jesus but whom everyone called Chucho, warned that I was also making a mistake. He worried that my internship working among the most brutal prisoners in the state was simply not a good idea. It was too danger-ous, he said. This from my father, who was a cowboy and had made his mark in the vaquero capital of Texas! He wasn't afraid of anyone. But I wanted more than the family ranch, which had been passed down from my grandfather to my dad, and where my family barely eked out a living. I had to leave the confines of my small Texas railroad town. I couldn't pass up the opportunity to experience my first real criminal justice job.

I packed only a few clothes for the trip as if to prove to my parents that I would soon be back, that this wasn't for-ever. I'd keep my promise to be by my mother's side to help her through the chemotherapy treatments that she was about to undergo in Laredo. But my parents turned their backs and refused to speak to me.

That's how I left my childhood home at eighteen, with a heavy heart and wondering if I would ever see my mother alive again. Looking back now, through the prism of so many years, I know they must have been just as sad as I was.

The tears came as soon as I put the key in the ignition and gripped the steering wheel of my 1974 Chevy Nova. I bought the two-door, sleek brown muscle car with the cash I had saved from picking watermelons during my summer breaks in Hebbronville, which is probably the world watermelon capital, surrounded by seemingly endless green fields of the fruit. I had been doing the grueling work since I was fifteen, squatting among the dusty vines every summer under a blistering one-hundred-degree sun. The workers' truck would come by my house at 6:00 a.m. and would deposit me and our crew of mostly Mexican migrants at the nearby farms, returning home at 8:00 in the evening. The melons averaged about ten to fifteen pounds each, and by the end of the summer, I had arms like Popeye's. Several times, I encountered rattlesnakes that liked to hide below the melons to cool themselves off from the sun. I never got bit, but I came close. One of them tried to strike at me, but I threw a watermelon on it and crushed it to death. To this day, I can't eat watermelon, and I have a real phobia of snakes.

By the time I was seventeen, I became so good that I graduated from picker to cutter—part of an advance reconnaissance team usually made up of older workers who scour the fields for the ripest fruit. Later, I became a stacker, helping to load the melons on a trailer—an art form, as each stack had to be a perfect layer of melons lined up hor-

izontally from the floor to about eight feet high. I earned
$300 for each trailer I stacked and could complete two in
a day, so my paychecks were huge. I gave a big part of my
pay to my mom and saved up the rest to buy my car.

On that long drive out of the place I knew so well, I
cried because on some level I must have known that I was
leaving my youth behind, driving past the watermelon
fields, the elementary and high schools where I'd played
football and baseball, and the dive bar where I drank my
first beer. Speeding north along U.S. 59, the tears rolled
uncontrollably down my cheeks, clouding my vision. The
miles of ranches dotted by dust-covered vaqueros on their
horses and herds of cattle outside my window played like
scenes on a film loop from some long-ago life.

I passed Houston and drove north to Huntsville, the
seat of the Texas Department of Criminal Justice,
which operates all the state's correctional facilities for
adults. Someone—I can't remember who—once called it
a recession-proof company town because the main eco-
nomic activity is housing criminals.

Indeed, of the thirty-eight thousand residents who
made up the city, about seven thousand worked in its prison
system. Thousands more worked at the local university.
There are seven prisons in Huntsville, housing more
than thirteen thousand inmates. Locals like to joke that
"half the population of Huntsville's under key, and the
other half gets paid for their time." It's all part of their
gallows humor, but it also underlies a pride that comes

from living and working in a place that has become a kind of national monument to criminal justice, despite what side of the death penalty debate you're on. There is a Texas Prison Museum, where the pistol Bonnie Parker was holding when she was gunned down by a sheriff's posse in Louisiana in 1934 is on display. But the main attraction is Old Sparky, the electric chair in which 361 prisoners were executed between 1924 and 1964. Before Old Sparky, prisoners marked for execution were simply hanged in different counties across the state of Texas.

I didn't know what to expect when I set out for Huntsville, and I was still red-eyed and raw from my drive from Hebbronville when I drove down the city's main streets. It was a nice enough Texas town, not unlike so many I had passed through as a kid—flat and sprawling, with rusty pickups parked outside the hardware store and the soda fountain. I stopped to stretch my legs and walked past what appeared to be the long-shuttered Old Town Theatre on Twelfth Street, near the Greyhound bus station, where later I would watch recently released inmates hesitantly waiting for buses, clutching beer cans wrapped in brown paper bags—their first taste of freedom after doing time.

On the Sunday afternoon that I arrived, a few diners were crowded with students from Sam Houston State University. Through the windows, I saw some of them lingering over pie and coffee, deep in homework assignments or animated conversations. But I knew I was in the most sinister place that I had ever been when I looked up at my new place of employment, an imposing redbrick building that dominated the city's downtown. Built in 1849, the 225-cell Huntsville Unit has the distinction of being the state's oldest prison. And since 1982, when Texas reinstated the death penalty, the prison, which is better known by its nickname—the Walls Unit—has housed the country's most active execution chamber.

I had nowhere to stay and checked into the cheapest hotel room I could find. The next morning, I reported too early for my internship and was assigned to the Ellis Unit, a prison twelve miles north of Huntsville, which housed the toughest death row inmates. Walking back to my hotel after filling out the necessary paperwork, I found a small, dilapidated trailer parked about a block from the Walls Unit. It was barely twenty feet long and was falling apart. It looked like it hadn't been cleaned in years. But I rented it on the spot from the old lady who owned it. Maybe she noticed my bloodshot eyes. Were my cheeks still stained by tears? I don't know why she seemed to trust me on the spot, sheepishly asking for only a hundred dollars a month. On my days off, I could walk from the tiny trailer to the main prison and use my vouchers to get free lunch and dinner.

My first day of work, I drove to Ellis Unit and was assigned the death row roll call. I received no training or warnings about what this would entail, and as I took hesitant steps on the three-foot-wide metal catwalk that separated the inmates' cells on either side, I'm not ashamed to admit that I was scared to death. My hands were clammy, and my heart was pumping too fast in my chest with every move down the catwalk, not daring to peer into any of the cells. I kept my gaze fixed on the list of names I had to call out on my clipboard. I was sure that the prisoners could smell my fear and hear the hesitancy in my voice as I began the roll call, careful to focus on the correct pronunciation of all the names. They must have known I was the new guy and totally in over my head, for when I called out the third name and heard nothing but deafening silence, someone suddenly yelled out a loud "Boo!"

That "Boo!" sent me over the edge, and I bolted. I whipped around and ran back across the catwalk as fast as I could.

When I came to my senses, everyone—the guards and the other prisoners—seemed to be falling over themselves laughing at my expense.

I breathed a sigh of relief, but I couldn't help feeling uneasy. After all, the brutality of the crimes that these inmates had committed was no laughing matter.

And there were dangers lurking everywhere in the prison. I arrived at Huntsville a few years after the July 1974 hostage taking—the longest siege in U.S. prison history—when Fred Gómez Carrasco, a notorious drug trafficker from San Antonio known as El Señor, took sixteen hostages at the Walls Unit library. Carrasco, then thirty-four, was one of the most notorious heroin kingpins, responsible for the deaths of as many as fifty-seven people throughout

Texas and parts of Mexico. Carrasco and fellow inmates
Rodolfo Dominguez and Ignacio Cuevas had bribed
prison workers to smuggle three .357 Magnum pistols
into the prison in a can of rotting ham. More than three
hundred rounds of ammunition were smuggled in cans of
peaches.

The kidnappers negotiated with prison officials for
eleven days, threatening to kill hostages who ranged from
other inmates and librarians to a prison chaplain. Carrasco
requested that authorities provide him and his two accom-
plices with bulletproof vests, suits, and, bizarrely, Nunn
Bush shoes for their daring escape. On August 3, they left
the prison protected by a makeshift shield of two rolling
blackboards, reinforced with fat legal books and cardboard
taped to the outside for added protection. They christened
their contraption "the Piñata" and "the Trojan Taco." The
convicts handcuffed themselves to three women—librarian
Julia Standley and teachers Yvonne "Von" Beseda and No-
vella Pollard—and took them inside the chalkboard fortress along with the prison chaplain, Father O'Brien.
Around the Piñata, they wound a rope and handcuffed
four other hostages as a human buffer in case Texas authorities decided to shoot. The plan was to make it to the
courtyard, where an armored car Carrasco had demanded
was waiting.

But as the blackboard caravan descended a ramp from
the third-floor library under cover of darkness, police
turned on a high-pressure hose that dispersed the hostages

on the outside. Immediately, shooting from inside the shield began as police demanded that the inmates surrender. For an intense fifteen minutes, the shooting continued. In the chaos that followed, Dominguez shot Standley four times in the back. She died instantly, before Dominguez himself was gunned down by authorities. Carrasco killed Beseda and then turned the gun on himself. Cuevas shot and wounded Father O'Brien before fainting and falling on top of Pollard. Cuevas, the illiterate son of a Mexican peasant who was serving a forty-five-year sentence for murder, was the only hostage-taker to survive the dramatic prison break. He was convicted three times of capital murder in the death of Standley, a forty-three-year-old mother of five. Although two of the convictions were overturned on appeal, Cuevas was tried for Standley's murder under a Texas law that makes an accomplice liable for crimes committed in the same incident. On May 23, 1991, Cuevas was executed by lethal injection, only a few yards from where the dramatic prison break had taken place.

My internship also coincided with the incarceration of a fat white guy everyone on death row called the Candyman. I soon learned that the press had dubbed him "the man who killed Halloween" because he poisoned his own young son with cyanide-laced candy to collect a fat insurance payout.

His name was Ronald Clark O'Bryan, and he was an optician from the Houston suburb of Deer Park. After he was convicted of murder, parents across the country panicked, thinking twice about allowing their children to accept Halloween candy from anyone—strangers as well as family.

On a drizzly Halloween night in 1974, O'Bryan and another neighborhood dad took their children trick-or-treating in suburban Pasadena. O'Bryan, then thirty, lagged behind his friend and the children and came back holding several treats that he claimed had come from a home on their walk that had been dark and shuttered when they had tried to ring the doorbell. O'Bryan distributed the treats—Pixy Stix—to his own two children—eight-year-old Timothy and five-year-old Elizabeth—and the three others who accompanied them. When they got home, O'Bryan urged his son to try the poisoned Pixy-Stix. But after little Timothy gulped down a mouthful of the poisoned powder, he complained it tasted bitter and began vomiting. He died soon after.

O'Bryan told police that he got the candy from the darkened house on their trick-or-treat route. He claimed that after he rang the bell, he had just seen a hairy arm holding out the candy. The alibi was quickly proven to be false when the owner of the house produced time sheets from his job as an air traffic controller. He was working Halloween night and had several witnesses to prove it.

Police arrested O'Bryan days later, after they found that he had taken out tens of thousands in insurance policies on his children. He was $100,000 in debt and was about to lose his home and his car. He was also about to be fired from his job after his employers found him stealing. Timothy's death alone was worth $31,000 in insurance cash.

I wasn't around for O'Bryan's execution. After winning two previous stays of execution, O'Bryan was condemned to death in 1984, several years after my internship at Huntsville. He maintained his innocence even as he was being strapped to the gurney, just before receiving the lethal injection. He was thirty-nine years old.

"We as human beings do make mistakes and errors," he said in his final statement. "This execution is one of those wrongs. But it doesn't mean the whole system of justice is wrong. Therefore, I forgive all—and I do mean all—those who have been involved in my death."

As much as I deplored their crimes, I did come away from that experience thinking that O'Bryan was right on one thing: All the inmates—even the most brutal convicted criminals—are still human beings. This is one of the most valuable lessons I have taken away from law enforcement, and I learned it from a Huntsville prison trustee—a prisoner who was assigned to help the guards in exchange for special treats, such as telephone use or extra food. Be strict with them, yes, but be compassionate as well, he told me.

In the end, though, that same compassion didn't filter down to me at Huntsville. Just before my three months were up and I was scheduled to return to college, I found myself on the receiving end of an ugly racial slur that almost ended my career before it had even started. It was so nasty and unexpected that it still haunts me all these years later.

Back home in Hebbronville, my only cousin was getting married, and her wedding fell on the last day of my shift. I summoned up the courage to ask the commander of the prison for a day off. The Captain, as he was known, was a heavyset white man with an intimidating presence. At Huntsville, he was an anomaly because most of the people I worked with were decent and caring, many of them criminal justice majors working on their degrees at Sam Houston University. As I sat in the prison's executive office and stammered out the details of my family situation and asked him to allow me to make up the time by working extra hours—I proposed to work nine consecutive days instead of our usual seven-day shifts to make up for the day off—he flew off the handle. He started screaming at me, calling me "a lazy Mexican" among other things that I have blocked out of my memory. He ordered me out of his office, and he told me he was going to write me a negative recommendation, which could ruin my law enforcement opportunities in the future.

That was it! Three months of hard work, where I felt I had learned so much to advance my criminal justice career, and my fate appeared to be in the hands of a racist who couldn't control his temper. I thought I was doing the right and proper thing by letting him know about my personal situation, but I left his office in a shambles. I worked the seven-day shift, and then without a word to anyone, I got in my Chevy and drove back to Hebbronville. I made it to my cousin's wedding and then headed back to school.

I was barely nineteen and felt my career in policing was over. Later, when I applied for work with the sheriff's office in Laredo and to become a special agent with the DEA, I was too afraid to include Huntsville on my résumé.

STEVE

I saw the headlights of the oncoming car as it barreled into my lane. I was still a rookie cop with the Bluefield Police Department. That night, I was on patrol, driving through leafy, residential streets of the historic railroad town in the heart of the Appalachians, about twenty minutes outside of Princeton, where I still lived with my parents.

With a population of just over twenty thousand, Bluefield was the largest town in southern West Virginia and western Virginia. The primary industry was the Norfolk and Western Railway Company, which eventually became the Norfolk Southern Railway. The primary cargo coming through the town on the railroad was coal heading to Norfolk, Virginia, to be shipped to various places around the world. People from nearby villages and other towns would come to Bluefield for shopping and entertainment, and every Saturday night, there was dancing with a country and western band at the Bluefield City Auditorium.

There were usually three to five off-duty police officers working these events, and it wasn't unusual for us to arrest quite a few people each week—most of them for picking fights or breaking into parked cars while they were drunk. That's when things in Bluefield could turn ugly. A lot of the folks who descended on Bluefield were from areas that didn't have much in the way of a police presence, if any at all. They were not accustomed to having to obey any rules or being told by a police officer what they could or could not do. Back then, most of these out-of-towners worked hard during the week and wanted to play hard on the weekends. And for many of them, fighting was part of life, so it wasn't unusual for them to resist arrest when confronted by a police officer. The following morning, after they'd sobered up in the drunk tank at the precinct, they would either apologize for their behavior or they'd say something like, "Man, that was a great fight, wasn't it? I can't wait to come back next weekend for another try."

When I wasn't patrolling the parking lot of the auditorium, most of my duties consisted of driving through Bluefield's main streets, looking for any crimes in progress and checking commercial doors and windows for signs of break-ins.

I loved my job and felt I was making an important contribution to the community. One cold, winter night, I was sure I had saved three small children from freezing to death in the back of a pickup truck. Their parents had left them in the car, which was busted-up and missing windows, so that they could catch a few dances in the auditorium. I was horrified by the sight of the trembling little children. After my partner and I put the children in the back of our heated police cruiser, I marched into the auditorium. I made my way up to the stage, grabbed the microphone from the singer in mid-song, and demanded that the parents of the children come forward or I would be forced to take the children to Child Protective Services. After a few tense moments, the parents came forward and were loudly booed by the crowd. They were dirt-poor and said they had just wanted to enjoy a few dances. I could tell that when they were reunited with their children that they were good parents who had just temporarily screwed up because they wanted to enjoy a few moments alone on the dance floor. So we let them off with a stern warning that if we ever caught them doing something like this again, we would make sure to call the proper authorities to have their children taken away from them.

On another blustery winter's night, while a reporter who was following me on my rounds waited outside, Officer Dave Gaither and I charged into a burning house, frantically going from room to room until we saw a mother and her young daughter. Dave helped the child's mother escape, and I picked up the child and ran like hell out of the burning home.

I truly believed then as I still do today that a police officer is a public servant, a title that I carry as a badge of honor. As a public servant, an officer is expected to serve and help the public. It's not always about chasing bad guys, writing traffic tickets, and working accidents.

But when the good deeds were done, we returned to our routine and the often monotonous patrols on the midnight shift.

It was on a routine midnight shift that I saw the Cadillac that raced in my direction—a near accident that did a great deal to set my own views of small-town policing on its own collision course.

The crusty, seen-it-all senior officer who sat beside me in the passenger seat instinctively grabbed the steering wheel and cursed loudly as I swerved the police cruiser onto the sidewalk to avoid a head-on collision. The driver behind us wasn't so lucky. From my rearview mirror, I could see the speeding Cadillac sideswipe the vehicle behind us before continuing at breakneck speed into the night.

I put on my siren, made a precipitous U-turn, and gave chase.

When the car finally stopped, I was surprised to find that the driver was a well-dressed, middle-aged woman. She was also falling-down drunk. We placed her in custody and had her car towed. In her high heels and fur jacket, she was wobbly and had trouble standing still. She had no idea why we'd stopped her and said she didn't recall striking another car. She wasn't combative or argumentative but displayed an air of affluence and importance that was about as subtle as the slightly sweet smell of alcohol mixed with her strong French perfume. When I told her she was being arrested for drunk driving and leaving the scene of an accident, she seemed to stand straighter, looking down at my partner and me.

"Do you know who my husband is?" she asked, slurring her words.

On our way to the police station to test her on a breathalyzer, my partner told me that I would be alone handling this case to see how I did. I found this strange but didn't realize the significance of his gesture until much later. And then, lowering his voice to a whisper, he informed me that the prisoner sitting in the back of our cruiser was extremely wealthy and married to a prominent attorney in town. She also had a family member who was a local judge. Then he started laughing to himself.

I was so naïve and inexperienced that I picked up on none of these clues. For me, no one was above the law.

When we arrived at the station, I began the booking process, just like we did with every other prisoner. But things were different—the shift commander, a lieutenant, arrived at the station to witness the process, and I noticed that the desk sergeant was also acting very differently with this prisoner. They watched in silence as I conducted the breathalyzer test. The results showed her blood alcohol level at 0.20, which was double the limit for driving under the influence in those days.

As I got ready to escort the prisoner to the lockup, the lieutenant and sergeant told me to wait with her in the booking area. At the same time, the chief of police arrived—an extremely rare occurrence. He was accompanied by a well-known attorney. After a brief huddle, the prisoner left with the lawyer. I couldn't believe my eyes.

Several days later, at the trial, I presented my case. Normally, because this was city court, the chief sat in on all hearings to observe how we handled ourselves in court. But this time, he wasn't there and had designated one of the detectives to sit in for him. When I asked the detective what was going on, he just laughed and demanded to know if I was ready to learn what really happens in court. Not quite sure what to expect, I went to the table where our city prosecutor usually sat, but he wasn't in the courtroom either. When I looked over to the defendant's table, I saw the attorney I had seen the night of the arrest. But he sat alone, *without* the defendant.

When the judge arrived, the defendant still hadn't arrived. The judge, another local attorney, called the case and then told me to present my evidence. I nervously described how the woman had driven into our lane of traffic, forcing me onto the sidewalk. Then she hit the car behind us and continued driving, leaving the scene of an accident until I turned around and pulled her over. I told the court about her demeanor and inability to pass a field sobriety test. I read out the breathalyzer results and told the judge that was all the information I had available.

I waited for the defense attorney to rebut the evidence or ask me questions, but nothing happened. The judge ruled that the evidence was not sufficient to support a charge of driving under the influence. He then reduced the charges to "public intoxication and reckless driving" and found the defendant guilty. The defense attorney closed his notebook with what seemed like a single congratulatory clap and smiled at the judge without saying a word. The case was adjourned.

The look on my face must have been one of pure disbelief because the judge came over to me and made a point of shaking my hand, telling me I had done a fine job and that I had a very bright future ahead of me. He introduced me to the defense attorney.

After everyone left the courtroom, I found myself alone with my partner, the seasoned cop who had sat in the passenger seat of my cruiser the night that I thought I was doing a noble and good thing—taking a dangerous driver off the streets of Bluefield.

Boy, did I feel like a boob.

"Welcome to the world of small-town politics," said my partner as he walked out of the courtroom ahead of me.

JAVIER

We moved my mother from the ranch in Hebbronville to my grandmother's house an hour away in Laredo after I got my first job at the sheriff's office there. The cancer had returned with a vengeance, spreading from her breasts and consuming her entire body, and she needed to be close to the hospital where she was being treated.

I accompanied her to her oncologist's appointments and chemo sessions as often as I could, taking turns with my grandmother to care for her.

But nothing helped. My mother died at just fifty. I was glad that she was able to make it to my college graduation and to see me get my first job in the Laredo sheriff's office. She told me that she was very proud of everything I had accomplished.

Her death was the hardest thing I'd ever endured, partly because we were so close and because I had always looked to the women in my family as sources of incredible strength.

I was very close to both my mother and grandmother, who never missed any of my high school baseball or football games. My grandmother was the toughest woman I knew—the anchor of our family. She spoke only Spanish and knew only a few words of English, but she always managed to get by. Her name was Petra, but everyone called her Pete, including my grandfather. A chain-smoker, she stood five foot eight and was more than 180 pounds. I never saw her without a pack of Winstons, even when she developed respiratory problems and her doctor told her the smoking was killing her. She claimed she never inhaled, but we all knew that it wasn't true. My entire family begged me not to buy her cigarettes, but she pleaded with me, and I always capitulated. I could never say no to my *abuelita*.

That's what my brother and I called her—little grandmother! And when it came to us, she had the kindest and most understanding heart. We always got the best Christmas gifts from her. When I was seven, she bought me my first bicycle—a red Texas Ranger with two headlights.

We were also quite close to my grandfather, who had deep blue eyes and a weak constitution—the opposite of my fierce *abuelita*. My grandfather's name was Francisco, but everyone called him Pancho. Unlike my grandmother, he was an intellectual, a title searcher, who worked for a local abstract company. He never smoked or drank, and he was a health nut before it was fashionable to be one. His dinner of choice was often a boiled apple in a bowl of milk with granola. I wondered how and why they had ever fallen in love because their personalities were so opposite. When their house in Laredo was robbed, my grandfather went to shut all the doors and windows in the house and then found a hiding place. My grandmother confronted the crooks with a hammer.

In Laredo, my deeply religious grandmother also opened up her home for church socials and became a confidante of the local Spanish parish priest. Every Sunday afternoon, he made a beeline to her home to sample her tamales—delicate meat- and pork-filled pillows of soft masa, steaming when you unwrapped them from their corn-husk jackets.

My grandmother was a brilliant cook, and she never used a cookbook. Every Sunday when I was a kid, we would make the one-hour drive from Hebbronville to Laredo to visit my grandparents and feast on her cooking. My mother especially cherished those visits, spending hours in the kitchen cooking with my grandmother. Their specialty was *cabrito en su sangre* (baby goat in blood). My mother, aunt, and grandmother would often cross the border into Nuevo Laredo and bring back a freshly killed goat. They insisted upon watching the animal being slaughtered to make sure that its blood was packed in a separate plastic bag so that it would not contaminate the goat's meat, or be mixed from the blood of another goat which could also spoil the meat. Later, the blood was mixed into a fragrant sauce with ancho and green chilies, garlic, cumin, and oregano. The smell of the dish filled my grandmother's kitchen, and after hours of slow cooking, the blackened stew was heaped on earthenware plates atop steaming Mexican rice. The meal was always accompanied by homemade corn tortillas.

I happily moved into my grandparents' home when I got my first law enforcement job in Laredo at the Webb County Sheriff's Office. They were so happy that I was moving in with them that they built me a separate extension onto their house, complete with my own bedroom and bathroom.

My grandmother proudly told everyone about my first job at the sheriff's office, even though I didn't spend much

time going after bad guys in one of the country's most po-
rous and busiest border regions, where in those days, traffickers easily smuggled drugs from Mexico in the tractor
trailers that clogged the bridges across the Rio Grande. In
my first real job in law enforcement, my main duties were
limited and mainly consisted of supervising prisoners at the
local jail. They ranged from petty thieves to entitled drug
traffickers and politicians who were used to getting what
they wanted.

The Aranda brothers were the worst. Arturo Daniel
Aranda and his brother Juan José were probably the first
drug traffickers I ever met, and they always gave me a hard
time. They were extremely violent, and they didn't care
about anything, probably because they were looking at
spending the rest of their lives in jail. I have to admit that
pretty much everyone who worked for the Webb County
Sheriff's Office hated them for gunning down a young cop
from the Laredo Police Department. Pablo Albidrez Jr.
answered a call just after midnight on July 31, 1976, from
undercover narcotics officer Candelario Viera, who was
following a station wagon with out-of-town license plates
heading toward the banks of the Rio Grande, a well-
known crossing point for drugs from Mexico. Viera had
been assigned to help a DEA task force and saw the Aranda
brothers loading burlap sacks into the trunk of the car. The
sacks contained more than five hundred pounds of marijuana.

Driving in an unmarked car, Viera followed the station

wagon and radioed for assistance. At a city intersection, Albidrez's police cruiser came to a screeching stop in front of the station wagon. Viera pulled up from behind.

"Police officers! Get out of the vehicle! Step out of the car!" yelled Viera, clutching his 9 mm Browning pistol.

But there was no sound from the station wagon, and the two officers decided to approach cautiously. That's when the Arandas began shooting wildly. Bullets pinged off every surface and in every direction.

When the shooting stopped and officers who had arrived on the scene arrested the brothers—Arturo had suffered wounds to his left shoulder and hand—Viera looked back where Albidrez was crouched in front of his police cruiser, clutching his heart. He had been shot straight through his police badge. Albidrez, twenty-eight, died on his way to Mercy Hospital. He left behind a young wife and two toddler daughters.

Another man incarcerated at the jail while I worked my first job at the sheriff's office was the powerful Laredo political boss, J. C. "Pepe" Martin. Pepe Martin was a legend in Laredo. His father, J. C. Martin Sr., was a wealthy landowner who had been elected Webb County sheriff. J. C. Jr. followed his father into public life and became the ultimate "patron"—a Democratic political boss who promised jobs in exchange for votes and wielded almost absolute power in office. He won six four-year terms as mayor, ruling the city between 1954 and 1978, when he decided he'd had enough of politics and declined to run for another term. Pepe had numerous large-acre ranches and thought nothing of using city workers and machinery to take care of them. A month after the reform candidate, Aldo Tatangelo, was elected mayor, Martin was indicted by a federal grand jury on mail fraud. He pleaded guilty and paid a $1,000 fine in addition to $200,000 to the city. He also had to serve a "prison sentence," where he spent thirty weekends hanging out at the jail.

But despite his conviction, Pepe Martin still wielded a great deal of power in southern Texas. My job was to let him into a downstairs jail cell every weekend after they dropped him off at 6:00 p.m. on Fridays. But I was under strict orders to let him stay in the cell by himself and never to lock him in. He was a nice, charismatic older gentleman, and he would come out and talk to us during the day. In fact, he had pretty much the run of the jail and would shoot the breeze with us and act like a regular guy. Every Sunday morning at 7:00 a.m., a black Suburban would idle outside the jail, and I would release him to his driver. It was politics at its best!

When I wasn't working, I was crossing the Rio Grande into Nuevo Laredo, hitting the bars where there were no age limits on drinking and everything was much cheaper than on the American side. You didn't need a passport to cross the border in the 1970s and 1980s, and the city was still relatively safe. A decade later, violence from the drug wars would result in the closure of a lot of the bars and restaurants in Nuevo Laredo. The violence was fueled by

Los Zetas, a criminal gang originally made up of deserters from the Mexican Army's special forces units. The group eventually became the armed wing of the Gulf Cartel in the 1990s, brutally murdering the group's rivals in a bloody turf war and engaging in sex trafficking and kidnappings. Years later, they turned Nuevo Laredo into a virtual war zone as the group became increasingly powerful and fought for control of lucrative drug-trafficking routes. By the mid-1990s, the Zetas took control of a lot of the Mexican businesses. Many more closed down because of the "tax" imposed by the Zetas. After a series of massacres in the city, many Mexican businesses ended up relocating across the border to Laredo and San Antonio.

But when I was working at the sheriff's office, most of us headed to the Mexican side for beer and fajitas, and I spent most of my time off hanging out at the bars and discos. There was the Lion's Den, where the gold-colored swizzle sticks featured an imperial lion's head. The disco catered to rich kids from South Texas. Nearby, the Cadillac Bar featured live music and a more upscale menu. Originally founded in New Orleans, the restaurant was moved by the owners to Nuevo Laredo during the early days of Prohibition in 1920. The moneyed drug traffickers and Laredo politicians who frequented the joint had a famous Super Bowl pool. Shares ran at a minimum $1,000 apiece. Even at this price, the pool always sold out quickly. The place was too rich for me, and most of the time, my buddies and I would head to Boy's Town, the red-light district, where the nearby cantinas and brothels had the cheapest beer.

Years later, when a bad guy held a gun to my head, it was my knowledge of the brothels and bars in Boy's Town that ended up saving my life.

When I was still working at the sheriff's office, my best friend was Poncho Mendiola. He was older and retired from the Texas Department of Public Safety. Like me, he taught at Laredo Junior College, where he was chairman of the law enforcement department. We spent a lot of time together drinking beer and barbecuing. People in Laredo would complain that they had little money, but they always seemed to have a cooler full of beer and plenty of fajitas on the grill. In fact, beer and meat often became a currency on the border, where there was a real sense of community. When I dented my police cruiser a few times, Poncho helped me get it fixed without my supervisors ever finding out. Poncho and I headed to an old garage that was also a police hangout in Laredo. The owner, Nando, would fix police and government cars in exchange for beer and steak, which they would barbecue on the spot, even as they were fixing the car. Nando would also do deals with regular customers by overcharging their insurance companies for the work and then giving back some of the money to the customer. The body shop doesn't exist anymore. It closed down after Nando's death.

For a while at least, I felt I had it made in Laredo. I had my own place, rent-free. I came and went whenever I wanted, and my grandmother doted on me and cooked my favorite meals. She was also my gatekeeper, and when I broke up with a girlfriend, my *abuelita* proved a capable enforcer. I realize now it was a cowardly way to treat women, but in the macho, cowboy culture of South Texas, I never gave it a second thought.

Still, my grandmother couldn't fix everything in my romantic life. And maybe if she had, I never would have ended up applying to the DEA.

In fact, it was all because of a woman that I ended up at the DEA. I was all set to do the right thing and marry my girlfriend in Laredo back in 1982 when she told me she was pregnant. But on the day before our wedding when she called me and told me she had gotten her period, I packed my shit and left Laredo as fast as I could!

I clambered into my Chevy and took off at the crack of dawn like a fugitive, terrified that her brothers would come after me. I waited until I was nearly four hours out of town before I called her to break the news.

"You're going to leave me?" she said, incredulous.

"Well, actually, I already have," I said.

She had manipulated me so well. She had even taken me to a clinic where a nurse told me she was pregnant.

After I left her waiting at the altar, I became persona non grata in Laredo, where her family was pretty well connected. My former fiancée's friend was an administrator at Laredo Junior College, where I was still teaching in the criminal justice program. After the incident, he told me that I should resign and leave Laredo because I was no longer a good example for my students or the community as a whole.

I got the message and started to look for ways out.

Months later, I applied to the DEA.

STEVE

I'd pretty much had it with small-town police work, and at the dawn of a new decade, I also found myself scrambling to support two young sons in a doomed marriage.

In November 1981, just months after my second son, Zach, was born and my marriage had come to a definitive end, I took a job as a special agent with the Norfolk and Western Railway and relocated to Norfolk, which was more than a five-hour drive from my home in Princeton.

The job paid double what I was earning as a cop in Bluefield. I had to remind myself of how much money I was finally making, because after a few months as a railroad cop, I was miserable.

For as long as I can remember, I had dreamed of doing hard-core police work, of going undercover to catch drug pushers and other bad guys. Now, I felt like a glorified security guard sitting outside the entrance to a multimillion-dollar pier where coal was loaded onto ships. I appreciated having the job with the railroad, but it wasn't what I really wanted to do.

Adding to my misery was the fact that I had just met the woman of my dreams back in Bluefield—a nurse with a passion for motorcycles and muscle cars—and now I was unable to spend any time with her because I was so far away.

Just before I took the Norfolk job, I met Connie, who was introduced to me by a mutual friend. She arrived at the station house with a group of other women while I was on one of my last midnight shifts for the Bluefield Police Department. I was in the squad room for roll call when the desk sergeant called back to our lieutenant, "Murphy has a carload of ladies waiting for him on the ramp."

I can no longer remember the wisecracks from the other officers in the room, but when I made my way to the ramp, I knew why they were all jealous. Checking my reflection in a glass door, I did my best tough-guy swagger to the car—a light blue Chevy SS with nice wheels, driven by the most beautiful woman I had ever seen. Connie, a registered nurse, had very long hair and a dark tan. Like me, she was recently divorced and worked the night shift—in her case, the emergency room and trauma wards at the hospital in Myrtle Beach—and then spent most of her days at the beach to relax. Which was why she looked to me like a bronzed beauty.

After we started dating, I realized that she was incredibly handy around cars and motorcycles. I had a motorcycle at the time, and when I learned that she owned her own motorcycle, that was a big attraction. As a guy who loved adventure and excitement, how could I not fall in love with a woman who owned her own motorbike?

Her fascination with cars and bikes probably came from growing up with two older brothers, and her father was a mechanic. She always drove a very nice sports car—vehicles that most would consider a muscle car, like the Chevy SS or Chevy IROC. And she knew what to do with a wrench, which was incredibly empowering and sexy! One day, I returned home to find her installing new speakers in her car, a sleek Camaro Z/28. The very ambitious project involved removing the dashboard, an enterprise I would never even have dreamed of undertaking on my own.

I could tell from the outset that Connie loved her job, which was why she was able to recognize the same passion I had for my own work. Early on, I confided to her my dream of doing serious police work, cultivating informants, and going undercover to capture bad guys, especially those who were trafficking drugs. I dreamed of being a DEA special agent before I even knew that such a position existed.

Before starting my career, I'd read several books and articles about officers working undercover, infiltrating groups and organizations. To me, that sounded like a real challenge, and it certainly had to be exciting.

Also, I'd seen the danger and devastation caused by illegal narcotics—how drugs overwhelmed users' lives and changed their personalities, how they could go from promising lives to ones of utter despair and agony. Equally important was how this negatively affected their families, friends, and others around them.

Illegal narcotics had long been a problem in the United States, but it wasn't until the 1970s that federal authorities decided to get tough and create a law enforcement agency whose sole purpose was ending the menace by going after the traffickers.

Illicit drugs were nothing new in the United States. In the 1930s, heroin started to enter the country from the South of France. The raw material was opium poppies grown in Turkey and the Far East, which arrived on ships docking at Marseille, one of the busiest ports on the Mediterranean. The heroin was produced at underground labs in the city and trafficked by the Corsican gangsters and the Sicilian Mafia who made up the so-called French Connection. The heroin was shipped from Marseille to New York City in what seems today like quaintly modest quantities. The first major heroin bust took place in New York on February 5, 1947, when police seized seven pounds of the drug from a Corsican sailor.

Years later, a Republican congressman from Connecticut began to sound the alarm that heroin was becoming a scourge, leading to high addiction rates and crime in the United States. In April 1971, Representative Robert Steele began to investigate reports of rising addiction rates among U.S. soldiers returning from Vietnam. Reports suggested that 10–15 percent of U.S. soldiers were addicted to heroin.

Those findings coupled with rampant marijuana use among counterculture hippies alarmed many in law enforcement, who predicted that these were but the early signs of a coming epidemic. Indeed, drug abuse was exploding in the country, as U.S. and South American traffickers began to follow their Corsican and Sicilian counterparts to feed the increasing U.S. demand for marijuana, cocaine, and heroin.

In this charged climate, President Richard Nixon declared "an all-out global war on the drug menace" and began the process of setting up an agency exclusively devoted to federal drug law enforcement. In the past, the federal government had relied on myriad different authorities that simply couldn't wield the muscle to wage Nixon's all-out war.

"Right now, the federal government is fighting the war on drug abuse under a distinct handicap, for its efforts are those of a loosely confederated alliance facing a resourceful, elusive, worldwide enemy," Nixon declared. "Certainly, the cold-blooded underworld networks that funnel narcotics from suppliers all over the world are no respecters of the bureaucratic dividing lines that now complicate our anti-drug efforts."

Nixon called for a centralized command to deal with the scourge. To this end, the Drug Enforcement Administration, a federal agency devoted to cracking down on drug use and ending drug smuggling, was established by executive order on July 1, 1973. There were certainly ulterior motives attached to Nixon's focus on drugs as he fought to take media attention away from the scandal that would eventually end his presidency. But at the time, the creation of a federal law enforcement group that would act as a powerful strike force seemed like a good idea.

When I wasn't working, I was missing Connie. We started a long-distance relationship after I moved to Norfolk and only managed to see each other about once a month. Eventually, Connie took a nursing job at a hospital in nearby Virginia Beach so that we could be together. It was the first of many occasions that she would sacrifice her career for mine.

After about two years with the railroad police, I applied to return to my law enforcement roots and transferred back to Bluefield. Both Connie and I wanted to be closer to our families. But the change of venue didn't do anything to make me any happier about my job, even as Connie managed to get a nursing job at nearby Princeton Hospital. Although I truly enjoyed working with the other railroad officers, who were very talented investigators, I was still working in what I considered a dead-end position.

I first heard the initials *DEA* at an all-night diner over eggs and bottomless cups of black coffee after I'd finished a midnight shift in Bluefield. Between mouthfuls of scrambled eggs doused in ketchup, Pete Ramey, a fellow railroad cop, told me about working undercover to bust drug dealers. Pete was a large, towering figure with an easygoing personality. A former Virginia state trooper, he had spent time working narcotics throughout Virginia and as a task force officer with the DEA in Roanoke. After Pete joined the railroad police, I took him under my wing, and when we shared the same late-night shifts, we headed after work to the local Hardee's, where I peppered him with questions about his narcotics background. I must have asked him the same questions over and over, but he always took the time to answer them and fill in the blanks.

More than anyone, Pete knew that I wasn't happy working as a railroad agent, and he started to encourage me to apply to the DEA. At first, I didn't think that anything like that was possible for me. I'd applied for two other federal law enforcement agent positions in the past and was put off by the fact that the process was excruciatingly slow. It always left me discouraged. But Pete persisted, encouraging me to complete my college degree so that I could qualify for a spot with the DEA.

In the spring of 1984, things started to look up. Connie and I were married in a small ceremony surrounded by close family and friends. Shortly after the reception, we left for our honeymoon, a Caribbean cruise that departed from Miami. It was my first time flying on a plane with more than one engine.

When we returned from our honeymoon and I began to settle into my new duties of inspecting trainloads of freight in Bluefield, a life-and-death incident would suddenly put my whole career in sharp focus. It would force me off the safe path and into the perilous but also exciting unknown.

One Saturday night as I was patrolling Norfolk and Western property in downtown Bluefield, checking buildings and vehicles to ensure that none of them had been broken into, I heard what sounded like the pop of gunfire and faint screams in the distance. As I got closer to the shooting, I saw a Bluefield cop crouched behind a police cruiser. He had a gun in his hand aimed at the third floor of the building directly in front of him, where a gunman was firing shots that sounded like cannons going off. I recognized the thumps of a .44-caliber Magnum and saw the bullets ricocheting off the police cruiser, missing the young police officer by mere inches. The screams were closer now, and I saw that they were coming from a man lying on the sidewalk, a dark patch of blood spreading across the concrete where he lay.

I immediately ran to the cop and asked if backup was on the way, but he was so new to the force that he hadn't thought to call in his position. I told him to radio the police department before I rushed to help the wounded man. I dragged him into a recessed doorway so that he was out of range of the gunman upstairs. Then we exchanged shots with the gunman on the third floor.

Once reinforcements arrived, the police officer was able to persuade the gunman to surrender with no further injury. Later, I assisted detectives at the crime scene, taking statements from witnesses. We soon learned that the gunman had returned to his apartment to find his wife with the man. The enraged husband had pulled out his Magnum and shot the other man in the butt as he fled the third-floor flat.

I returned to railroad police headquarters at about 6:30 in the morning, confident that I had done the right thing in helping a fellow officer in a potentially deadly situation. I was proud of what I had done and proceeded to inform the division chief about my involvement in the shooting.

"Just what did that shooting have to do with railroad business?" he asked, becoming increasingly hostile as I tried to explain that I considered it my duty to come to the aid of a fellow officer. It was an unwritten rule: Street cops always helped each other, especially if one of them was in mortal danger. Law enforcement is a closed society—a close-knit fraternity, quick to protect its own.

But the division chief was a bureaucrat who had never worked the street. Enraged, he was buying none of my explanation. He drove to our office and demanded that I turn over my weapon—a Smith & Wesson Model 15 .38/.357-caliber snub-nosed revolver. Before giving him my revolver, I removed the bullets from the cylinder, which is a common safety practice with any firearm.

The chief became apoplectic. He began yelling at me that I shouldn't have emptied my weapon because now he wouldn't be able to determine how many rounds I had fired. I asked him if he really thought I would not have reloaded my weapon after being involved in a gunfight. Then I handed him the empty casings from my pocket so he could see how many rounds I'd fired.

He berated me for an uncomfortable fifteen minutes. But I stood my ground and told him that given the same circumstances I would respond in exactly the same manner, that I would never leave a fellow police officer in danger. And the same can be said for almost every other railroad police officer working in Bluefield, as well as around the country.

That's when he threatened to "get my job" over the incident.

I had already decided my time was up with the railroad. Later, I was interviewed by BPD detectives as well as the hierarchy of the Norfolk and Western police over my part in the shooting. Luckily, those higher-ups had been street cops prior to becoming railroad cops, and they understood. The Bluefield Police Department was so pleased with me that they awarded me a commendation for bravery and for coming to the aid of a fellow officer.

Of course, the division chief was not happy with the way things turned out.

Following the shooting, I decided I'd finally had enough of small-town policing—again. I continued with trying to finish my college degree, which had been interrupted during my first marriage and birth of my sons. When I finally graduated and got my diploma in May 1985, I immediately submitted an application to become a special agent with the Drug Enforcement Administration.

I waited and waited for a response. I had no idea it would take two years.

I whined, I complained. I called DEA headquarters countless times. And I also met with Pete. He listened and never wavered in his encouragement, remaining enthusiastic about the career that he knew to be just around the corner for me.

I learned that a former college classmate, Dave Williams, was working as a DEA agent in Miami. Dave and I had taken that first police test together in 1975. While I went to work for the city police, Dave opted to work at the sheriff's department. After a few years there, Dave moved to Charleston, South Carolina, where he became a highly decorated police officer there. I called Dave in Miami to see if he had any advice on what I should do. As an old friend, Dave was very supportive, but he wasn't in a position that would help with the processing of my application.

I panicked. And after waiting more than eighteen months after I'd submitted my application, I decided to drive to the DEA division office in Washington, D.C., determined to speak to the DEA recruiter in person.

Special Agent Charlie West met me at the reception area wearing a slightly bemused expression.

"Do you have an appointment?" he asked.

I blurted out that I really wanted a job with the DEA and had taken the chance of catching him in the office because I hadn't heard anything from the agency. Charlie was clearly shocked. He probably thought I was an idiot for driving that far—it was over five hours from Bluefield to Washington—on the chance that he might be there.

To his credit, Charlie checked on my status and returned to tell me that my application was still being processed. Charlie said he would see what he could do to push things along, and I left.

Within a few weeks, I received a call from Charlie, who told me to return to Washington for an interview. I was elated, but I think Pete was even happier for me. My interview went well, and Charlie initiated the investigative process, one of the first hurdles on the road to being accepted into the elite federal agency.

But after a few months, I received a shocking letter from the DEA stating that my application was turned down due to medical reasons.

Several years earlier, I had had problems with a stomach ulcer. Although I hadn't had any issues for years, this was enough to disqualify me from becoming an agent. Needless to say, I was completely devastated, and it was Pete who came to my rescue yet again. I also thought about my father and his desire to get into the army—an urgency that caused him to cheat on his eye exam. For more than a split second, I considered doing the same, but in the end, I didn't have to.

Pete told me that the DEA had a process that allowed me to challenge their findings. And after speaking with the DEA physician at the agency's headquarters, I went to two other doctors and underwent the required screening and submitted my results to the agency, asking them to reconsider my application.

In May 1987, I transferred back to Norfolk from Bluefield with the railroad police. I'd only been there for a couple of weeks when in early June 1987, I finally received the phone call from the DEA recruitment office, congratulating me on being accepted as a candidate to attend special agent training and asking if I could report to the DEA office in Charleston, West Virginia. A week after that, I would report to the DEA Training Academy located on the U.S. Marine Corps base in Quantico, Virginia. I didn't hesitate. When that call came in, I immediately accepted and agreed to report to Charleston the following week. After calling Connie, I handed in my resignation with the railroad, packed everything up in the temporary apartment I had rented in Norfolk, and drove back to Bluefield. Fortunately, I had three weeks of vacation time pending with the railroad and used that to give notice that I was resigning.

In the end, I was so sure I would be accepted into the DEA that I had refused to sign my lease.

JAVIER

I did my DEA training at the Federal Law Enforcement Training Centers in Glynco—a 1,600-acre campus in southeast Georgia, located between Savannah and Jacksonville, Florida. It was the spring of 1984, and the crack epidemic was just beginning to sweep across the United States. Overnight, it seemed that drugs were everywhere.

I couldn't help thinking about this as I started the intensive eighteen-week program that would turn me into an elite soldier in America's war against drugs.

Those weeks at DEA training camp were the hardest I'd ever endured, much more difficult than the training I had undergone for certification for the Webb County Sheriff's Office in Laredo. For one thing, the instructors at Federal Law Enforcement Training Centers (FLETC) were all veteran agents, drawn from the FBI and the DEA. They brooked no nonsense. If you failed two tests, they simply threw you out.

We lived in apartment-type housing with four men to an apartment. The four of us quickly became friends and looked out for one another. We helped each other study in the evenings, which became a real discipline after a day of grueling exercise and "practicals"—scenarios led by professional actors, which were supposed to teach us basic surveillance skills. The practicals started off easy but then advanced to complex cases. Each case practical was different, and each agent would be assigned as the lead agent preparing us for situations in the real world. There was always a lot of pressure because the instructors could suddenly send you home for messing them up.

One of our roommates—an attorney who grew up in a rich New York family—got off on the wrong foot with one of the agent instructors. The agent disliked him from the start and proceeded to make life miserable for him. We encouraged him not to drop out, and he eventually graduated from the program. But back in New York after a few months with the DEA, he realized the agency was not for him.

During the training, I never left the base. My stomach was in knots most of the time because of the numerous academic tests and practicals, which lasted until about 10:00 every night, after which you had to go back to your room and study for the next one. It was the first time in my life that I worried that I was simply not cut out for this kind of law enforcement work. In fact, in our class of forty-five cadets, only thirty made the cut. Many simply flunked out or left of their own accord when things got too difficult. I studied hard and tried to maintain a positive attitude because the instructors seemed to follow our every move and mood.

Every Sunday, I would call my father in Hebbronville and tell him about the week. Talking to him about the training and what was going on at the ranch calmed me down and gave me enough confidence to face yet another grueling week of tests and physical activity.

One of the things I did like was the communal mess hall that was open to cadets from various federal agencies. I had never seen so much food in my life—tables full of salads, steaming trays of mashed potatoes, vegetables, roast chicken, and beef. Still, with so much food, I managed to lose weight. I went into the academy weighing about 200 pounds and came out at 180.

The last week of the academy, I knew I had passed and remember my class coordinator telling me I had done well and would graduate in the upper third of my class.

No one came to my graduation. A lot of the guys had their families and wives at the ceremony, but I was single, and it was too complicated for my family to make the trip from Texas. Still, I was on top of the world when they gave me my new credentials and a gun, and I simply couldn't wait to show off.

I flashed my shiny new DEA badge at the tiny airport in Brunswick, Georgia, as I checked in for my flight back to Texas. But I guess I wasn't the first one to have that idea. Over the years, airport personnel must have dealt with hundreds of new DEA and FBI recruits heading home after their training.

In any event, I was deeply disappointed that as I held up my badge during check-in, no one bothered to look up.

STEVE

After undergoing the bureaucratic formalities in Charleston, I headed to Quantico in a suit and tie. Or more accurately, my suit was in a garment bag in my car as I drove the three hundred miles to the DEA Training Academy. There is nothing I hate more than having to wear a suit and tie. The blazer reminds me of a straitjacket, making it difficult to move my arms. The starched shirt feels like cardboard cutting against my skin, and the tie is, in a word, suffocating.

But I was a newly minted basic agent trainee (BAT), and the training manual required that we show up in business attire. At the last exit before Quantico, I stopped at a McDonald's to change into my suit, and then I drove the last few miles to the academy. When I arrived at the U.S. Marine Corps base that was to be my home for the next thirteen weeks, I noticed several other BATs in jeans and shorts. They were promptly told to leave and return in the proper attire.

I had stepped into the DEA firmament and was determined to follow every rule, even though I missed Connie terribly, and I didn't get along with one of the three counselors that I was assigned to. After my second week at the academy, I received an urgent call from Connie that my father had suffered a heart attack and the prognosis was not good. The doctor suggested that family members who wanted to see my dad again should do so immediately. During the first five weeks of DEA training, BATs are not allowed to leave the academy, including on the weekends. To leave the academy, I needed to obtain permission from our counselors and the academy staff. The only counselor available that Friday evening was the one I tried to avoid because of his caustic personality. When I approached him about my family situation, he was predictably difficult.

"I've got a baby agent who can't handle his own problems, so what do you expect me to do?" he asked me.

I was shocked because I thought I had entered the most elite police force on earth—the ultimate fraternity where officers were tough but kind and had each other's backs.

Even after I explained the gravity of my father's situation, the counselor remained unmoved, but in the end, he did provide me with the clearance for the drive to Princeton. The next day, just before I left for the hospital to visit my father, I received a phone call from my regular counselor asking how my father was doing and if there was anything he could do for my family and me. As I learned later, this was more in line with the fraternal DEA I had dreamed about. My father survived that heart attack and lived several more years before finally succumbing to another heart attack.

Our weeks in the classroom consisted of reviewing the U.S. federal code associated with narcotics violations, money-laundering statutes, writing reports and drug identification, and testing as well as dealing with informants. There were also courses in firearms and physical training—both of which were taken very seriously at the academy. We learned how to handle weapons and focused on marksmanship and how to engage multiple targets. We also practiced with using available objects to protect ourselves under fire and how to deal with malfunctioning weapons.

After nearly twelve years of police work, I was a good shot. I'd won recognition in various state and national competitions, and when I was at the academy, the instructors asked me to work with some of the other BATs who were struggling to meet the DEA standard in firearms.

Every Wednesday evening was Agent Enrichment Night, which required BATs to wear business attire to dinner and was always followed by a guest speaker in the auditorium. It was also steak-and-wine night, which made wearing a suit bearable. The only problem was that the dining hall was located above the firearms cleaning room and the sickeningly sweet alcoholic smell of Hoppe's solvent permeated everything we ate.

Just before graduation, BATs are expected to attend a ceremony to announce their new assignments. The ceremony is held in a classroom where each BAT is called to the front of the room and asked where they would like to be stationed and where they think they will end up before being handed a sealed envelope by one of the instructors. The envelope is opened in front of the entire class. It's also another occasion at which a suit is unfortunately required.

At the beginning of training, each recruit is asked to submit a wish list of five offices around the country where they would like to work. My list included Norfolk, Virginia; Wilmington, North Carolina; Charleston, South Carolina; Jacksonville, Florida; and Miami, Florida. Recruits are required to sign a mobility agreement that says that you are willing to be stationed anywhere in the United States at the DEA's discretion.

When it was my turn, I stood up and said I would love to be stationed in Norfolk but that I was likely to get Jacksonville.

Sweating, and with my heart pounding through my starched white shirt, I tore open the envelope and read, "Miami."

Later that day, I called and told Connie about my assignment. I can't say that either of us was all that excited. Not at first. We were both concerned about being so far from our families, but we didn't have any other choices. Once again, Connie would leave her job to follow me. We had no idea then that it was a sacrifice that would go on for the next twenty-six years.

Moving across the country may sound routine for many people whose jobs require them to transfer frequently, but as I would quickly come to learn, being a DEA agent is not a job; it's a lifestyle. It requires long hours at work and away from home, with days often stretching between twelve and twenty hours, or longer. Agents make many sacrifices to get the job done, which in turn sometimes requires even greater sacrifices from their families. It takes a strong spouse to tolerate the amount of time the agent is gone, to run a household, keep up with the kids and their activities, and hold down their own careers. I already knew that the marriages of many agents ended up in divorce because of the stress and strain on the families from the requirements of being a successful agent. The stress extended to the concern over an agent's safety while working one of the toughest jobs in law enforcement. I knew I would be away from home for long periods, that Connie would probably be facing a lot of things on her own.

But as we spoke on the phone about the adventure that awaited both of us, neither of us could really get a grip on what we were in for. That single word—*Miami*—hit us gently like a warm ocean breeze. We would be moving to Miami, and we would just get on with it.

My dad was too sick to attend my graduation from the DEA Training Academy, but Connie came along with her parents. At the ceremony, after the speeches and the jokes, I pledged to support and defend the Constitution, enforce the drug laws, and protect the United States against foreign and domestic enemies.

In my woolen suit and starched white shirt, I noticed that I raised my right hand with a new sense of freedom and dexterity of movement. For after thirteen weeks of the hardest training I had ever known, I had lost twenty-five pounds, and my only suit was now far too big. But as I clutched my gleaming new badge, I have to say that I never felt more comfortable in my own skin.

JAVIER

I was headed to the DEA office in Austin, Texas, but first, I had to deal with some unfinished business in Laredo, where I returned after my DEA training.

I worked my first narcotics job on the international border I had come to know so well as a cop. But entering the murky undercover world of drug traffickers and cooperating informants left me confused. Sometimes, it was hard to know just who were the bad guys and who was on your side.

For instance, there was Guillermo González Calderoni, the head of the Mexican Federal Judicial Police—an agency roughly equivalent to the FBI. Calderoni was known as El Comandante and was probably the most powerful cop in Mexico. But part of his success in capturing some of the biggest Mexican drug cartel members lay in his profound relationships with the bad guys. El Comandante was particularly adept at playing both sides against each other for his own personal enrichment. He had grown up with José García Ábrego, the brother of Juan García Ábrego, who was the head of the Gulf Cartel, and considered him a friend. Of course, all of this came out much later when U.S. federal agents found that while he was going after some of the biggest dealers of the day and working as an informant for the DEA, he was also protecting others, going so far as to collect millions for setting up hits on rival drug lords.

I met Calderoni several times as a young cop and then as a DEA agent, and I never trusted him. By 1993, he was fired in Mexico over accusations that he was helping to ship drugs to the United States. Calderoni fled across the border, where he convinced a U.S. federal judge to deny

Mexico's extradition request on charges of torture, illegal enrichment, and abuse of power. Calderoni, who eventually settled in a gated community in the border city of McAllen, Texas, accused former Mexican president Carlos Salinas de Gortari and his brother, Raúl, of doing business with the country's biggest drug traffickers. He also accused Salinas of ordering the killing of two rival politicians during the 1988 presidential campaign. The fifty-four-year-old former cop became a marked man, and in 2003, he was killed with a single bullet as he sat in the driver's seat of his silver Mercedes-Benz outside his lawyer's office in McAllen.

Like I said, I never trusted Calderoni, and my gut told me to stay far away from him even as he was the top cop in Mexico. But on my first undercover job, we couldn't avoid him. At least my partners at the time needed to seek his cooperation to bust a heroin dealer in Nuevo Laredo. On that first assignment, Raúl Perez and Candelario Viera (we all called him Candy) were my partners. These were the same guys who had been involved in the shoot-out with the Aranda brothers when I had first joined the Webb County Sheriff's Office. Candy and Perez were both strong-willed, no-nonsense cops who had gone on to work some of the biggest drug seizures on the border. Working with the DEA for more than a decade, they knew the identity of every drug trafficker who operated on the border, and they knew who was cooperating with the Mexican feds. They may have even known about Calderoni's unsavory connections, but they weren't about to rat him out, since they knew they needed his cooperation to do anything.

I'm not ashamed to admit that I was nervous as we crossed the border into Nuevo Laredo, where I was scheduled to meet the target. Even in the short time that I had been off the beat at the sheriff's office, the Mexican border town that I had come to know so well was in dangerous flux. In a few years, the drug violence would reduce it to a virtual ghost town. Los Zetas were consolidating their control, and their cartel boss, Heriberto Lazcano, dealt harshly with his rivals. In one instance, he dispatched Miguel Treviño Morales, better known to us as Z-40, a federal informer and one of the most brutal members of the group, to wipe out his rivals in Guatemala. In Mexico, Z-40 was responsible for the massacre of hundreds of people. In some cases, he forced his victims to fight each other to the death. He subjected others to the notorious *guiso,* or stew—which consisted of dumping them into vats of oil and then dousing them with gasoline before lighting them on fire.

In the shadowy world I now inhabited, there were few formalities and little respect for the rules. I was shocked that we seemed to be breaking the law by crossing into Mexico—another country!—without any of the proper authorizations! Candy, Perez, and I simply drove over the bridge to Nuevo Laredo without obtaining any of the requisite country clearances from federal authorities in Mexico

City, which at that time entailed writing a teletype and waiting for their go-ahead—a process that usually took a few days. But Candy and Raúl had friends among the Mexican feds in the city and simply coordinated with them. And since I was new to the DEA and unknown to the drug traffickers on the Mexican side, I was the perfect agent to conduct the operation. As part of their sting, I was to pose as a heroin buyer. Their informant told the bad guy that I had the cash for the deal. Right before the sting, we met with the commander of the Mexican federal police to let him know about the operation. Then we drove to a grimy Church's Chicken restaurant, where I waited for my target. Five minutes after I sat down in a booth, a handsome and very cordial gentleman in his sixties appeared at my table. He asked me if I was Juan—my undercover name—and when I said yes, he motioned for me to walk with him outside the restaurant, where he showed me a ball of what looked like black tar. I picked up the heroin and told him the money was in my car. At that moment, six Mexican federal police agents swarmed him and arrested him without incident. I felt sorry for the old man. What was such a dignified and seemingly well-educated man doing selling heroin at a fast-food restaurant on the Mexican border?

Back in Laredo, the Mexican federal agents called and said that the heroin that we seized was pure, and they complimented me on a job well done.

Of course, I was happy that everything had gone well,

but if you want to know the truth, I was also pretty spooked.

As I drove to Austin and to my new life as a special agent with the DEA, I had the feeling that I had embarked on a dark journey to a strange new country, populated by UCs, CSs, and an alphabet soup of strange acronyms that I would come to learn along the way.

There was no map to guide me and no way to tell just whose side anyone was on.

PART TWO

PART TWO

STEVE

Most of what I knew about Miami, I learned from watching episodes of *Miami Vice*.

And once I heard that the DEA was sending me to South Florida on my first assignment, I joked with my police friends that I was going to become the new Sonny Crockett, the handsome detective at the Metro-Dade Police Department who was played by a dapper Don Johnson in the TV series.

Fond of unstructured linen blazers and his black 1972 Ferrari Daytona Spyder, Crockett worked undercover chasing Colombian drug traffickers. *Miami Vice* followed the exploits of Crockett and his partner, a former New York cop named Ricardo "Rico" Tubbs, played by Philip Michael Thomas. Sure, I knew that a lot of the series wasn't accurate, but I still loved the excitement, the conflict between the characters, and the tropical scenery of the city. At the back of my mind, I dreamed of the intensity of becoming an undercover narc in South Florida and the challenges of taking on some of the biggest drug dealers in the world. But I honestly didn't think it would ever become a reality.

By the time *Miami Vice* premiered on television in 1984, cocaine was already booming in the United States, and addiction was turning into a national epidemic. Two years earlier, beloved actor and comedian John Belushi died after injecting a combination of heroin and cocaine in his bungalow at the Chateau Marmont in Los Angeles. He was thirty-three years old.

But cocaine was not just reserved for celebrities and the wealthy. By the time Belushi died, crack cocaine—the cheap, smokable form of the drug—was beginning its sweep of U.S. inner cities, leading to high crime and overdose deaths. Made with cocaine residue, water, and bicarbonate of soda, a single dose could be purchased on the street for about $2.50. Crack ravaged entire communities. According to the DEA's own statistics, crack-related hospital emergencies increased by 110 percent in 1986, rising from 26,300 to 55,200 across the country.

In the early 1980s, cocaine production was through the roof. According to the DEA's own Narcotics Intelligence Estimate, the manufacturing and distribution of cocaine had risen by 11 percent. In early 1984, the supply of cocaine on the U.S. market was so plentiful that there were significant price drops. The price per kilo in the early part of the year was $16,000 in South Florida and $30,000 in New York.

But prices soon went up when the supply was temporarily halted after one of the biggest raids in DEA history. In March 1984, the Colombian National Police, with the assistance of the DEA, dealt a historic blow to cocaine production and distribution in Colombia with the destruction of Tranquilandia, a complex of nineteen cocaine labs and eight runways buried deep in the jungle near Caquetá. The sprawling encampment, complete with luxurious accommodations and mess halls for hundreds of workers, was a joint creation of José Gonzalo Rodríguez Gacha, the Ochoa family, and Pablo Escobar—all names that I heard for the first time in Miami. I didn't know it at the time, but in years to come, I would become obsessed with all of them.

Undercover CNP and DEA operatives found the jungle facility, which was guarded by heavily armed militia, after placing satellite tracking devices on tanks of ether purchased through a chemical distributor in New Jersey in 1983. Ether is a major chemical in the processing of raw coca leaves into cocaine, and the bad guys were buying up vast quantities and transporting them deep into the Colombian interior. During the raid on Tranquilandia, law enforcement arrested hundreds of workers and seized an astounding 13.8 tons of cocaine, with a street value of more than $1.2 billion. Despite the enormity of the haul, it made barely a dent in the Medellín Cartel's profits, which were estimated at more than $25 billion in the mid-1980s.

I didn't really receive any briefings about Miami from my DEA bosses before my new assignment began in

November 1987. Typically, all agents receive the same training and are expected to be able to function anywhere in the United States. Prior to arriving at a new post, agents and analysts don't really know what cases they'll be assigned to work. When you arrive in a new city, you try to get your bearings and help your family settle in. Then you are expected to hit the ground running. While I might have been a little naïve about different cultures and knew little about the United States outside of my own hometown, I was experienced in law enforcement.

Still, Miami was exotic to me, imbued with a sense of mystery. I had only been through the touristy parts of the city with their quaint pastel-colored houses and imperial palms on my honeymoon and had once spent a few days in Fort Lauderdale on spring break with a group of fraternity brothers. Most of what I knew about Miami—a center of the cocaine and marijuana trade from South America and the Caribbean—was what I had learned from the press and on TV. Like many Americans, Connie and I watched the gory spectacle of cocaine-addled Colombian and Cuban drug dealers battle for dominance, spraying each other with machine-gun fire on Miami street corners in the movies and on TV. Before we arrived in Miami, we often wondered if it was real or the stuff of elaborate fiction.

Did drug traffickers really threaten their rivals with bloody chain saws, as they did in Brian De Palma's *Scarface*? The movie, released in 1983, followed the violent adventures of Cuban refugee and ex-con Tony Montana, who arrives in Miami as part of the infamous Mariel boatlift, which saw the migration of nearly 125,000 Cubans to South Florida between April and September 1980. The exodus started after a bus driver crashed the gates of the Peruvian embassy in Havana, and thousands of would-be refugees swarmed the embassy grounds seeking asylum from Fidel Castro's repressive Communist regime. Facing a riot, Castro outmaneuvered everyone and announced that Cubans wishing to leave the island could assemble at the Mariel harbor, twenty miles west of Havana. Boatloads of refugees sailed to Key West and overwhelmed South Florida. Among the refugees were convicted criminals that Castro freed from the island's jails. There were also patients from insane asylums who were so dazed when they arrived in Key West that many didn't realize they were in a different country.

The refugees added an estimated ten thousand killers and thieves to South Florida, according to officials at the Miami Police Department's Homicide Bureau. Between January and May of 1980, the bureau documented 75 murders. Following the arrival of the Marielitos, there were 169 murders in the last seven months of the year, according to police statistics. By 1981, Miami had the highest murder rate of any city in the world, and just about everyone in the United States was aware of how dangerous South Florida had become. So many bodies piled up in the city as a result of the escalating cocaine wars that the Miami morgue couldn't cope, and the medical examiner's office ended up renting a refrigerator van to deal with the overflow. In real-life scenes that could have been taken straight out of *Miami Vice* or *Scarface*, Colombian and Cuban dealers would pull up alongside each other in their fancy cars and shoot each other up with automatic weapons.

Despite the violence, both Connie and I were very excited about this new opportunity. Strangely, we didn't worry so much about our safety. We were concerned about being so far away from our families. We were small-town folks, and we both knew that moving to a large city would be a bit of a culture shock. Connie had an aunt and uncle living in Plantation, about thirty miles from Miami, so we rented a two-bedroom apartment there to be close to them. It allowed us to feel like we still had family just down the street, and to learn more about this exotic and crazy place called South Florida.

At first, we found the traffic challenging! But we also found people to be very friendly, and everything was beautiful year-round. Cold, dreary West Virginia winters seemed such a distant memory as we sped past the picture-postcard vistas of swaying palms set against impossibly blue skies that now made up the backdrop of our new lives.

And of course, there was the beach! Miles and miles of sandy coastline, dotted with colorful umbrellas and roadside fish shacks where we gorged on grilled sailfish, conch fritters, and deep-fried shrimp.

During our free time, we explored neighborhoods,

looking for a more permanent house next to the ocean. But our favorite pastime was simply watching people. When it grew too hot to be outside, we whiled away many afternoons people-watching at the Broward Mall. The sprawling shopping center in Plantation never disappointed, and we saw some pretty strange sights. Coming from small towns, we were fascinated by the way some people dressed and interacted. There were smartly dressed women whose faces were stretched from too much plastic surgery, walking little dogs with jeweled leashes. There were overweight men in guayaberas, smoking fat cigars, and Latin American tourists with their suitcases, stuffed with new clothes from the Gap and Old Navy, as well as electronics that were prohibitively expensive in their home countries because of high tariff walls.

At first, we thought we had landed in a different universe, but the longer we lived in South Florida, the more we came to realize that most people were just like us—transplants from another place. Very few people we met were actually born in the area.

In those early days, we were on a strict budget. We didn't go out to eat much. If a good movie was playing at the mall theater, we'd go to the afternoon matinée to save money. We were always the youngest people in the audience, surrounded by retired couples, commonly referred to as "turtles," who were obviously living on fixed incomes. When the house lights went down, we could hear the other moviegoers rustling through their purses and backpacks, pulling out bags of homemade popcorn and opening cans of soda that they'd brought with them to save money.

One evening, Connie and I went to a local Pizza Hut for dinner, when an elderly couple came to sit at the table next to us. After reviewing the menu, we could hear them discussing what they planned to order for dinner. We could hear the wife telling the husband that they couldn't add extra toppings to their pizza because of the cost and were ordering only one salad to share and drinking water to save money. This was pretty heartbreaking for us to hear, so when our bill came, we asked the waitress to bring us the bill for the other couple so we could treat them to dinner. We asked the waitress not to say anything to the couple until we had left the restaurant. The waitress teared up as we were talking to her and took our payment for both meals. Connie and I hurried out of the Pizza Hut. As we were driving out of the parking lot, we saw the waitress standing at a window with the older couple waving to us. The smiles of appreciation on their faces is a memory that still remains with us today. Although we didn't have much ourselves, we felt that we'd done a good deed for people who were a lot worse off.

I never considered myself a prejudiced person, but during those first months in Miami, I am ashamed to admit that I had little tolerance for life in a city that was more than 70 percent Latino. I remember going to lunches with the other more experienced DEA team members and being annoyed that the menus were entirely in Spanish. I had no idea what I was reading. To be honest, I was appalled to learn that businesses in the United States had employees who couldn't speak English and were running restaurants without bothering to translate the menus. For the longest time, I resisted learning any words in Spanish, believing it was *their* responsibility to learn our language. But as we continued to work and live in Miami, I developed a sense of tolerance and understanding. Like I said, most people we met in South Florida were from somewhere else, and in many cases, they had escaped crushing poverty and brutal dictatorships in places like Cuba, Haiti, and other parts of Latin America to build better lives for themselves and their families. They may not have been able to muster up enough English to write out a restaurant menu, but like us, they were all just trying to earn an honest living.

At work, I wasn't exactly Sonny Crockett—for one thing, I lacked a Ferrari—but I was still living the dream of a narcotics agent at the epicenter of the cocaine wars. I was immersed in dope: I tracked drug traffickers, I pored over books and reports about Colombian drug dealers and trade routes, and I was proud to be attached to Group 10—one of the DEA's most elite squads. The cases coming out of Miami included some of the largest cocaine seizures of all time. The first seizure I participated in was for four hundred kilos of cocaine. Let me just pause for a moment to underline what an enormous quantity that is. Four hundred kilos of cocaine! It took up the whole inside space of a twin-engine aircraft. It was the new normal for me. I no longer described busts in terms of ounces or grams. Kilos and tons were now the norm.

And in those early days in Miami, the quantities of cocaine kept mounting. In another case, we seized 300 kilos of cocaine from an airdrop by one of our informants off the coast of Puerto Rico, followed by another 440 kilos. When our own work slowed down, several of us younger agents would volunteer to assist other DEA enforcement groups on drug busts.

But life at the epicenter of cocaine trafficking was not without its risks, and on the very first case in which I worked as the lead investigator, I began to receive death threats.

In August 1988, we worked jointly with U.S. Customs investigators to seize hundreds of kilos of cocaine arriving through Haiti. One of our informants owned a coastal freighter—*Dieu Plus Grand*—that regularly hauled both legitimate and illegitimate cargo coming from the Caribbean country. He tipped us off that he was moving nearly 500 kilos of cocaine into the cargo piers in downtown Miami. We found the dope packed in cartons of vegetable oil and stashed in the freighter's forward ballast tanks, but we left it alone, waiting for the smugglers to unload the vessel. With help from our counterparts in Customs, we kept the freighter under continuous surveillance until we saw a group of men transferring boxes from the vessel to a van idling on the dock, late on a Saturday night. We followed the van to a duplex in northwest Miami, where two of the men unloaded some of the boxes and carried them into the house. The group changed drivers and a short time later the van drove off, which meant we were forced to split our surveillance team to cover the duplex and the moving van. When the van stopped at a Miami apartment building and more guys emerged to unload boxes, we moved in for the arrests. We apprehended seven smugglers and seized 491 kilos of coke. Among the seven men we arrested were Jean Joseph Deeb, a Haitian, and his accomplice Serge Biamby, the brother of Haitian brigadier general Philippe Biamby. Three years later, the general, who was chief of the army, would help lead the military coup that would oust President Jean-Bertrand Aristide from power.

When we arrested Biamby, he had a lot of information in his briefcase on HIV, and we later found out he was in the advanced stages of the disease. Still, he agreed to testify against Deeb in exchange for a reduced sentence. Deeb had been released on bond, but became a fugitive. He was later arrested in the Dominican Republic.

Accompanied by assistant U.S. attorney Ken Noto, I flew to Atlanta, where Biamby was being held in federal custody. Our plan was to debrief him, but we were shocked when he arrived at the federal courthouse; his face was gaunt, and his arms were covered in open sores. The federal marshals were angry at us because they had to transfer Biamby to the courthouse in such an obviously advanced stage of the disease. In the late 1980s, HIV still carried a huge stigma, and many felt that exposure to anyone with HIV could result in instant infection.

Biamby was so ill that we were unable to debrief him, and I flew back to Atlanta two months later to conduct the interview at the federal penitentiary where he was held. Deeb's attorney was also present for the debriefing, which we videotaped. Biamby was so sick that he was eventually released from prison and died a short time later. When Deeb finally went to trial in 1990, Biamby's videotaped testimony was entered into the record—the first time this had ever been done in federal court. As a result, Deeb was convicted and sent to prison.

I never knew where the death threat came from. Someone with a Caribbean accent called the DEA Miami office during Deeb's trial and said that a group of Haitians planned to kill me at the federal courthouse in Miami. I admit that as a new agent up against some of the biggest organized crime syndicates in the world, I was a little rattled.

I arrived in Florida just as law enforcement was discovering the enormity of the Colombian cocaine cartels. As Connie and I were settling into our new home in Plantation, the U.S. attorney's case against Colombian drug smuggler Carlos Lehder Rivas was going to trial, providing a glimpse into the power and scope of the Medellín Cartel for the first time.

Lehder, a former car thief, was charged in a 1981

indictment with smuggling 3.3 tons of cocaine from Colombia to Norman's Cay in the Bahamas and then shipping it to airports in the southern United States. Lehder, who counted the unlikely triumvirate of Adolf Hitler, Che Guevara, and John Lennon as his heroes, had dreamed of becoming the king of cocaine transportation. His plans for an elaborate cocaine distribution network were hatched while serving a two-year marijuana-smuggling sentence in federal prison in Connecticut in 1974. While in detention, he met George Jung, a fellow prisoner and small-time marijuana smuggler who would become instrumental in helping Lehder set up his Bahamian empire after the two were released from prison.

At first, the two business partners recruited young women to spirit a few kilos of cocaine at a time out of Colombia in their suitcases. They soon realized they could transport hundreds of kilos at once by using small aircraft and turning the Bahamas into a transshipment and refueling point for cocaine into Miami.

By the late 1970s, Lehder was well on his way to setting up his vast distribution network on Norman's Cay, a tiny island some two hundred miles from South Florida that featured a marina, a yacht club, and a few dozen private beach houses. Lehder set about buying up the homes so that he could be master of the entire island. He built a 3,000-foot runway guarded by attack dogs and a private army. Lehder grew so wealthy that he offered to pay Colombia's multibillion-dollar external debt more than once.

Just before his capture in 1987, the debt hovered at about $14.6 billion.

Lehder's downfall began after a bombshell news report exposed how he had bribed local officials, including Lynden Pindling, the prime minister of the Bahamas. Suddenly, Lehder was on the run and out of cash, unable to return to the Bahamas after the government froze all his assets. In 1987, Lehder was found hiding in Colombia after neighbors ratted him out to police, and he was extradited to the United States several months before I arrived in Miami.

By November, he was just five hours away in Jacksonville, standing trial in a frigid federal courtroom, where the air-conditioning always made you feel like you were stuck in a supermarket meat locker. Four years later, Lehder would cooperate with the U.S. government and provide evidence and testimony against former Panamanian leader Manuel Noriega and others who were involved with the importation and distribution of cocaine to the United States. As part of his plea agreement, the U.S. government agreed to relocate his immediate family in the United States to protect them from being murdered by other drug traffickers. That duty was eventually assigned to me. But I am getting ahead of myself. We didn't really cross paths until I was assigned to Colombia in 1991.

While I was still in Miami, Lehder was convicted on eleven counts of drug smuggling and sentenced to life without parole, plus an additional 135 years—a development that was watched closely by Colombia's powerful cartel leaders thousands of miles away. Extradition to the United States was a sore point for them, and they had already begun to wage a bloody civil war in Colombia to pressure the government to change the law.

Like everyone else in the DEA Miami office, I read the classified memos on Lehder and followed the trial, but I could never have imagined how a ruling by a U.S. federal judge would influence the next few years of Colombian history and dominate my own life.

JAVIER

I couldn't wait to work as an undercover narc.

I was determined to make a big impression, to hit the ground running when I arrived in Austin as a newly minted DEA special agent in 1984. I hung out at the seediest bars trolling for drug dealers and hoping that I could turn them into informants. I pored over DEA reports about the manufacturing of methamphetamine and the steady growth of cocaine trafficking by Mexican cartels that were beginning to use the Texas capital as a major distribution center.

I was pretty eager to impress in those days—always volunteering for crazy jobs and taking a lot of chances. In many instances, I was reckless.

And it was that sense of abandon coupled with too much ambition that nearly cost me my job. It very nearly got me killed.

I was the only Hispanic in the office, so I was being used for a lot of undercover work. I was young and single, so I had no problem working round the clock. The Austin Police Department's narcotics unit started calling me to work weekends and nights to help them out with their drug investigations.

After work, I hit the bars on the gritty east side of Austin. I drank pretty hard and regularly got into situations I would rather forget. One night after too many beers and whiskey shots, I picked a fight with the guy sitting beside me. I was saved by Joe Regalado, a local cop who would become my best friend. Joe was a stocky, good-looking guy with a mustache and black curly hair. Like me, he was twenty-eight, single, and Hispanic. We had pretty much the same personalities, and we liked to run clubs in Austin, drink beer, and go after girls. We also ended up doing a lot of undercover work together. He was street-smart because he grew up dirt-poor in east Austin at a time when it was mostly populated by drug addicts and prostitutes. His father died at an early age, and his mother scraped by raising the family. Joe had eight other siblings, and after a few years in Austin, I got to know the entire family pretty well. Almost immediately after he started working with Austin PD, he bought his mother a house. It was old and pretty much falling apart, but we spent many happy times there, drinking beer and barbecuing. After the city built a new convention center next door, its value skyrocketed to nearly $2 million!

I got pretty close to him and Austin PD sergeant Lupe Trevino, a tough-talking cop with big ambitions. Lupe was a good-looking guy with a heavy black mustache. He seemed ancient to us because he was in his forties and the leader of one of Austin PD's narc squads. He was brash and cocky and pretty much hated by police hierarchy. We looked up to him because he knew the streets and he knew the crooks. In hindsight, I think he knew them too well.

Still, his guys loved him, even though he expected fierce loyalty and hard work. If they did a big drug bust, Lupe would celebrate by buying beer and sandwiches for the crew. Lupe was very ambitious, as he was always trying to outdo the other Austin PD narc squad, headed by his rival, Sergeant Roger Huckabee. Lupe would call me to assist them with drug investigations, and I learned a lot from him, even though I knew he had ulterior motives for bringing me onto his squad. The presence of a federal officer allowed him to operate outside Austin city limits. Not that I ever complained about that. I knew that it was also good for me because I got involved in a lot of cases and built up my stats. Lupe helped me become a bit of a star at the DEA.

But there was a lot of petty jealousy in law enforcement, and my relationship with Joe and Lupe didn't sit too well with many of the other cops in Austin. One time, Joe and

I were drinking at one of our regular hangouts when I got into a scuffle. Joe jumped the guy who pushed me, and the whole thing soon turned into a melee we never expected. The bartender panicked and called the cops. In the end, nobody got hurt and nothing was broken, but the responding Austin PD officer—a cop named Mark, who seemed to have it in for us—started to arrest us. We were hauled into police headquarters and sat fuming at the station house when Lupe arrived to bail us out. He was completely pissed and took us into a conference room to read us the riot act. He drove us home in silence. I worried I would be fired before I had even gotten the chance to prove myself and do real undercover work.

The next morning when I told my DEA boss, he laughed the whole thing off and told me to continue doing my job. But things didn't go quite so easily for Joe, who was suspended for two days. That was just crazy since I was the one who had started the fight. In fact, Lupe's response to the whole incident annoyed me to no end, since I always saw him cutting corners when we were on the job. I never saw him do anything illegal, but he was always looking out for himself and trying really hard to have the best stats in the police department. In hindsight, maybe that's why we got along so well. I was equally if not more ambitious. But there were limits to what I was willing to do, and I would never have treated a fellow officer the way Lupe treated Joe.

It wasn't until years later that I learned that Lupe appeared to have no such concerns.

In 2013, I would remember that crazy night of our arrest in Austin. This time it was my turn to arrest Lupe Trevino. I was working as the special agent in charge of the Houston field division, which oversees the Texas/Mexico border, and it was my job to haul in Lupe, who had run afoul of the law. By then, he was the Hidalgo County sheriff in McAllen, Texas, accused of taking illegal campaign cash from drug traffickers. His son Jonathan, whom Lupe always bragged to me about being a good undercover narc, was also arrested for shaking down drug dealers. He got seventeen years, and Lupe served five in prison.

I can't say I was surprised by Lupe's arrest. Like I said, he always played fast and loose with the rules. And in the mid-1980s, when I was trying to prove to my DEA masters that I was a rising star, some of Lupe's work ethic seemed to rub off on me.

At one of our regular watering holes in east Austin, I started talking to a tall, lanky, and very drunk drug dealer who pulled up to the stool next to mine. On the spot, I decided that I was going to use him to make my first big drug bust. Of course, I knew it was reckless because to initiate any DEA operation, an entire bureaucratic process needs to occur that begins with filing what always seemed to me countless reports. We were also required to set up backup—agents who would come to our defense if anything went wrong. But I'd been at the bar for a while and had had a few drinks, and this guy—he told me his name was Marvin—was boasting about his connections to the drug world. So without hesitation, I asked him if he had any connections for multi-ounce quantities of coke. His eyes lit up, and he said that he had a connection in Houston who could deliver on the drugs. Then he took out a gram of coke from his pocket and told me he was selling it for a hundred dollars. I had some cash in my pocket and took it off his hands. Then I shakily wrote my number down on a matchbook, squinting at the numerals to make sure I got them right, and asked him to get in touch. Marvin did not give me his phone number in return. I knew I was operating outside the DEA rule book, but if you want to know the truth, I really hate paperwork. Marvin presented me with an opportunity, and I was damned if I was going to let it slip by me because I was obliged to fill out a bunch of forms first.

Still, I knew I had broken the rules, and when I had time to sober up, I realized that I was in deep shit. I was still on probation at the DEA, and I was sure that my boss would suspend me after I told him what went down. The next day, I sheepishly told my boss what I had done. I got off with a stern warning, but a few months later, Marvin started calling me at home. (I had given him my home number because for the life of me I couldn't remember the secret undercover number we used at the DEA office! That's probably how drunk I was.) By then, I had pretty much forgotten about Marvin, but I called him back. He said he could get me as much coke as I wanted. At that time in Austin, coke was not so readily available, and even getting your hands on an ounce of the stuff was a big deal.

This time, I did things right. Like I said before, I'm not a paper guy, but I filled out the forms and opened a proper investigation into Marvin. Later, Joe and I met him under the guise of buying an ounce of coke. The price was $1,600. DEA surveillance agents provided backup as we waited for the target in the parking lot of a run-down housing complex in east Austin. Marvin showed up with another Hispanic guy named Pedro and sold us the coke. I immediately liked Pedro because he was soft-spoken and very respectful to me. We made plans to purchase a pound a week later—on the night before Christmas in 1985.

I always remember that particular drug bust because it occurred at Christmastime. That's when I started to get insistent calls from Pedro about the cocaine, and I started to become annoyed. The guys in my office were also annoyed because it meant we would probably have to do the arrests on Christmas Eve, when everyone wanted to get home early to be with their families. I tried to convince Pedro and Marvin to meet the following week, but Pedro told me it was urgent. If we waited, he would have to sell the coke to some other client. There was a great deal of demand in Austin, he said. We were under a lot of pressure at the DEA Austin bureau at the time because our stats were so low. With all this information weighing on me, I ignored the complaints of my fellow agents and went ahead to set up the bust for noon, Christmas Eve. That way, if everything went well, everyone could get home early to spend the holiday with their loved ones.

At high noon, we met in the same parking lot where our pre-surveillance guys were already in place. From their parked cars, they watched a man drive up to Pedro and Marvin and hand them what looked like a shoebox. It was only later that we found out that the courier was Pedro's brother, Juan. Our guys tracked him down in Houston and arrested him a few weeks later. Juan turned out to have a law enforcement day job; he was an active parole officer for the state of Texas.

When Pedro and Marvin handed us the pound of coke, I told them I was a DEA agent, and we arrested them on the spot as the parking lot began to fill up with local police and federal units in riot gear. We caused a lot of commotion, and people started pouring out of their apartments to have a look. Among the curious neighbors were Pedro's wife and three small children, who lived in the housing complex. When they saw their father in handcuffs, the little children began weeping and tried to help their dad.

The whole scene broke my heart. When I arrested Pedro, I searched his pockets as per DEA rules and found $3,000 in hundred-dollar bills. We both knew it was drug money, but as his kids were standing there in tears, he took me aside and asked me in Spanish if I could give his wife the money because it was all they had. And it was Christmas.

I knew that Pedro was going to jail and wouldn't be able to spend any time with his wife and children. And I knew that I was about to break DEA policy. What I should have done was seize the cash and include it as part of my report on the bust. Instead, I glanced around me to make sure none of the other officers in my group were watching. Then I clutched the rolled-up cash and stuck my hand in a pocket, and I headed in the direction of Pedro's wife. I pretended to interview her and casually slipped her the money, which she hid in a pants pocket.

No one ever found out what I did. I told only Joe Regalado, who has kept my secret all these years.

STEVE

On my first undercover operation with the DEA, I volunteered to pose as a deckhand on a boat. Not just any boat but a sleek, fifty-three-foot Hatteras Sportfish that the DEA had seized from other dopers. I'm not sure what possessed me to get involved, since I had never been on a boat in my life. I knew absolutely nothing about sailing. Just about the only thing I knew how to do was swim, and I was confident I could pull off a couple of miles in the ocean if something went terribly wrong on board. But I rationalized my complete inexperience as a minor inconvenience, and I wasn't going to let anything stop me from my life's dream of going undercover on a major drug bust!

As with all law enforcement jobs, the more progress the youngest agent makes on supervised cases, the more freedom and responsibility they have. With a bunch of successful cases under his or her belt, senior staff can then feel good in their decision to allow the junior agent to fly solo. But the smartest recruits know that they need to check their ideas and tactics with a mentor before taking any action.

Special Agent Gene Francar was an important influence on me. He was a heavyset man with an impossible baby face, and he was my first DEA partner. He wore guayaberas with polyester trousers and loafers, and he was one of the smartest people I had ever met. I valued his wisdom and experience so much that I pretty much ran everything by him. Gene knew more about distribution channels than anyone in the agency at a time when southern Florida was the primary entrance point into the United States for cocaine coming from Colombia.

When I arrived in Miami in November 1987, Gene was already working on a major case that targeted a group of Miami Cubans who were smuggling multi-hundred kilo loads of coke through the Caribbean into South Florida.

Gene had two confidential sources whom he had nicknamed Cheech and Chong. The first time I went out to meet them, I had visions of a rendezvous in a fancy restaurant or a swanky club. I also expected to meet two street-smart guys who would be dressed like Crockett and Tubbs from *Miami Vice*. I imagined we would all be driving unbelievably nice sports cars. Instead, I climbed into Gene's g-car, after he had cleared the passenger seat of food wrappers, clothes, and other accumulated junk. Then we drove to a Denny's near Miami International Airport, where I finally met the two men whom Gene had code-named after the pot-smoking comedy duo who were popular in the 1970s. Gene's "Cheech" was an older white guy, and his "Chong" was a middle-aged, slightly overweight Asian guy. Both had gray hair, and I imagined they were not so far off from relying on walkers to get by.

Cheech and Chong were experienced pilots who were rumored to have worked for the CIA in the past. They had an import-export business in the warehouse area adjacent to Miami International, and Gene had their office wired with hidden video and audio devices so that their meetings with the bad guys could be recorded. At that first meeting, Gene and the informants discussed the possibility of the delivery of five hundred kilograms of cocaine, coming from Cuba and landing in the United States. You could have knocked me over with a feather. Despite being on the job for a few months and participating in big drug seizures, the sheer volume was still staggering to me. But by now, I had already learned to keep a poker face to hide my surprise. When the meeting with Cheech and Chong ended and we were driving back to the office, Gene asked me my thoughts on what I'd just heard. I told Gene I thought the informants were full of crap. Being a professional, Gene asked why I thought that. I told him that I simply couldn't believe that anyone could deliver five hundred kilograms of coke in a single shipment.

"Where are you from again?" asked Gene, laughing.

Once I got involved in the case, I learned that Gene was directing Cheech and Chong to offer transportation— via boat or airplane—to move massive loads of coke through the Caribbean for the drug cartels. The Cuban case was an important priority.

At Gene's behest, Cheech and Chong conducted several meetings with the bad guys, who contracted them to move the coke from the Turks and Caicos to Miami via boat.

Our undercover boat had a living room with couches, chairs, tables, and lamps and was wired with hidden video and audio. Below the main seating area, there was a small kitchen and a refrigerator, a freezer, a small bathroom, and two tiny bunk rooms. There were sliding doors in the rooms, but they were quite small and rather claustrophobic.

On the outside areas of the boat, there was a primary area for fishing at the back, complete with a fishing chair strategically placed in the middle. A ladder connected you to the bridge, which contained the steering mechanism, radios, and radar units. The bridge was covered by a canvas canopy and surrounded by thick plastic sheets that could be zippered closed in bad weather.

At the front of the boat, there was a great deal of open space where you could lie quite comfortably on the deck, but the entire space was taken up with a Zodiac motorized rubber raft, which was our lifeline if the boat went down. We also used it to get to shore when the Hatteras was moored off the coast.

I was given a crash course in sailing from fellow agent John Sheridan, who knew his way around boats. The DEA had two special agents on board who were trained and certified by the U.S. Coast Guard as captains. Still, to look the part of an experienced deckhand, I let my beard grow and spent weeks working on my tan. But by the time we sailed, I still couldn't pull off the sun-weathered look of someone who had spent their whole life under the elements. I didn't care. This was the most exciting thing I had ever done in my professional life.

As was customary for these types of transportation services, the bad guys fronted the cooperating informants—Cheech and Chong—with $50,000 in cash to cover some of the expenses associated with getting the boat to Providenciales—Provo, for short—and to pay off the necessary officials to allow the load to go through. The typical transportation fee in those days was between $3,000 and $5,000 per kilo for this service. We were charging $3,500 per kilo, so our total transportation fee would have been $1.75 million. This is a great example of why so many people were willing to risk their freedom for money, right?

In early February 1988, we were finally ready to make the trip and were scheduled to sail from Fort Lauderdale to Provo—a distance of more than six hundred miles—to pick up the dope. But just as we were ready to sail, the bad guys stopped us because they didn't have everything ready at the Turks and Caicos end. We cooled our heels for two weeks in Miami until we finally got the green light to sail.

On our first day at sea, we made it as far as Treasure Cay in the Bahamas—189 miles from Fort Lauderdale—before hitting a reef. The crash bent one of the propellers on the boat, and as our vessel began to shake and shudder, the captains immediately cut the engines. After much discussion, the younger captain went into the water to examine the propellers and found that one of them was indeed bent. We couldn't use it because of the damage, but we still had one engine, so we made our way to Treasure Cay. It was our first day at sea, and I wasn't at all comfortable with the situation, but I was the new guy and decided to trust the captains.

A great deal of arguing ensued between the two captains, but on the following day, we sailed to Nassau. Using our boat's radios, they made arrangements for the DEA air wing to fly a new propeller to Nassau.

We were all at pretty close quarters, and for that reason, I got to know the two captains pretty well. They were complete opposites. The senior captain was older and had the ruddy look of someone who had spent most of his life in the sun and on open water. His boat shoes were well-worn, and he mostly dressed in faded T-shirts and shorts. He could easily pass for the owner of a charter fishing boat from a South Florida marina. His voice was gruff, and most of the time, he used foul language. The second captain was tall and blond, and he looked like someone who sailed luxury yachts for a living.

The two captains spoke in heated conversations. It

wasn't exactly arguing, just differences of opinion on how to sail the Hatteras. And they were never bashful about voicing their own views about how things should be done. But after a few days at sea, I have to say that I trusted the opinion of the older captain, although I preferred speaking to the younger one, only because the younger one was less gruff. But since I had no experience working on a boat, I really just kept my mouth shut and tried to learn from both of them.

In Nassau, we took delivery of the propeller that the DEA air wing had left at the marina. As luck would have it, there was a U.S. Navy submarine tender in the area, and two navy divers came over and replaced the propeller for us.

This was a real revelation for me. It was a great demonstration of cooperation between federal agencies, and it was an example of how much influence the DEA had. And at that moment, I finally saw just how important the so-called war on drugs really was. I couldn't get over the fact that the DEA and navy would commit such resources to complete an investigation. I was thoroughly impressed!

The following day, we set sail for our intended destination, Providenciales, on the Turks and Caicos Islands.

But the tension in the confined quarters on our boat was just getting worse. It was exacerbated by the repair to the damaged propeller, which put us behind schedule by two days, perhaps even three. The captains couldn't agree on the simplest things and were no doubt annoyed by the non-sailor among their number. Not only was I new to the ocean and this boat, I'd only been a DEA agent for less than a year. And then as the waves got bigger, we all got sick.

Although we were all pretty ill, I was able to recover faster, partly because I had had more time to rest than the captains had. Because we were so far behind schedule, we continued throughout the night toward our destination. I could tell that the captains were exhausted from being ill and forced to be awake for so long.

By the third day, the situation with the captains was pretty grim. I could see that they desperately needed some downtime and rest. I went up to the bridge and volunteered to help, telling them I would handle the boat during the night so that they could both get some sleep. We all decided I would watch the boat, and I was given a crash course in navigation, the radar, and radio systems. I was told not to touch anything on my watch. The boat was equipped with autopilot, so basically, they set the speed and course and told me to leave everything alone. My biggest responsibility was to check the radar several times each hour to make sure there were no other vessels in our path that we might hit. And then off they went to sleep.

It was a simple enough assignment that even a landlubber like me could handle. My biggest challenge was staying awake throughout the night, but after several hours and multiple radar checks—the boat's radar scanned out to seventeen miles in all directions—my mind started to wander. Sleep-deprived, I started to become paranoid and panicked that we would collide with another vessel or hit a reef. I imagined other catastrophes. And if something did happen, we were seventeen miles away from any kind of help! What if we hit another reef and this time became food for the sharks that were just lurking under the water? Just then, I heard them—the sound of hundreds of fish jumping up into the boat. It was then that I realized how vast the ocean was, and I started to worry even more.

Despite my fatigue, I managed to follow instructions and keep the boat on course. When the captains awoke several hours later, the older one rushed upstairs and asked me what had happened. He acted as if something was wrong. We were still on course, and I really hadn't touched anything, but he began accusing me of changing our speed and heading. Although I tried to explain that nothing had changed, he didn't want to hear it and told me to get off the bridge. Needless to say, this did nothing to improve the tension and stress that we all felt.

By the fifth day on the water with the seasick captains at the helm, I also got sick but managed to keep it together, although it did nothing to temper the tension that developed between me and the boat captains.

But as we got closer to Provo and I started to feel less queasy, I decided to try to make peace. While both captains were busy with navigation, I grilled us all some steaks, baked some potatoes, sautéed some mushrooms, and surprised them with a decent meal. While I thought this was a great idea, neither of the captains were happy with me. They didn't say much other than they thought it certainly wasn't the right time for this steak dinner, when we still hadn't reached our destination. Obviously, their attitudes didn't sit well with me, and to be frank, I was more than ready to get off the damn boat and get away from these two guys.

When we reached Provo, I asked them to take me to shore in the Zodiac. I had packed my bag the night before our arrival and wanted nothing more to do with them. I met up with Gene and several other Group 10 agents who had flown in ahead of us to participate in the operation. That night, I slept on the floor of Gene's hotel room because I didn't want to get back on the boat with the feuding officers.

We waited by the pool of Gene's hotel in Provo, but because we were late arriving in Provo, the bad guys decided to postpone the delivery for another couple of weeks. We all returned to Miami, and the two captains stayed with the boat while we rescheduled the delivery. I was perfectly happy to be returning to Miami. I couldn't imagine staying with those two in tight quarters ever again. When everything was set up again, we flew back to the Turks and Caicos.

A few days after landing on the island, I drove in a battered pickup truck with the boat captains and a local police officer (we coordinated everything with the Turks and

Caicos police) to the Provo airport to finally await the
shipment of cocaine. We hid at the far end of the runway,
on a small road, away from the airport terminal. Eventually, a twin-engine plane landed and taxied to the far end
of the runway where we were waiting. At that point, I still
had no idea where the plane had taken off from, but I pre-
sumed it was Cuba. As the plane turned away from us
and headed in the direction of the terminal, the door
opened, and someone threw down several green duffel
bags. I got a glimpse of the two pilots, who were Hispanic
and looked like they were in their twenties. They wore
guayaberas and loose-fitting trousers. The plane looked
like any other aircraft, except that all the seats were removed to give them more storage space for the coke and
to reduce the weight of the aircraft. This was common with
drug dealers, and it was a significant indicator for us to
know that a plane was most likely being used for smuggling
purposes.

We had arranged to roll out to the end of the runway
when the plane landed. Once it got to the end of the runway and a nearby hangar, it would turn around, and we—
the two DEA boat captains, a local police officer, and
myself—would emerge from hiding to collect the coke. We
had additional personnel located a short distance away in
case assistance was required.

The pilots didn't even acknowledge us, and we didn't
speak to them. The unloading process took less than a

minute. After all the bags were off-loaded, the plane proceeded to the terminal area, where it refueled and departed
a short time later, presumably for Cuba.

Once we'd collected all the duffel bags, we took them
to a safe area to examine their contents. We weighed the
baggage and verified that we were dealing with four hundred kilos of coke.

Once we tested the dope to make sure it was genuine,
a DEA airplane arrived, and we loaded the duffel bags
onto the aircraft to fly the dope to Miami. I stayed with
the duffel bags during the entire time to maintain our
chain of custody. There was so much coke on the plane that
there was almost no place for me to sit. I had to crawl on
top of the duffel bags and nestle among them all the way
back to Opa-Locka Airport in Miami. On the ground in
Florida, other Group 10 DEA agents were waiting to assist in the transport of the coke to our secure storage facility, where we bagged and tagged the drugs as evidence.

While the coke was safely in DEA custody, Cheech
and Chong lied to the bad guys, telling them that they had
hidden the coke in secret compartments of the Hatteras
Sportfish and that the shipment could take as long as two
weeks to arrive in Miami, depending on weather conditions and the location of patrol boats. The Hatteras still
had to appear to be a fishing vessel out on an extended
fishing excursion.

Two weeks later, Cheech and Chong called the Cubans

and reported that the load had arrived safely in Miami and was ready for delivery. We conducted an "international controlled delivery" of the coke to the bad guys in Miami and surveilled the drop-off point until we felt the time was right and we could arrest the bad guys with the coke.

While I was escorting the cocaine back to South Florida, Gene, along with officials from the U.S. Attorney's Office in Miami, was busy preparing an indictment against Raúl Castro, Cuban vice president and the younger brother of Cuban dictator Fidel Castro. They believed that he was the mastermind behind the shipment of the cocaine load. Later, I learned that the plane transporting the four hundred kilos had indeed originated in Cuba. The pilots flew to Provo, dropped off the drugs, and returned to the island. After it took off from Provo, the plane was tracked by a U.S. military AWACS plane all the way back to the Communist island.

But just as the indictment was about to be presented to a grand jury, our first-line supervisor surprisingly ordered us to stand down.

Stop pursuing Raúl Castro, he said, offering no further explanation.

Months later, Cuban military man and highly decorated revolutionary hero General Arnaldo Ochoa Sánchez was accused of having taken bribes from Colombian drug dealers to transport thousands of kilos of cocaine through Cuba, a place that Fidel Castro had proudly

118 STEVE MURPHY and JAVIER F. PEÑA

proclaimed to be drug-free since the 1959 revolution. In what many Cuban experts characterized as a show trial, Ochoa and thirteen other codefendants were tried before an extraordinary military tribunal and convicted of conspiring to ship tons of cocaine and marijuana to the United States. Testimony at trial seemed to confirm what we already knew at the DEA—that the Cuban authorities had allowed their island to be used as a transshipment point for cocaine destined for the United States. But it was the Castro brothers who were in bed with the cartels. Even if Ochoa had been involved, he would have participated at the direction of the supreme leaders of the revolution. No one in Cuba acted without the knowledge of the Comandante.

Nevertheless, Ochoa was sentenced to death. At dawn on July 13, 1989, the highly popular general and three other Cuban army officials were executed by firing squad at the Tropas Especiales military base in Havana.

I never found out if Ochoa's trial and execution was precipitated by our seizure of the cocaine in the Turks and Caicos, but Ochoa proved to be a convenient scapegoat for the Communist rulers.

It wasn't until years later that I learned the truth.

Our orders to scupper the Castro indictment came not from the Department of Justice but straight from the White House. President Reagan himself. Needless to say, we were all stunned.

But making sense of the geopolitical realities of the relationship between the United States and Cuba was beyond our pay grade, and in the end, we knew just to leave it alone.

JAVIER

Sometimes, I was so scared on the job that I prayed. I've never been a good Catholic, but I still remember the prayers that my mother and grandmother used to recite. And I no longer remember how many times I prayed to the Virgin or repeated the Lord's Prayer at the various moments in my career when I really thought I was going to die.

I guess the first time that I felt that clammy sense of dread was in the mid-1980s when I was still in Austin. The senior agents in the office set me up on an undercover operation in which I was to play the role of the Mexican owner of five hundred pounds of marijuana. My assignment was to negotiate with a group of bad-guy distributors and lure them into a trap. We had spent a lot of time conducting negotiations over drinks at Austin strip clubs before I was scheduled to make the drop-off with a pilot who was acting as an informant. He was nice enough, but he had what seemed to me a tiny one-engine plane that looked like it was held together with masking tape.

After a great deal of paperwork—the dreaded paperwork!—and red tape, we got permission from DEA headquarters in Washington to load the five hundred pounds of grass—which came from several of our own seizures in Austin—onto the plane. The marijuana was in burlap sacks that we stuffed into the baggage compartment of the plane, which was parked at a small airfield outside Austin. To make everything look as real as possible, our informant, an older white guy who worked as a smuggler, said he would buzz the airstrip and tell them to roll out toilet paper strips onto the makeshift runway—the traffickers' signal that it was okay to land.

I was already nervous even before climbing into the impossibly small plane that didn't seem at all stable to me. Our informant, who was also the pilot, told me the plane was safe and that it had carried him through numerous smuggling operations. Crammed into the passenger seat, I held my breath as the aircraft lurched off the runway and seemed to hover over patches of dry brush at the western edge of Austin. The plane rattled and spurted as it headed for a very short, dust-covered runway with its white toilet-paper markers. I was sweating profusely and gripping the edge of my seat as the pilot began the approach. But as soon as he got close, he pulled the plane back up and abruptly took off again. The sudden movement and the resulting turbulence sent me into a sudden panic, and that's when I was sure I was going to die. Sensing my fear, the pilot tried to reassure me. He explained that it was a maneuver meant to indicate that it was safe to land. As we got closer to the ground, the small plane jerked from side to side, bouncing off the dirt before it touched down. It finally came to a stop, which I thought it would never do. I said another prayer, thanking the good lord and the Virgin of Guadalupe that we had not crashed.

On the ground, I saw a group of men standing next to their cars on the edge of the strip. At first, I recognized no one, and the happiness of finally having my feet firmly on the ground quickly dissipated as I worried that maybe I had landed in a trap. But relief set in as I recognized the two undercover agents who rushed to the plane, opened the baggage compartment, and began unloading the burlap sacks filled with marijuana.

I walked slowly on shaky legs to a shack at the edge of the runway, where a black Suburban and a dark gray pickup were idling. The main undercover agent and the real crook, who was the buyer of the marijuana, started coming fast at me, and the show was beginning. I spoke in broken English and shook the hand of a crook, who told me his name was Steve. He was very courteous and was treating me with respect because he thought I was the owner of the dope. Steve was accompanied by an undercover agent named Larry. Once pleasantries were exchanged, we got into the Suburban and left the runway. The marijuana had been stacked into the pickup truck, which looked like every other pickup truck in Texas. You could never imagine that there were five hundred pounds of grass inside.

On the road to Austin, Larry kept up the façade. He talked Steve's ear off about how this would be the beginning of a beautiful friendship, that he knew lots of potential buyers who needed large quantities of marijuana on a regular basis. He kept repeating to Steve that I was the undisputed king of marijuana and I could deliver it by the ton. I did my best to convince everyone that I could deliver. As long as they were paying cash.

Steve had already given us about $200,000 in up-front cash but still owed us another $700,000, which he had promised to pay upon delivery. Steve told us that he had other buyers with the cash scattered throughout south Austin. Our first stop was a ramshackle hotel, where we began unloading the marijuana. As Steve began to count out $100,000, we moved to arrest him. He tried to run, but we captured him a few minutes later. Some of the other buyers who were waiting to buy their dope at the hotel saw the arrest and began to run. As two of the buyers got into their cars, I snapped into action and got into a rental car—a Lincoln Continental that belonged to one of the crooks. It was like a car chase from the movies. At one point, I headed the wrong way down a one-way street, my adrenaline pumping, furiously honking for people to jump out of the way.

I came to a screeching halt in front of one of the bad guys, who I boxed into a corner. I flew out the door of the Lincoln and cuffed him in a few seconds flat. There were five arrests in total that day, and we seized more than $800,000 in cash.

Steve was the only one to go to trial, and he hired one of the best civil rights lawyers in the country to defend him. Tony Serra, a self-described hippie lawyer from San Francisco who wore his long white hair in a signature ponytail, had already defended everyone from the Hells Angels to members of the Symbionese Liberation Army, the group that kidnapped heiress Patty Hearst in 1974. His biggest and most politically charged case was his defense of Black Panther Huey Newton. In 1970, Serra successfully appealed Newton's manslaughter conviction for shooting an Oakland cop who had pulled him over in a traffic stop three years earlier.

But in the mainly white, Baptist city of Waco, Texas, which is home to the ultraconservative Baylor University, Serra was more of a liability than an asset in his defense of the drug dealer. On top of that, he was extremely arrogant during the court proceedings. At the time, the assistant U.S. attorney and the DEA had offered Serra's client Steve very good terms if he was willing to enter into a plea deal. Serra refused, and the case went before Judge Walter Smith, who would later gain national notoriety when he presided over the trial of the Branch Davidians who had escaped the bloody 1993 standoff with federal agents that left eighty members of the apocalyptic cult, including twenty children, dead. During Steve's trial, I took the witness stand and relived the conversation that Steve and I had had in the Suburban about supplying him with large quantities of marijuana. The only question I remember being asked by Serra was whether I lied as part of my job. I remember answering him that I only lied while working in an undercover capacity. Maybe my answer stumped him because there were no further questions from Serra.

Steve was found guilty and sentenced to thirty years in jail.

STEVE

Sweat dripping down my face, I shouldered the Colt 9 mm submachine gun and nudged the bullet-riddled bedroom door slightly open, warning my DEA colleagues to hang back.

It was high summer in the Miami suburbs, and our hiding place in the master bedroom of a low-rent house in Hialeah had just been discovered. My partner Kevin Stephens, a fellow DEA agent and former Marine from Indiana, had just been shot twice in the arm by one of our targets—a Cuban cocaine dealer who had gone on a shooting rampage when our buy-bust scheme turned deadly.

I'd heard a commotion in the living room of the house. As I peeked out the bedroom door, I saw that the two bad guys were holding handguns, and our undercover agent and the informant were lying on the living room floor begging for their lives. I closed the door and radioed our two backup teams for assistance. As Kevin opened the bedroom door, one of the bad guys was opening the same door from the outside. Kevin yelled, "Police!" and the bad guys started shooting at Kevin with pistols. Kevin managed to fire a few rounds from his 9 mm pistol before being hit twice in the right arm. As he fell backward, Kevin managed to slam the door shut!

Now with the sweat pooling on my face and my hands sticky with Kevin's blood, I pointed the machine gun in the direction of the suspects in the living room. Out of the corner of my eye, I could see our confidential source trying to hold himself upright, thick rivulets of blood coursing down his fingers as he clutched his throat in an effort to stem the blood that was spurting out in all directions. The CS had been shot with a round from the second bad guy's .357-caliber revolver while escaping out the front door. Pete, the undercover agent, was on the floor yelling for someone to get help for our source.

How did it all go wrong?

We all thought it would be a quick undercover deal, and on the surface, it seemed pretty simple: Show up at the house we had rented in a blue-collar neighborhood for the buy-bust, offer the crooks a bunch of cash, and while they are counting the money, arrest them and seize the "package"—seventeen kilos of cocaine, valued at $26,000 per kilo.

Easy, right?

That stupid thought raced through my mind when our hastily planned buy-bust turned into a bloodbath.

It was 1989, two years into my assignment with Group

10, the Caribbean Enforcement Group. Our specialty had been those big-time seizures involving hundreds of kilos of cocaine making their way to the port of Miami from Medellín by way of tiny Caribbean islands like Haiti and Cuba and, most memorably for me, the Turks and Caicos.

So conducting a small operation involving the seizure of only seventeen "keys" was in no way considered a significant event. My partners, Pete, Lynn, and Kevin, looked upon it as more of a way to get out of the office for an afternoon and have a little fun with a case that didn't require a lot of investigative preparation.

Kevin and I had worked difficult situations in the past. We were both young agents, willing to take on any assignment, eager to advance our careers. A year before the ill-fated Hialeah bust, we worked on a "blue on blue" assignment—a potentially deadly situation in which the bad guy we were after was an undercover law enforcement officer looking to identify the cocaine traffickers, build a case on them, and have the traffickers show up with the cash to purchase the cocaine. The undercover cops or federal agents would then arrest the trafficker and seize the money for themselves.

In the late 1980s, during the worst of the drug violence, South Florida was pretty much crawling with undercover law enforcement personnel from every federal agency. There were also undercover local cops. They all carried weapons, were pretty well trained, and were all trying to outdo one another. No one ever wore a uniform; they were all in plain clothes.

In late 1988, a year before we found ourselves in an impossible situation at the ramshackle Hialeah house, Kevin and I interviewed a CS who told us he'd met a cocaine distributor who was in the market to sell multi-kilogram quantities of cocaine. We debriefed the CS and obtained as much information as we could. Even though we knew little about our potential targets, we were eager young agents and felt that with our Miami senior agent Gene Francar's help, we had enough information to set up a bust.

Based on Gene's advice, we instructed the CS to meet the bad guys at the Denny's near Miami International Airport. For some reason, that particular restaurant was a popular rendezvous spot for traffickers, perhaps because of its anonymity and proximity to the airport. The parking lot across the street from the restaurant would give us and our surveillance units the opportunity to see who the CS met with and what types of cars they were driving. And if everything worked out as planned, we would follow the bad guys to learn more about where they lived and the places they frequented.

Kevin and I arrived with the entire surveillance team and took our places in the parking lot across the street from the Denny's. And we waited. I was driving an old, beat-up Oldsmobile with tinted windows, which wasn't so uncommon in South Florida, where most vehicles had blacked-out windows.

I pulled into the lot, positioning myself so that I could have a good look at the front door of the restaurant. I parked next to a pickup truck, also with blacked-out windows. The restaurant was to my east, and the truck was to my west.

Just before we were ready to send the CS into the restaurant for the meeting, the truck parked next to me started its engine, and I sat up with a jolt. In addition to watching the front door of Denny's, I was also watching other vehicles in the area, but I hadn't seen any movement in the truck and assumed it was unoccupied. Just then, the truck pulled out of its parking space and repositioned itself between me and the front door. I could no longer see the Denny's. But no one got out of the truck.

That's when it hit me that something was very wrong, and I realized with a start that while we were watching for the bad guys, they were probably doing their own surveillance. They were watching us!

Was this a hit team poised to ambush us or our own CS? Maybe this was a jealous husband or boyfriend spying on his wife or girlfriend?

I contacted Gene for advice, and we made the decision to approach the truck in the parking lot. We needed to know who was inside—a potentially deadly situation. Kevin and I, along with other surveillance agents, drove to a nearby lot and strapped on our raid gear—bulletproof vests, gun belts, and raid jackets—that we always carried in the trunk. We got into our undercover cars and drove back to the lot in front of the Denny's. Based on our plan, three of our cars pulled into the lot together and stopped in front of the truck. Other surveillance units screeched into positions flanking the truck. We turned on our flashing blue lights and got out with our weapons drawn. We identified ourselves as police and ordered the occupants of the truck to step out. The doors of the truck opened slowly, and we saw hands go up in surrender on both sides of the truck. They were holding police badges.

Our "bad guys" turned out to be undercover narcotics officers from the Hialeah Police Department. They were working their own investigation based on information from one of their informants. There was so much competition between agencies, with many officers and special agents becoming territorial about their cases. On top of that, they wanted to keep their cases secret from other law enforcement personnel so that they would get the credit in the end. Here was a "blue on blue" incident, but one that turned out with a happy ending. Needless to say, we were very disappointed with the outcome of this potential investigation. It is very painful and aggravating to work months on a single case only to have someone else's case take precedence over your own. We hadn't caught any bad guys, but we all breathed a huge sigh of relief that no one was hurt.

Kevin and I were lucky that day, but unfortunately, our luck didn't last. During the tense moments of the Hialeah bust, I glanced at my hands, stained copper with Kevin's blood, and I thought we were both going to die.

How had we found ourselves in such an impossible situation? What had we done so wrong?

Our confidential source was a short, stocky Cuban-American who had been an informant for the DEA for nearly fifteen years in Miami. I don't think he was ever a drug dealer, but I don't know. We never fully trusted these people. The CS didn't drive fancy cars or dress in flashy clothes. He liked moving around in the shadowy under-world of the cocaine dealers where he could blend in, but he was involved with lower-level dealers—people who could move maybe fifty kilos of coke or fewer. It may sound funny that someone who could move fifty keys would be considered a lower-level dealer, but again, there was so much coke flowing through South Florida during the late 1980s that it was impossible to keep up.

The CS arranged the meeting with the two suspects at the house on a Thursday afternoon. But when the musta-chioed, guayabera-clad suspects arrived, they refused to get out of their car.

"Something doesn't seem right," said one of the suspects after he drove around the neighborhood—a collection of sad stucco houses with bars on their windows and bare patches of lawn facing a concrete wall—in a hasty effort at reconnaissance.

Pete and the CS shrugged and arranged to meet them the next day.

Friday dawned humid and stifling—a typical summer day in South Florida. By the middle of the afternoon, when we had arranged to meet the bad guys, the smog and the intense heat made it difficult to breathe. In the living room of the bungalow, which reeked of mold, Pete and the CS pretended to examine the two kilos of cocaine that the suspects had brought as a sample. The suspects said they would bring the other fifteen kilos when they saw the cash. When Pete and the CS told them that they didn't have the entire amount—more than $400,000—one of them whipped out a .45 semiautomatic pistol and ordered them to the floor.

Once we heard Pete and the CS yelling, we knew that the situation had taken a very dangerous turn. As I radioed our team for backup, Kevin opened the door and quickly became involved in a close-quarter firefight. When Kevin fell to the ground, he landed in front of me. I grabbed a pillow and placed it on his two wounds, using pressure to stem the bleeding. While I was making sure that Kevin was stable, one of the suspects unleashed a torrent of bullets, continuing to shoot through the closed bedroom door until he ran out of ammunition. Lynn, a tall former banker from North Carolina (the DEA always had an eclectic mix of people!), returned fire through the closed door. When the shooting stopped, there were twenty-three bullet holes in the bedroom door.

As it turned out, as soon as I got to the living room, my submachine gun poised on my shoulder, prepared to engage in a second firefight, the bad guys dropped out of sight. One of the suspects—the mastermind of the operation—sped away in a car driven by a third suspect, who was waiting in the driveway. When I saw the second suspect trying to limp away, I ordered him to stop. Later, we found out that suspect number two had just been diagnosed with HIV, and the disease had affected his mobility, which was why he moved with difficulty. He had already dropped his revolver on the sidewalk. The outside surveillance agents arrested him when he left the house. The driver of the car was picked up later that night in Miramar, a city in nearby Broward County, and the suspect who shot Kevin during the first gun battle surrendered to police three weeks later in New York City.

Outside the stucco cottage in Hialeah, a helicopter was preparing to land to take the CS and Kevin to Jackson Memorial Hospital trauma center in Miami. Kevin was rushed into lifesaving surgery, but the CS, who was almost completely covered in blood, died just as the helicopter landed at the hospital.

We later learned that the drug dealers had been planning to rip us off all along. They didn't have the seventeen keys they promised; they were just planning to steal the cash.

During my entire career with the DEA, I would remember the important lessons of that buy-bust gone bad.

Lesson number one is this: There is no such thing as

honor among thieves. Lesson number two: No drug deal should ever be considered "routine."

JAVIER

I was a big fan of a particular Tejano superstar who could really belt out a song. So it was a real bummer when I found myself slapping a pair of handcuffs around his wrists.

I was stunned! He was a fixture in my home, his melancholy tunes beloved by most of the people I knew in South Texas, especially my grandmother.

It was one of the oddest coincidences of my life, really, when I found myself in the back seat of a Lincoln Continental Mark IV filled with boxes of his CDs. Odder still was that the heavyset driver with the droopy mustache was none other than the legend himself!

I was working undercover on a meth bust that my buddy Joe Regalado at Austin PD had started investigating. In the mid-1980s, meth was a big problem in Austin, with dozens of meth labs scattered in impoverished neighborhoods throughout the city. We always looked for the telltale signs of trash receptacles filled with empty cans of paint thinner and battery acid, and burned patches of lawn outside the home labs. Meth makers usually dumped their excess chemicals outside decrepit houses in impoverished neighborhoods. Inside, we looked for glass cookware on the stove, stained with powdery residue.

Methamphetamine in crystal or powdered form is one of the most highly addictive drugs. Like cocaine, it attacks the central nervous system and can be snorted, injected, or swallowed. It immediately affects the dopamine levels in the brain, heightening pleasure but also putting the user at serious risk of death because of the hazardous chemicals that are used in its production. Unlike cocaine, meth is man-made and fairly cheap to produce.

I had an informant who worked at an Austin "chemical house"—a fat, middle-aged Hispanic man named Johnny. The chemical house was in a bad area of town in east Austin where a lot of Hispanic traffickers lived. When you walked into the warehouse, there was a long counter that prevented access to the back of the building. Customers would place their orders with Johnny, who would bring the chemicals up to the counter.

The chemical house was located in an old, whitewashed cement warehouse surrounded by trees in a residential neighborhood of ramshackle houses. The trees were good cover for surveillance, and sometimes, I would sit in my car for hours, hidden behind a clump of green to watch who came in and out of the building. I worked a lot of meth cases just by following the customers of the chemical house. Before I started with the DEA, I had never heard of a chemical house, but I soon found out that it was a legitimate business that sold industrial chemicals like ether, sodium, ammonia, and other types of cleaning solvents and chemical glassware such as beakers. They also sold phenylacetone, more commonly known as P2P, the main ingredient in the manufacture of meth. If someone ordered it, we knew that they were probably using it to make the drug in a basement lab.

Once Johnny became my informant, he told me that the owners—a father-and-son team—made a lot of money. They had their own company truck with a logo and delivered large orders to local businesses in fifty-five-gallon drums. But there were problems with the enterprise. The father was getting old and losing his grip on the business, and the son was taking advantage of his elderly father and running a crooked company. Edgar, the son, was middle-aged and lanky and very white, and he stood out in a neighborhood that was mostly black and Hispanic. According to Johnny, Edgar was also stealing money from the company and selling chemicals to known drug traffickers to support a lavish lifestyle. Edgar knew me and was very cooperative when I asked him questions about the business. He told me about the company's legitimate customers but denied that he ever did business with crooks. He never suspected that I had recruited Johnny as my informant.

Of course, Johnny knew what his bosses were up to, selling glassware and meth-producing chemicals to the bad guys, which was why Johnny was more than happy to give me information just in case we locked up his bosses. It was his insurance policy so that he wouldn't end up in jail if we ever raided the warehouse.

On top of that, I paid Johnny every time he gave us a

tip. He called me whenever a crook came in to buy a particularly large quantity of chemicals. It happened a lot, and
Johnny would call me as the crooks were at the counter
paying for their haul. I would drop whatever I was doing
and rush over because the DEA office was close to the
chemical house.

I remember one time Johnny tipped me off to a customer who looked like he was pretty legit. He was white,
tall, and well-dressed, and when we followed him home,
we saw that he lived in a big house in an exclusive Austin
neighborhood and ran a string of legitimate businesses in
the city. But he came off immediately as suspicious because
he ordered a fifty-five-gallon barrel of P2P. We watched
him come to the warehouse and saw Johnny use a forklift
to place the barrel in his pickup truck. We followed the
buyer to a professional trucking carrier company and
traced the delivery to Waco. Later, we arrested him and
were able to prove that he was aiding other meth traffickers and had facilitated other chemical deliveries to the
bad guys. His case took a long time to wind its way
through the courts, and I was already in Colombia by the
time he was convicted. But in the end, he went to jail and
lost everything, including his big house.

On another occasion, Johnny called me to say that his
bosses had just purchased hundreds of glass beakers and
pots to cook meth. The glassware, which the owners of the
chemical company had bought at a government auction,
still had the DEA evidence stickers on them. I couldn't

believe what I was seeing! Our people had seized the drug-making paraphernalia that they had gotten off the streets only to be put back on the streets by our own government! Had we not seized the glassware, the crooks would have resold everything to the traffickers. I made a huge stink with the U.S. Marshals, whose idea it was in the first place to auction off the glassware.

Back in 1985, when I started working the meth case with the Austin PD, meth was about $1,500 an ounce. Joe Regalado and I went undercover and started buying up meth from a guy who bragged that he could come up with huge quantities. We bought up a few ounces from the same trafficker before we ordered up a pound of meth, which was going for about $20,000. The Austin PD didn't have that kind of money, so the DEA kicked it in, and we prepared to make an arrest, hoping that the trafficker would take us to meet his supplier.

The crook told us to meet him in a parking lot of an upscale diner on Austin's west side. Lupe Trevino, Joe's boss who was supervising the bust, specifically told us not to "trip." We were not allowed to go anywhere if we got inside the dealer's car. We were simply to give him the bust signal when we had the pound of meth in our hands, and Lupe would send backup to block the traffickers and move in for the arrest.

But things went immediately wrong when Joe and I drove into the restaurant parking lot and saw the bad guy motioning us to get into his car. I admired the Lincoln with the spare tire in the well of the trunk because in those days not many people had that car. As I made my way into the back seat with Joe, I pushed aside several boxes of the CDs out of my way to sit down.

We never noticed that the man whose picture was on the cover of the CDs was the driver of the car. In fact, we didn't even notice that there was a driver until the bad guy slipped into the passenger seat and the car suddenly jerked into reverse and took off. Joe and I panicked. We protested loudly that we did not feel safe driving to an unknown location. Just then, the trafficker pulled out a package from under the front seat and threw it at us. It looked like the pound of meth, and I quickly said that we needed to go back to the restaurant parking lot because I had left the cash in my car. The driver made a U-turn and we headed back, which was lucky because as soon as we had left, the surveillance units had lost us. I breathed a sigh of relief when I saw our guys milling in the parking lot. As the Lincoln came to a stop, I took off my cap, which was the signal for arrest, and Joe and I got out our guns and quickly arrested the two men. Backup police and DEA agents arrived as I was placing the cuffs on the driver. He never put up a fight and sheepishly admitted that he was the great Tejano legend. I was shocked and told him that he was beloved of my family in Laredo and Hebbronville. When my DEA boss sent the teletype to headquarters, he made a point of saying that we had arrested a famous Tejano artist.

The two men each did four years in prison. Before I arrested him and put on the cuffs, the legend took out a CD from one of the boxes in the back seat of the Lincoln. He took out a felt pen from his pocket and signed his autograph with a flourish.

STEVE

Shortly after the guy who shot up Kevin was arrested in New York City, the DEA sent me on a temporary duty assignment to get me out of Miami while Kevin recuperated. Kevin's full recovery lasted a year, but he eventually returned to full DEA duty. They sent me to the Bahamas for three months to work on Operation BAT. This was a joint operation between the DEA, the Royal Bahamas National Police Force, the U.S. Coast Guard, and the U.S. Army. In a nutshell, we were flying helicopter patrols throughout the Bahamas island chain looking for go-fast boats and other vessels involved in smuggling activities. After spending a week in Nassau at the U.S. embassy in the DEA office, I went off to Freeport for the daily, and often tedious, reconnaissance missions.

As the Lehder trial showed, the Bahamas and the entire Caribbean were absolutely crucial to drug traffickers. Before his arrest, Lehder had set up a virtual military operation on Norman's Cay, complete with landing strips, small aircraft, speedboats, and lodging for his army of pilots and sailors and traffickers who were importing cocaine into South Florida around the clock.

Despite the importance of the Bahamas for big cocaine cartels, I was shocked to find that there was only one other DEA agent in Freeport when I arrived. That meant we worked twenty-four hours on, twenty-four hours off, seven days a week. It wasn't a bad thing; I was still excited to be an agent even if it meant that we would be flying helicopters every day, looking for suspicious activity below. Routinely, we flew two patrols per day, one in the morning and the other during the late evening. But if any calls came in about suspicious activity, we would head to the airport right away.

One day after the morning patrol, I'd gone back to the house we were renting in Freeport to do some paperwork. While there, I received a call from DEA group supervisor Pat Shea, the agent in charge of Operation BAT. Pat said they'd received information that a Colombian drug trafficker named Pablo Escobar Gaviria was spotted on Treasure Cay and was using a private jet to travel. Pat gave us a Mexican tail number for the jet and instructed us to proceed immediately to the Freeport airport. He sent out additional backup agents and helicopters from Nassau, but we knew that we would arrive much sooner and be on the front lines of this particular operation.

Pat then asked if I knew who Escobar was. While I had certainly heard his name and knew something about his reputation from some of the cases we'd been working on in Miami, I had no real sense—not back then—as to the scope of his involvement in cocaine trafficking. At the time, I had just started reading *Kings of Cocaine* by *Miami Herald* reporters Guy Gugliotta and Jeff Leen. The book has a picture of Escobar in it, and Pat told me to take the book with me to assist in identifying Escobar if we encountered him.

When I arrived at the airport in Freeport, the Coast Guard ground crew was already busy prepping our helicopter for takeoff. The two pilots and two crew members were going through their preflight checklists. When the two Bahamian police officers arrived, we took off for Treasure Cay. During the flight, we all wore headsets so that we could speak to one another. Typically, I would sit in the jump seat between the two pilots, and the Bahamians would sit in the back. I made sure that everyone knew who we might be facing if the tip paid off. I also made sure that everyone was aware of Escobar's reputation for violence.

Pablo Escobar was known to travel with a large arsenal of weapons, far more firepower than we could muster. I was carrying a Smith & Wesson 9 mm pistol; the Bahamian officers each had a .38-caliber handgun and extremely old machine guns that looked like they had been salvaged from the Second World War. For their part, the Coast Guard did not typically carry weapons, but stored them in a locked compartment inside the helicopter. These consisted of two .45-caliber pistols and two 12-gauge shotguns. While this might have seemed like a great deal of firepower, I knew that Escobar would have far more. We were no match for him.

We flew very low that day—maybe fifty to one hundred feet above the ocean. As we approached Treasure Cay, the pilots let us know that they had spotted a plane on the runway that was moving into the position for takeoff. As we flew closer and over a clump of trees, we could all see the private jet on the taxiway, poised for takeoff. The pilots slowed down so that I could read the tail number. Although the plane did indeed have a Mexican registration number, it was one numeral off from the one Pat had given us. But I decided to take action anyway and told our pilot to block the runway to prevent the jet from taking off.

When we landed, we prepared for a tense face-off. The Bahamian police officers and I immediately got out of the helicopter with our weapons drawn. I approached the Mexican jet and slid my finger across my throat, indicating that they should cut their engines, but they revved up as if they were about to take off. The Bahamian officers went prone and pointed their machine guns at the jet. I knelt on one knee and pointed my pistol in the jet's direction. Our pilots remained in their seats with their .45 pistols and shotguns at port arms. Their primary responsibility was to protect the helicopter, but based on our mutual trust and respect, I felt confident that they were ready to offer us assistance if a firefight erupted.

Finally, the jet cut power, and the pilots raised their hands. We approached gingerly, not knowing what to expect. When the door opened, one of the pilots was standing in the doorway with his arms raised and speaking rapid-fire Spanish. Knowing that the universal language for pilots is English, we ordered the pilot to calm down and exit the plane where we could speak. He said he had delivered some executives to Treasure Cay and allowed us to search the plane's interior. The pilots had never heard of Pablo Escobar, and after we showed them his picture from *Kings of Cocaine*, they claimed never to have seen him before. It was only after we had parked our helicopter that we spied the other plane with the tail number Pat had given us. The Mexican pilots assured us that the jet belonged to the same company as theirs and had been used to transport another group of executives to Treasure Cay.

After our backup units arrived, we questioned everyone who worked at the Treasure Cay airport, showing them the black-and-white photograph in the book. Not one person could recognize the mustachioed chubby man, dressed casually in a short-sleeved shirt and blue jeans. After a few hours, we finally returned to Freeport.

Was Escobar on Treasure Cay, and did he fly on one of those jets? We'll never know.

JAVIER

I almost walked off the job the first time I felt the cold metal of a revolver against my temple.

An informant had told me about the sale of a pound of black tar heroin. It was a simple undercover deal in which my DEA partner—a veteran agent who had previously been stationed in Afghanistan—and I would pretend to be interested in buying the dope, and we would bust through the door and arrest the crooks. Just like in the movies.

The deal would go down on the south side of Austin, a desolate, sun-parched stretch of pawnshops, crack houses, abandoned storefronts, and used car dealerships. We had little time to pull together a backup team because it was a long weekend, and no one wanted to work. Looking back, we probably should have canceled the whole thing, but like I said before, I was still eager. I still wanted desperately to impress.

We drove up to a down-at-heels motel, and I held my breath as I knocked on the door. One of the drug dealers let us in. I barely had time to take in the grimy motel room with its flowered, polyester bedspread, the stained broadloom, and the tired air conditioner churning stale air, when one of the men—the short one with the beard—grabbed a gun from under a flowered pillow and cocked it against my head.

"If you're a cop, you're the first to die," he said in Spanish.

I swallowed hard. I didn't want to die like this, with a bullet in my head, over a pound of heroin. I fantasized about confessing. I would tell them that I was an actor playing a part, and we would shake hands, laugh it off, and walk away. Just a misunderstanding. I didn't want any part of this. Sweat beaded on my forehead, and I willed myself into stillness, repeating my schoolboy prayers by rote as the drug dealer (I'll call him the Mexican) started to go on about Mexico and Nuevo Laredo.

Nuevo Laredo?

Of course I knew everything about Nuevo Laredo! It was across the border from where I grew up. Suddenly, without even thinking about it, I went into overdrive, talking about La Zona. I babbled about all the dive bars, bragged about hanging out at the Papagallo and the 123—clubs that were also pretty hard-core brothels. The crook started to let his guard down and finally eased his grip on the revolver.

I guess all those times hanging out with my high school buddies and hitting the red-light district had finally paid off!

The blood pounding in my ears, I got back to the business of the bust. Somehow, I convinced the Mexican to allow us to inspect the heroin. I broke off a piece of the black, gummy brick and rolled it through my fingers. I put it up to my nose and inhaled tar.

My partner went out to the car to get the $10,000 in cash we had brought for the operation. And then I braced myself for what I thought was going to result in a huge firefight when the backup agents came flying through the motel room door. We had planned that as soon as my partner left the motel room to get the cash, the arrest team would swoop in behind him. I scoped out the room, desperately trying to figure out how I would inch my way into the bathroom, where I could get in some shots at the crooks. I felt for my .38, which the Mexican had either overlooked or no longer cared about now that he'd decided I was no longer a cop. My heart was pounding when my partner returned a few minutes later holding a paper bag with the cash. The arrest team hadn't noticed him in the parking lot, so he returned to the motel room without any backup. He threw the bag on the bed, and the crooks dropped their weapons and rushed to count it. My partner and I looked at each other. This was our chance. I positioned my gun without them noticing anything.

"Get down on the floor!" I yelled in Spanish, pulling out my .38-caliber, five-shot pistol.

When the arrest team finally burst through the door, I had already grabbed my crook, and I was screaming at him because I had nearly died in that room. I also got a few shoves in at him, but he didn't say anything because he knew I could have killed him.

"The next time you sell dope, don't fucking bring a fucking gun!" I screamed at the Mexican.

I learned a lot that day, and I promised myself I would never get into a dangerous situation like that—in confined quarters, in a motel room—ever again.

Of course, I broke that promise as soon as I arrived in Colombia.

PART THREE

PART THREE

JAVIER

I had never heard of Pablo Escobar before I got to Colombia. The truth is that I never wanted to go there in the first place. I had put in for Mexico City after my time in Austin ended. I got Bogotá instead, and I was bitterly disappointed.

And once I set foot on Colombian soil, I couldn't escape Pablo Escobar Gaviria. In our internal communications at DEA, he was "TKO 558 case number ZE-88-0008." He was my new assignment, to be sure, but after the night of August 18, 1989, Pablo Escobar also became my obsession.

Escobar controlled the Medellín Cartel—which, by the time I arrived in 1988, was the most powerful group of drug traffickers in the world. Eighty percent of the world's cocaine came from Colombia, processed from coca leaves and paste that originated in Peru and Bolivia. In Colombia, Escobar's army of *sicarios*—most of them small-time teenage crooks from the *comunas,* or shantytowns, of Medellín—waged a war of narcoterrorism. By the time I arrived on the scene, they had already killed hundreds of cops, jurists, reporters, and their own rivals in the drug trade.

Escobar and the other members of the Medellín Cartel fought fiercely against the Colombian government's plans to extradite drug traffickers to stand trial in the United States. In 1984, elected officials debated a treaty that would allow the federal government to extradite any Colombian even if they were merely *suspected* of a crime. Cartel leaders, who were used to bribing or killing their opponents in Colombia to avoid arrest, knew they could never exercise the same power in America, and any trial there would surely lead to a lengthy prison term.

So they fought back in the most brutal way they could: The grisly deaths of their opponents meant to serve as a warning that *Los Extraditables*—the Extraditables—would brook no interference. *Plata o plomo*—silver or lead—was the guiding principle of the Medellín Cartel. With Escobar, either you negotiated and accepted a bribe to look the other way, or you got a bullet through the head.

In the early days of the terror, most of those who stood in Escobar's way, lobbying for extradition, got several bullets through the head.

One of the earliest proponents of extradition was Colombia's crusading justice minister Rodrigo Lara Bonilla, a member of Nuevo Liberalismo, a progressive faction of the Liberal Party he'd cofounded. A former lawyer, the thirty-seven-year-old politician was not afraid of denouncing Escobar, exposing how he financed all the community projects that had earned him comparisons to Robin Hood in Medellín through corruption and murder. Those exposés, which came to light when Escobar had been elected to the Colombian congress as an alternate, became the main reason that Lara lasted only eight months as the federal government's top cop. He was gunned down by two of Escobar's henchmen as he sat in the back seat of his chauffeur-driven Mercedes on his way home from work on the night of April 30, 1984—three days after he denounced Escobar as a criminal in Congress and moved to seize his assets. The U.S. government had warned Lara that his life was in danger, and the embassy had even given him a bulletproof vest. The vest was found next to his corpse in the back seat of the car. His body was so riddled with bullets that it's unlikely the vest would have saved his life.

Colombian lawmakers were so appalled by his brutal murder that they immediately approved the extradition treaty. The Reagan administration had long pressured Colombia to pass the legislation putting the treaty into force, and the United States immediately demanded the extradition of one hundred Colombians. But to tell you the truth, we could not have cared less about the small-time drug dealers who were on that list; our focus was on the leaders of the Medellín Cartel—José Gonzalo Rodríguez Gacha, the Ochoa clan, and Escobar.

As the Colombian government increased the pressure on the Medellín Cartel, the bad guys unleashed a brutal campaign of terror. On November 6, 1985, the cartel backed the disastrous siege of Bogotá's Palace of Justice. Dozens of M-19 guerrillas stormed the building, holding all twenty-five of the country's supreme court justices and hundreds of others hostage. The leftist group's goal was "to denounce a government that has betrayed the Colombian people." Their plan was to force the judges to take the country's president to task for violating a peace deal with the rebels that had been signed a year and a half earlier. They were also angry over the extradition treaty and agreed with the leaders of the Medellín Cartel that no Colombian should have to face justice in another country. Later, it emerged that Escobar himself had financed the assault. But the government of President Belisario Betancur refused to negotiate and sent in the army to rescue the hostages. Over the next two days, the Colombian military launched a bloody assault, complete with tanks and explosives, that resulted in the deaths of eleven judges, thirty-five guerrillas, and forty-eight soldiers. Eleven others—most of them cafeteria workers—remain missing. A fire broke out—or rather, was set—that destroyed thousands of documents that the court was using to determine the extradition of drug traffickers. According to news reports, many of the files pertained to the case of Pablo Escobar.

Despite the violence, Colombian leaders continued to risk their lives to fight against the drug traffickers. A year after the Palace of Justice assault, Guillermo Cano Isaza, editor and part owner of *El Espectador,* the country's second-largest daily, was shot dead by two gunmen on a motorcycle as he left the newspaper's printing plant in an industrial suburb of Bogotá. Cano's newspaper had been the first to document Escobar's life of crime, beginning in 1976. The paper carried a story about his arrest on drug-smuggling charges, along with his cousin and confidant Gustavo Gaviria Rivero and his brother-in-law Mario Henao. Cano reprinted the original article years later when Escobar was elected to the Colombian congress in 1982, although he was forced to resign in disgrace after attacks from his own party and Cano's columns denouncing his role in the Medellín Cartel.

Escobar swore he would get even with his enemies, and the killing continued.

Two years after Cano's murder, on January 25, 1988, the country's attorney general, Carlos Mauro Hoyos Jiménez, was kidnapped and killed by Escobar's goons. According to Jhon Jairo Velásquez Vásquez, the Medellín Cartel's most important henchman, who was known as Popeye, Escobar wanted Hoyos tried for treason and accused him of taking bribes from the DEA for supporting the extradition of Colombians. According to Popeye, Escobar also said that Hoyos had accepted bribes from members of his own outlaw group.

I arrived in Bogotá right after the killing. The news of Hoyos's death was huge, especially because he was killed in the Medellín area—the stronghold of the cartel. I knew almost nothing about the violence that was engulfing Colombia, and I knew very little about Escobar, the man who would come to dominate my thoughts for the next several years. We had no DEA briefings on new assignments in those days, and so little of what was going on in the country ever made its way into newspapers in Texas.

It took me a while to get my bearings and wrap my head around my new assignment. I was a frontline soldier in America's war on drugs, but I only really began to realize that much later. For the moment, I was simply shocked at how inadequate my reinforcements were in what was then one of the most dangerous places in the world.

It's hard to convey how eerie it was to arrive in a city at war. The streets were mainly deserted at night, and soldiers in riot gear wielding AK-47s and accompanied by ferocious-looking German shepherds tethered to short leashes stood sentinel at every major hotel in the city.

The DEA office was in the basement of the old U.S. embassy, a low-rise bunker surrounded by a cement wall and topped with spiked iron bars in downtown Bogotá. Our headquarters were very small, dingy, and located right next to the embassy garage. The ambassador's car was parked right outside our door, and I felt like we breathed in exhaust all day. The office itself was very cramped, and it sometimes flooded during a rainstorm. We were careful never to leave documents on the floor for fear they would be destroyed by the water. We had pods with makeshift walls that only went up halfway. If you stood up from your desk, you could see what your neighbor was doing, and it became impossible not to listen in on every conversation.

When I got selected for Bogotá, the rumor was that there was deadweight at the DEA office and that many agents had simply stayed on, which was easy to do in a place like Colombia, where agents made 50 percent above their regular salary, most of that in "danger pay." But statistics on drug busts were way down, and there was almost no coordination with local authorities. One of the constant negatives was that you could never trust the Colombian cops and military. We soon found out that was dead wrong.

I was part of a group of six new agents hired from all over the United States to infuse the Bogotá office with vigorous, go-getter talent. Our new leader was Joe Toft. The DEA's agent in charge arrived in Bogotá at the same time I did. He was a hard-nosed veteran who had worked his way up from posts in San Diego, Rome, Madrid, Dallas, Washington, and San Antonio. Toft was my boss in Texas, and I had a tremendous amount of respect for him. At more than six feet tall, he was a towering presence in the office. He was raised in Bolivia, and he spoke Spanish like a native. He was demanding and deliberate—a hard-ass and in-your-face type of guy who had no time for slackers. Toft made people work because he came to Bogotá with marching orders from DEA headquarters to turn the office around. When he arrived in the city, he started denying tour extensions to do-nothing agents. Typically,

DEA special agents are sent abroad for two years at a time and then can extend their tours up to a maximum of six years. Despite the danger, Colombia was a sought-after assignment because of the extra pay.

Toft didn't have many friends at the embassy, and he rarely socialized with us agents. He spent his weekends playing tennis, and occasionally he would invite a few of us to games of pickup basketball or volleyball, but he was extremely aggressive and very intense. He would yell at you if you made mistakes on the court. During one indoor volleyball game, Toft and the ambassador had a violent shouting match over whether the ball had gone out of bounds.

Toft was a workaholic, and when he did socialize, it was with his friends in the Colombian police and military. He spent a lot of time building relationships with the country's top law enforcement officials, and he demanded that the agents under his charge create their own networks among the Colombian National Police (CNP) and the military operatives who were at the front line of the battle against Escobar. At our first meeting, he told us that if there was a big coke seizure or a major arrest, he wanted the Colombian cops to call us first at home and give us the details. He did not want to read about it in the newspapers the next day.

This in itself set Toft apart from his predecessors, who rarely consulted Colombian law enforcement. In turn, all the leaders of the CNP respected him and regularly sought his advice. Toft became very close to Major Jesús Gómez Padilla and General Octavio Vargas Silva, both of them leaders of the CNP during the search for Escobar. He also knew Hugo Martinez, the CNP colonel who would prove instrumental in the Escobar searches. But Toft and Martinez were not particularly close because Martinez seemed a little jealous of Toft's relationship with Vargas. For his part, Toft also formed a strong bond with the counterintelligence chief Miguel Maza Márquez, the head of DAS, which was the Colombian equivalent of the FBI. When Toft visited both agencies, they would have guards ready for his arrival. They would escort him up via the private elevators that only the generals were allowed to use. With Vargas, who would later become a commander and architect of the Escobar Search Bloc, Toft would visit him at his home on Saturday mornings for strategy meetings. Sometimes, I would accompany Toft to these encounters. All this networking made our jobs a lot easier. In hindsight, I don't think we would have gotten anywhere in the search for Escobar had it not been for Toft.

Under Toft's leadership, we were soon building important relationships with the local authorities, all of them veterans of a brutal drug war that had seen many of their own friends and colleagues killed. Toft felt that the Colombian anti-narcotics cops and federal agents would never take us seriously unless we volunteered to go out with them on enforcement operations, demonstrating that we were willing to put our own lives at risk in the battle against the cartels.

Gary Sheridan was my first partner in Colombia. We arrived in Bogotá at the same time. We knew from the get-go that we were there to start kicking some ass in the drug war under Toft's very capable leadership.

A former agent for the Bureau of Alcohol, Tobacco, Firearms and Explosives, Gary was slim with a touch of silver hair. He looked distinguished, with a serious air about him. While he could seem aloof at first, he was really a common-sense type of guy. We got along really well, and shortly after we both arrived in Colombia, we took Toft's lead and spent a lot of time cultivating sources in the Colombian law enforcement community.

Gary was with me the night both of our lives changed, and the search for Escobar took on its most urgent dimension.

August 18, 1989, was a Friday, and after a long week at work, we headed to our favorite bar and restaurant. Mr. Ribs was a popular eatery in the fancy northern part of the city. It was a favorite among American expats, local politicians, and wealthy Colombians. The restaurant specialized in succulent ribs, grilled steaks, American-style burgers, and fries. The beer was always ice-cold, and Mr. Ribs was packed on the weekends. Gary and I ordered burgers from a pretty waitress with long brown hair and a trim figure. We were just settling in to drink our beers when our waitress approached the table in a state of shock, tears beginning to roll down her cheeks as she interrupted our drinks.

"Galán was murdered a few minutes ago," she pronounced in a hoarse voice. "We have to close now."

Stunned by the news that the leading presidential candidate, Luis Carlos Galán Sarmiento, had been gunned down while campaigning in nearby Soacha, a working-class suburb of Bogotá, we filed out of the restaurant in a mass exodus with the other patrons. Nobody paid their bills. The murder of the most progressive candidate for president, who was expected to win with more than 60 percent of the popular vote, was far more important than any restaurant bill in a country that had endured years of terror. Like just about everyone else in Colombia, the proprietors of the restaurant were in a deep state of shock and mourning.

It was Galán's third attempt at the presidency. A senator of the progressive wing of the ruling Liberal Party, he was one of six candidates seeking the party's presidential nomination for elections slated for May 1990. He ran on an anti-corruption and anti-narco platform, and he was pretty much public enemy number one of Escobar and Rodríguez Gacha.

The tough-talking, mustachioed politician was determined to extradite the drug traffickers, and he denounced the cartels every chance he got, calling them "the worst threat against liberty and justice" around the world in his campaign speeches.

Of course, Galán had received numerous death threats, but he was recklessly unafraid and always eschewed the bulletproof vest that his campaign manager, César Gaviria, pressed upon him on the campaign trail. In fact, Gaviria, who would later go on to be president himself, warned Galán that it was much too dangerous for him to campaign in Soacha on that fateful summer night.

Although he ignored Gaviria's advice not to speak at Soacha, Galán ironically donned the bulletproof vest for the first time. As he took to the stage and began to address a crowd of ten thousand people, seven gunmen who were dispersed throughout the crowd opened fire. Two bullets penetrated Galán's stomach just below the vest because Galán had raised his arms above his head to greet the adoring crowd. A photographer who was standing next to the presidential candidate when he fell onto the stage said he asked to be taken to the hospital, but Galán died soon after, a month shy of his forty-sixth birthday.

The assassination came on the same day as the murder of Colonel Franklin Quintero, a police commander for the Antioquía province where Medellín is located. Quintero, who fought against drug traffickers for years, conducting huge raids that resulted in the seizure of several tons of cocaine, had left his home without his regular entourage of bodyguards. He was gunned down before his chauffeur-driven car had barely left his driveway. A witness told Caracol Radio that the colonel had been hit more than one hundred times, and the car was destroyed by gunfire.

Outside Mr. Ribs, Gary and I hurried through chaotic streets as police and military scrambled to set up road-blocks. Bogotá was on lockdown, with army tanks blocking major intersections and police in full riot gear directing the crowds as the country's president, Virgilio Barco Vargas, immediately took to the airwaves, declaring a state of siege and reestablishing the extradition treaty with the United States. The treaty had been temporarily suspended by the country's supreme court on a legal technicality in April 1988. After Barco called a national state of emergency in the wake of Galán's and Quintero's murders, he could use his extraordinary powers to bring back the treaty without congressional approval. He also ordered a series of raids across the country that resulted in the capture of some ten thousand suspected drug traffickers. Under the state of siege, police could hold suspects for seven days without charge.

I will never forget that wild night. I walked home, flashing my carnet—the little red book that contained my diplomatic pass—to get through police barricades and the crowds of ordinary Colombians who had taken to the streets, some of them openly wailing, others wandering around in a deep, almost zombielike state of disbelief and mourning. I felt Barco was a real hero for using Galán's death to bring back the treaty and for going after the cartels as aggressively as he did. At Galán's funeral a few days later, Barco blamed his killing on the millions of people in Colombia and around the world who consume drugs, thereby sustaining and empowering the country's cartels.

"Each Colombian or foreigner who consumes drugs should remember that he is helping those who assassinated Luis Carlos Galán," said Barco as tens of thousands lined the streets of Bogotá for Galán's funeral procession. "Colombia is the greatest victim of an international narcotics organization dedicated to narcotics trafficking—a great and powerful organization the likes of which has never existed in the world."

More than anything, it was Galán's assassination that led to the downfall of Pablo Escobar and the Medellín Cartel. I knew the killing had been directed by Escobar, and I think all of Colombia knew it too. In any event, he was the most wanted drug trafficker in the United States—first on the extradition list charged with drug trafficking and ordering the murder of an American, his former pilot Barry Seal, in Louisiana in 1986.

We had an emergency meeting at the embassy to discuss strategy. Barco appealed directly to the United States for help, and in the days following the assassination, President George H. W. Bush earmarked $65 million in emergency aid to Colombia to help fight the drug cartels, with the promise of another $250 million in military aid to arrive in the near future.

"The package will include equipment for police and military personnel, with initial shipments to arrive as early as next week," the president said in a statement issued at his vacation home in Kennebunkport, Maine, shortly after Galán's assassination. "In addition, it will include aircraft and helicopters to improve the mobility of Colombian forces engaged in the antidrug effort." His administration also sent military advisors to help train Colombian law enforcement in what was building into an all-out war against the bad guys.

Working from our basement headquarters at the embassy, we intensified our search for Escobar and his cronies as they stepped up their attacks against the government.

Before Galán's death, there was no sense of urgency. We mainly collected information and set up a twenty-four-hour hotline to take tips on the fugitive billionaire drug dealer. We worked with Colombian law enforcement, talked to analysts, and, whenever the Colombians conducted a big raid, we were given twenty-four hours to copy as many documents as we possibly could. We had what we called Xerox parties, where we would rent out a warehouse and photocopy machines and work in shifts with embassy personnel in what became frantic copying marathons. We had ten such parties. The information we gathered later resulted in a series of raids on clubs and legal and accounting offices associated with the Medellín Cartel in Colombia and the United States.

In those first few months after Galán's assassination we brought in twenty additional analysts to help out. Under the new state of siege, we no longer needed any probable cause to go after suspects. As long as there was something suspicious, anything to suggest that a target was a drug trafficker, we wouldn't hesitate to hit. In the six months after Galán's assassination, we rounded up thirty suspected drug traffickers and extradited them to the States.

One of the first to be extradited was José Rafael Abello Silva, known by his underworld moniker, Mono Abello. He was a pilot for Escobar and the chief of operations for the cartel on Colombia's northern coast. It was largely thanks to his capture that we were able to track José Gonzalo Rodríguez Gacha—"the Mexican," and one of the country's most powerful drug lords—two months later.

Abello tried to pay off the DAS guys when they swooped in to arrest him at an upscale Bogotá restaurant where he was dining with his date. But as we found out later, they refused the cash. The informant was under my control, and while I still can't reveal who that was all these years later, I can say that they were loyal to us and delivered the target.

Abello was wanted in Tulsa, Oklahoma, of all places. He had been indicted by a federal grand jury there for conspiring to import and distribute cocaine. Abello was caught at a Bogotá restaurant on October 11, 1989, thanks to an informant working for Gary. Five days later, Abello was driven to a hangar at Bogotá's El Dorado International Airport in a convoy of about twenty police vehicles. I have to say that those early extraditions were sights to behold! And they were always captured on video to be shown on nightly news programs so that Colombians could see justice in action. Once at the airport, Abello, who was hand-cuffed, was handed over to a group of ten heavily armed U.S. Marshals, all of them wearing black and looking somber. The marshals led him onto a 747 en route to Tulsa. Under Colombian rules, a CNP officer had to accompany the prisoner on board the airplane. We would give the CNP officer a return ticket and a per diem.

With Abello out of the picture, it took less than two months to find his boss, Rodríguez Gacha. He was forced out of hiding to handle a shipment of cocaine aboard a ship at the port city of Cartagena. That may have been part of the reason that he came out of hiding, but the real story was that he was scared to death. At the time, he was probably the wealthiest member of the Medellín Cartel, making even more money than Escobar himself. He commanded a small army of mercenaries that he had im-ported from Israel to work as his bodyguards, but with Abello out of the way in the United States, he might have suddenly felt very vulnerable and exposed.

Known as "the Mexican" for his fondness for the coun-try's music and food, he was under indictment in the United States on several smuggling charges, but he had also made some unfortunate enemies in Colombia. Everyone from the Cali Cartel to the FARC (Fuerzas Armadas Revolu-cionarias de Colombia, or the *Revolutionary Armed Forces of Colombia*) guerrillas to the emerald mafia led by Victor Carranza wanted him dead. A few months earlier, he had detonated a bomb at Carranza's offices and had turned violently against Gilberto Molina Moreno, a former associate in the emerald business. To secure his dominance over the country's emerald fields, he sent twenty-five hitmen to kill Molina, who died in a bloody massacre during a party at his home with sixteen others.

In mid-December, the Mexican was suddenly on the run. He boarded a speedboat and tried to escape Colombian police with his son, who had been recently released from a DIJIN (Dirección Central de Policía Judicial e Inteligencia) lockup in Bogotá. Freddy, seventeen, had been briefly detained on weapons charges. I interviewed him while he was in jail. He wore a watch that was far too expensive for a teenager and tried to play the role of the flashy drug trafficker. But in the end, I just found him to be pretty naïve and incredibly frightened. The police eventually threw out his case for lack of evidence and then used him as bait to go after his father. We followed Freddy, and he led us to the same area of Cartagena where we had already dispatched our informant, a hitman named Jorge Velásquez, better known by his nickname, El Navegante— the sailor. Navegante was the captain of Rodríguez Gacha's speedboats and was well-liked and trusted by the drug dealer. We would meet Navegante in clandestine places in Bogotá—usually restaurants or a hotel room— and we had promised him $1 million in cash if he led us to Rodríguez Gacha.

Once Navegante had helped us find Rodríguez Gacha's exact location near the small resort town of Tolú, CNP

colonel Leonardo Gallego dispatched two artillery helicopters and set up roadblocks on rural roads leading to
Cartagena to trap the drug lord. With more than three
hundred cops under his command, Gallego stopped more
than ten of Rodríguez Gacha's guards. Among them was
a senator who tried to bribe Gallego with $250,000 in
cash. Gallego refused the cash and had the senator immediately arrested.

Alerted by the helicopters and the mounting police operation in the area, Rodríguez Gacha fled on the night of
December 14. He took his son and five of his most trusted
associates on his speedboat. The boat was abandoned on
the beach at a resort village called El Tesoro, where arrangements had been made ahead of time to have a vehicle waiting for their arrival. They were driven to a cluster
of beachfront cabanas, where they spent the night. According to a DEA report, "Rodríguez Gacha and company
remained at the small complex of wooden cabanas in El
Tesoro the remainder of the night." The next day, at
approximately 1:00 in the afternoon, the sounds of the
approaching helicopters forced them to flee. The police in
the helicopters, who had been following the boat, used
loudspeakers to demand that Rodríguez Gacha surrender
immediately. Disguised as farmworkers, Rodríguez Gacha and Freddy fled their hiding place in a red truck.
Freddy and a group of bodyguards then got out of the
truck, ran to a clump of nearby trees, and began shooting
wildly at the helicopters and lobbing grenades, but they

were overwhelmed by firepower. Both Rodríguez Gacha and Freddy died in a barrage of gunfire. Freddy was a bloody mess when they recovered his body. His father was unrecognizable. Rodríguez Gacha's face was shot off, reduced to a bloody pulp.

The next day, the bodies of Rodríguez Gacha, Freddy, and the five bodyguards were buried in the town of Tolú, in a common grave because no one imagined that anyone would arrive to claim the bodies, but on Sunday, December 17, Freddy's mother and the sister of Rodríguez Gacha arrived to do so. Ismael Rodríguez Gacha, a brother, was also present. A judge ordered the bodies exhumed, and they were flown by the family via private airplane to Bogotá, where they were buried in the town of Pacho, three hours outside of the Colombian capital. Relatives of three of the bodyguards also arrived to claim their bodies. The other two bodyguards remained in the grave.

Days later, we brought Navegante to the embassy to fill out the paperwork for the $1 million reward, promising him that we would have the cash in a few days. But after about a month of bureaucratic holdups, Navegante began to lose patience. He returned to the embassy to meet Gary and me, and we sat in an airless office drinking small, sugary cups of coffee. We told him not to worry, that the cash was on its way and was only delayed because of a lot of government red tape. But Navegante wasn't buying it. He leaped from his chair and told us to forget the cash as he headed for the door. He was so pissed! In a loud voice, he told us that the Cali Cartel had already given him $1 million for selling out Rodríguez Gacha.

I couldn't believe what I had just heard and asked him to repeat himself, which he did. And then we simply escorted him out. Gary and I reported the conversation to our bosses, and the decision was made not to pay him, as it would have been unethical for us to be effectively employing an admitted cartel member for his cooperation. In essence, we would have been guilty of working with the Cali Cartel in their dirty war against Escobar.

Despite the mess Navegante had made of the reward, we had reason to celebrate. With the death of one of the most important members of the Medellín Cartel, we felt nothing could stop us from bringing the whole enterprise down. Suddenly, a lot of the intelligence that we had gathered from raids started to produce great results.

Julio Corredor Rivera was a case in point. He was suspected of laundering money for Escobar. Our raids on his office in Colombia led to the seizure of many of the cartel's accounts in the United States. Later, he was murdered by Escobar's *sicarios* in Bogotá.

We also began to step up our intelligence gathering, and our work lives began to revolve around the secret data collection center at the CNP DIJIN office in Bogotá—the heart and soul of our investigative operations. The wire room was a hidden enclave located behind a row of secretaries and accessible through a bookshelf, which functioned as a clandestine door. The stuffy room was staffed by four analysts from Colombia's judicial police (DIJIN), who were local hires and who sat in front of a series of modules that monitored about fifty phone lines used by some of the biggest traffickers in the country. In those early days of our investigation, drug traffickers spoke pretty freely on the phone. Sometimes, they spoke in code about shipments of cocaine, but our analysts became pretty adept at figuring out the codes. For example, "I'm sending twenty head of whiteface cattle to La Playa" really meant "I'm sending twenty kilos of cocaine to Miami." Or "There are twenty melons coming through Las Torres" was code for "There is $20 million coming through New York City."

I would pay the analysts a visit every day, and they would allow me to listen to some of the more interesting conversations they had taped. In this way, I was considered the main liaison between the DEA and DIJIN. Sometimes, they would call me over with a synopsis of something they had found. I took copious notes in a steno pad and sent daily reports to my bosses. I made a point of numbering all the notebooks, and by the time I finished my assignment in Colombia, I had two hundred notebooks.

I got to know one retired sergeant pretty well. He was quiet but found a lot of good stuff for us that led to the seizures of massive quantities of cocaine. The intercepts were technically illegal, and when I wrote up my notes and sent them through the teletype to DEA headquarters, everyone knew that they could not be used to prosecute criminal cases.

Still, the intercepts produced a lot of great leads that we passed on to our counterparts in the United States. If an intercept led to an arrest, I would reward the analyst with an attaboy letter to their superior in the Colombian National Police, the force that was primarily tasked with going after Escobar. The letters meant a lot to them, as did our insistence upon giving them information that we got from our own sources in the United States. We gained their trust this way, as they realized that the operation was never a one-way street. A few of the really hardworking analysts received extra money from the DEA, so a retired cop making $200 a month could see his salary doubled if he worked hard for us. This was done in secret, and their own bosses never knew.

With intelligence that we gathered from the data collection center at the end of 1990, Gary and I were able to set up our first Colombian cop on a drug bust. Data analysts gathered intelligence that a trafficking group—the Coastal Cartel—was operating out of Montería, a dusty, sunbaked city of 150,000 in the northern part of the country near the Caribbean coast, and was planning to dispatch hundreds of kilos of cocaine to Miami. We both felt that Pedro Rojas, a captain with the national judicial police in Bogotá, was the man for the job. Rojas was the anti-narcotics chief for the DIJIN—tall, slim, and very committed to his work. He was also a serious equestrian, and he once showed me a photograph of himself on a horse. Somehow, that made him look even more like an upstanding man of the law.

Gary and I gave Rojas a per diem and expense money to go to Montería to catch the bad guys, who were working with their counterparts in the Medellín Cartel to store cocaine before exporting it to Miami. With its sparsely populated rolling plains and its proximity to a Caribbean port, Montería was an ideal center for drug traffickers, who carved out clandestine airstrips on the city's outskirts and hid pallets of cocaine in abandoned barns.

Rojas hadn't gotten very far when things went horribly wrong. On January 19, 1991, Rojas and his police driver, Juan Enrique Montanez, were following a car carrying four members of the drug-trafficking group to a farm on the outskirts of the city where tons of cocaine were reportedly hidden. And then they simply disappeared. We learned later that they were killed by Escobar's henchmen, and their bodies were cut up and thrown in the Sinú River that divides the city. Gary and I were devastated by their deaths, and we convinced the DEA to give the money that we had set aside for Rojas's work in Montería—about $20,000—to his family. Gary and I delivered it to Rojas's wife and father, who had also been a cop, at a small ceremony at DIJIN headquarters in Bogotá. It was an informal affair, held at the officers' mess. I remember his father, a retired cop, was in a suit. I also remember that his wife was there. Gary and I represented the DEA, and we made a short speech thanking the family before presenting his wife with an envelope with the cash.

We both felt bad because we had supported that mission, and we had given Rojas the operational funds to go to Montería.

Rojas's intelligence gathering eventually led to several arrests and drug seizures in the region, including 22,440 pounds of cocaine found on a farm called Manaos on the outskirts of Montería.

With the war against Escobar now at full throttle, I was sent to the front lines on a pretty regular basis. It was about an hour's flight from Bogotá's El Dorado International Airport to Medellín. I flew in on the DEA's Aero Commander. We had our own pilots, and during the Escobar manhunt days, DEA missions to Medellín had top priority over all other requests for DEA air service. There were times when we bumped other missions to get to Medellín as quickly as possible.

The first time I arrived, the police picked me up in a convoy of three armored vehicles. I sat between two heavily armed cops in the back of the second jeep. They looked at me, and one of them asked me if I had a gun. When I said yes, they told me to take it out and place it on my chest, my finger on the trigger, for the ride to the police academy, where I would live while I was in the city. Hitmen riding double on a motorcycle popped off hundreds of cops in those days, so we all had to be prepared to defend ourselves on the roads.

Nervously, I took out my 9 mm stainless steel Smith & Wesson semiautomatic and held it at my chest in the back seat of the police jeep for that stomach-churning half-hour drive through the mountains. The Medellín cops drove like Formula One racers. As we rounded each mountainous curve at breakneck speed, I swallowed hard to keep myself from getting sick.

My fingers became clammy gripping my gun so tightly. In that split second, I had some serious doubts about the operation to capture the elusive Escobar—a mafia don who commanded an army of loyal hitmen and had some eight hundred safe houses and hundreds of millions at his fingertips to defend himself, not to mention scores of leftist guerrillas he had coopted to fight against the government.

What the hell am I doing here? I asked myself.

But it was a momentary lapse. I knew I had been chosen to do a job—maybe even the most important job of my career—and I kept my eyes fixed on the winding road ahead.

STEVE

It was Connie's idea to move to Colombia. One day, after we'd been living in Miami for four years, she said, "Well, this has been really exciting! What's next?"

Don't get me wrong. We loved Miami. We loved the beaches, the warmth, and the interesting mix of people.

Miami is still our favorite city in the United States. We had also started building a new home in Fort Lauderdale, and there were times that we felt we'd live in South Florida for the rest of our lives.

But I guess once we'd settled in, we both came to the realization that something was missing. We longed for excitement and a new challenge. And when Connie asked me that question, I think she knew that the obvious next adventure in my career had to be Colombia. While I had worked on cases in Miami that involved Escobar and his crew, working in Colombia would finally be my opportunity to go after Escobar himself. If I was going to work as a DEA agent and target traffickers, I wanted to go after the biggest fish I could. Connie did have one condition: she would only go if she could take "Puff," her cat.

Shortly after applying for a transfer to Colombia, I was selected for the DEA office in Barranquilla, a historic city on the country's northern Caribbean coast. We were totally psyched about the move, but after a few weeks, I was notified that my name had been withdrawn and the position given to another agent who could already speak Spanish. I didn't think that was fair, and Connie and I were both disappointed.

After I complained, a staff coordinator for DEA called me a few months later and expressed some sympathy, letting me know that three positions were about to be posted in Bogotá and that I should apply. I did and was eventually chosen for one of them.

As Connie and I immersed ourselves in research on Colombia, we realized that going to Bogotá would indeed be the adventure of our lives. It would also be dangerous. Connie still has the booklet we'd received from the State Department complete with travel advisories, dictating that U.S. government families were only permitted to travel by air between major cities because any car travel outside Bogotá put you at high risk of carjackings and kidnappings. Country roads were high risk for roadblocks because checkpoints could be manned by criminals posing as police or military. Bombings were common, the brochure said. I noticed that Connie was actually checking on the paperwork necessary to take a cat to Colombia.

We had been following the news from the country quite closely over the years, and we knew about the jungle cocaine labs, the car bombs, and the murders of judges and politicians and even ordinary Colombians who were unlucky to be caught in the cross fire.

In addition to the drug traffickers, violence in the country also stemmed from guerrilla militants in M-19 and the Revolutionary Armed Forces of Colombia (the aforementioned FARC), who often worked in tandem with the cartels, providing security for their jungle operations.

I had seen a lot in my career in law enforcement, but I remember being shocked by TV footage of the distraught relatives of the dead and the smoldering debris of Avianca flight 203. The plane exploded five minutes after takeoff from Bogotá's El Dorado International Airport and crashed into the side of a mountain in the early morning of November 27, 1989. TV reports in the United States focused on the twisted metal of the wreckage, torn-up suitcases, and clothing strewn across a hillside on the outskirts of Bogotá. There were no close-ups of the mangled bodies, which were probably deemed too grisly for prime-time viewers in America. I was to see those images much later on Colombian national TV, which often flashed back to the disaster when they were reporting on Pablo Escobar.

The bomb, planted by one of Escobar's hitmen, killed all 107 passengers and crew. Later, I found out that two of our agents were scheduled to be on the flight, as was progressive presidential candidate César Gaviria. I also learned that we had no advance intelligence that the attack was about to happen, and it was by some miracle or crazy happenstance that the agents and Gaviria canceled their trips.

Hours after the crash shocked the world, an unidentified man called Caracol Radio and said the Extraditables had blown up the jet to kill several police informants who were on the flight. He told the radio station that the men had given information to the police that led them to an Escobar hiding place, forcing the drug kingpin to flee for his life.

But at DEA headquarters in the U.S. embassy, agents felt that the real target was Gaviria, Galán's former campaign manager. The Avianca bombing was a continuation of Escobar's sinister focus on the Galán campaign. Like the slain candidate, Gaviria was running on a tough line against the Extraditables.

As Colombians reeled from the senseless murder of civilians aboard the Avianca jet—the first time that a commercial airline was used in an act of terrorism in the country—their outrage and desperation grew. The Extraditables seemed unstoppable. A few days later, on December 6, they struck again—detonating five hundred kilos of dynamite outside DAS headquarters in Bogotá. The bomb killed sixty people, injured one thousand, and destroyed hundreds of nearby buildings over several city blocks. The target was DAS director general Miguel Maza Márquez, one of Escobar's biggest enemies. He escaped unhurt and in the years ahead would prove to be one of our most trusted intelligence sources in Colombia.

Five months later, in May 1990, the outlaw group continued their ruthless campaign of terror. The Extraditables were behind car bombs at two shopping malls in Bogotá that left twenty-six dead and scores injured. Hundreds of people were at the shopping centers in the upscale barrios of the city when the bombs exploded. Among the dead were a seven-year-old girl and a woman who was six months pregnant.

As chilling as these statistics were, we knew that nothing would deter us. Maybe it all just seemed surreal, watching those faraway scenes of carnage play out in our living room in Fort Lauderdale. We were both still young—in our midthirties!—and determined to go to Colombia. Nothing was going to stop us. Connie was with me every step of the way, even though it would mean uprooting yet again and leaving a job she truly loved. Of course, our families thought we were crazy, but Connie did a great job explaining to them that this was a voluntary assignment that we both wanted—the opportunity of a lifetime.

I got the job just as we finished construction on our home. We even managed to move in for a couple of weeks before heading to Washington for six months of language training. After four years in South Florida, I could still only speak halting Spanish. We rented out our house to another DEA agent and his family, who took really good care of the property, even as Hurricane Andrew swept through South Florida in August 1992, killing sixty-five people and causing billions of dollars in damage. Unlike many in the region who were left homeless, we were lucky and escaped with only the loss of a tree in our yard and some drywall damage from the 150-mile-an-hour winds shaking the walls. I have to say that we didn't really like the idea of leaving our new place in Fort Lauderdale, but it didn't stand in the way of our decision to move to Colombia. Nothing did.

On top of that, Connie and I wanted children. I already had two sons from my previous marriage, but they lived with their mother and we wanted to have children together as well. We tried unsuccessfully to have biological children, and Connie went through a battery of medical procedures while we lived in Florida, but those didn't work either, so we thought about adopting, but we soon found out that the adoption process in South Florida was a racket. It was extremely expensive, there were long waits, and no one really seemed interested in what was best for the kids unless you were famous and had a boatload of money. Maybe, just maybe things would be different in Colombia, although the possibility of adopting children in Colombia didn't really influence our decision to go either.

Even though we both spoke endlessly about our excitement in going to a new place, I have to admit that it was with some apprehension that I boarded our flight to Bogotá at Miami International Airport. As we flew over Central America and the Darién Gap, I glanced out the window at a darkening sky. I squeezed Connie's hand as she nodded off to sleep in the seat beside me.

Yes, Colombia would be a big adventure for both of us, but I was sure it would also be the most important mission of my law enforcement career, drawing on everything I had ever learned and testing my mettle as a narc.

I was determined to get Pablo Escobar. Months of research had convinced me that he was an evil monster. I knew I would have absolutely no problem putting a bullet in his head.

JAVIER

Joe Toft wanted me to be in the epicenter of drug violence as much as possible, and during my first year in Colombia, that even meant spending Christmas and New Year's in Medellín.

It was all part of Toft's grand plan—to prove to Colombian law enforcement that we were squarely behind them and taking the same risks as ordinary cops in the search for the world's most wanted drug trafficker. The CNP needed to be made aware that the DEA had finally selected the right agents for the job and that we were even willing to sacrifice our personal time to work this case no matter the obstacles we encountered. CIA and SEAL Team Six were also dispatched to Medellín on a regular basis, but our guys in the DEA were convinced that Escobar was uniquely our target.

It was a smart strategy, and I heartily embraced it. Most of the time. But that year, I had my own plans for the holidays—some of them involving an attractive woman—and spending them on a deserted military base with a handful of Colombian cops and U.S. special forces didn't leave me in the best of moods.

Don't get me wrong; despite the violence, Medellín was a beautiful city—warm and temperate and surrounded by verdant mountains, its streets full of some of the most attractive women I had ever seen. Before the cartel turned Medellín into an urban war zone, Colombia's second-largest city was also a sprawling industrial center of some two million people known for its exports of textiles and orchids. But after Escobar and his fellow Extraditables launched their war against the government and the police, the homicides were averaging twenty per day. In 1990, 350 police officers had been killed in the drug violence out of a total of 4,637 homicides. In 1991, the killings would rise to 6,349. There were so many people shot, especially on the weekends, that the city ran out of ambulances. Taxis and private vehicles often came to a screeching halt outside the public hospital's emergency entrance, the wounded lying on the back seats, which were often soaked in blood.

The car bombs were incredibly scary because you never knew where they were going to be detonated. In that case, you had almost no chance of surviving. One time, a bomb exploded next to the bullfighting ring, killing twenty young cops who were in the area on the back of a truck. At a funeral I attended for some cops I had befriended, there were eight coffins. The elite anti-narcotics cops who died in the line of duty would get religious services at the chapel at the headquarters of the Escobar Search Bloc before departing to their hometowns for burials.

In addition to car bombs, the Medellín Cartel had other methods for killing cops, who each had a bounty of about one hundred dollars on their heads. Often, the cartel hired pretty girls to entice a cop at a bar and then suggest going to her place, where a group of *sicarios* would be waiting to jump him. Often, there was torture involved before certain death.

The other common method was the tried-and-true drive-by consisting of two guys on a motorcycle, whereby the passenger carried a weapon and executed the target. Of course, this had been practiced on jurists and politicians as the drug violence swept the country in the mid-1980s. Many of my own informants were killed that way in Medellín.

It's difficult to convey the tension that hung in the air, the feeling that you were always a target. Medellín was so dangerous that we were only allowed to stay for a few days at a time. As a gringo narc, I was such an obvious target that the convoy that escorted me from the airport deposited me at what passed for the local fortress—the Carlos Holguín police academy on the outskirts of town.

The Medellín police academy was also the command center of the *Bloc de Búsqueda*, or Escobar Search Bloc—a group of elite, anti-narcotics officers from the Colombian National Police who spent every waking hour searching for Escobar and his goons. Set up by President Barco in 1986, the group went through a few leaders before the Colombians got really serious and appointed Colonel Hugo Martinez to lead the group in Medellín in 1989. General Vargas was the national leader of the group and its main strategist. On the ground in Medellín, Martinez was a no-nonsense cop and a natural leader. Thin and tall with broad shoulders and a commanding presence, he was known to everyone as Flaco, or Skinny. He was strong, and he demanded respect, although he didn't really associate too much with the other Search Bloc members and spent most of his time in his office poring over intelligence reports.

Martinez studied Pablo Escobar, knew his habits and his girlfriends, and mapped his safe houses in Medellín.

He knew that Escobar hired architects and contractors to build his hideouts and then killed them when the jobs were complete.

I had a rather formal relationship with Martinez; we met regularly to share intelligence. I would pass on leads that we had gathered about drug operations in the United States and do the paperwork to provide any funding assistance for the Search Bloc from Washington. In return, he shared with me the CNP intel his men were gathering on the Medellín Cartel. From the outset, I knew that if anyone had the brains and dedication to capture Escobar, it was Hugo Martinez. I guess Escobar knew it too. He hated the Search Bloc and Martinez because they were the only ones really fighting to get him arrested. He also knew that Martinez was incorruptible. That's why he placed car bombs close to the police academy and tried poisoning officers at Carlos Holguín. He also bribed police officers to snitch on the Search Bloc's activities, which was why Martinez prohibited anyone at the academy from making telephone calls before they went out on a raid. Despite attempts to bribe him and myriad threats on his family and his own life, Martinez never wavered from his duty to capture Escobar dead or alive. At least not in the early days.

When things got really dicey in Medellín, I was flown directly to the police academy aboard a Huey gunship with .30-caliber machine guns mounted in the doors. The chopper would be waiting at the Medellín airport to fly me to the base. This was about a fifteen-minute flight, and the landing on a grassy clearing surrounded by trees inside the Holguín school was always harrowing with both gunners hanging out the helicopter doors to make sure the pilots didn't clip any trees.

The police academy housed about six hundred cops and was more like a U.S.-style military base than a school. It featured several buildings behind a heavily guarded outer perimeter with two entrances for vehicles. There were no fences anywhere, although surrounding streets in the neighborhood were blocked off with concrete barriers. Located in the working-class Comuna Manrique, at nighttime, the base had breathtaking views across the valley and of the lights of one of the most dangerous shantytowns in the city, where Escobar regularly recruited his *sicarios*. If you didn't know what you were looking at, that vista of twinkling lights on a majestic slope of hill was truly magical.

Despite the heavily armed police presence at the base, security was problematic. One night, a *sicario* fired on us inside the perimeter of the Holguín base while we were sitting at the Candilejas Bar, eating burgers and downing beers. Undercover cops immediately pulled out their guns, and everyone started shooting, resulting in one undercover guy shooting a uniformed officer dead. During the melee, I left my burger and beer untouched on the table and immediately dove behind a car until the shoot-out was over, dragging two CIA operatives with me. They had wanted me to run down a dark alley with them to the main part of the base, but I told them that it was the surest way to get shot, and I ordered them to stay put behind the car. I'm sure I saved their lives that night.

I stayed in the CNP Officers' Quarters, a grandly named narrow building with no air-conditioning or heat. In the summers, we always slept with the windows open, which meant I fell asleep to the steady buzzing of mosquitoes and woke up covered in red bites. The rooms were just off the mess hall, and the cooks began clanging pots and preparing food at 3:00 a.m. Each room had a few bunk beds, and I often shared the space with a group of CNP officers. It was close quarters and sometimes uncomfortable, but that's also the way we became real colleagues, sharing a common purpose. And a bathroom. There was a bathroom for every two rooms, but soap and even toilet paper were not provided, and the shower consisted of a pipe in the wall—no showerhead and no hot water.

That first Christmas, I became intimately acquainted with one of those bathrooms.

On Christmas Eve, the base was pretty much deserted, and Colonel Jorge Daniel Castro Castro, a demanding, tough-as-nails officer who led the side of the uniformed police in Medellín and was responsible for mounting five to seven operations *per day* to capture Escobar, was the presiding commander. He and his men invited me to a Christmas party that turned out to be an initiation of sorts. The party was at one of the officers' houses on base, next to the main barracks where I was billeted. There were about fifteen people at the Christmas party, including wives and children, and everyone made me feel at home. That meant plying me with shots of Aguardiente Antioqueño—the local rotgut—all night, which I was only too happy to accept. But when I went back to the barracks at 2:00 a.m., I was violently ill and spent the better part of the next few hours throwing up in the communal bathroom. Castro must have heard me in the next room as he drifted off to sleep. He probably woke up with a start to the sounds of my dry heaving. Before I knew it, he had raised the alarm and woken up all the officers on the base.

"I need Alka-Seltzer now!" yelled the colonel as he ran through the barracks. "Give me Alka-Seltzer! Emergency! Javier is dying! Help me! Help me!"

I got my Alka-Seltzer.

"Merry Christmas," I muttered to the wild-eyed Castro as I stood sweating outside the bathroom door.

And then I immediately ducked back into the john.

STEVE

Connie and I arrived in Bogotá on June 16, 1991, three days before Pablo Escobar turned himself in to police.

It was late on a Sunday evening, and as we got off our American Airlines flight and entered El Dorado International Airport, we were confronted with drab, gray concrete walls with no advertising anywhere. We thought we'd arrived in a Soviet bunker. We were immediately disappointed.

There was a lot of noise and confusion, with authorities issuing instructions in rapid-fire Spanish, children crying, and families speaking loudly to one another. Other passengers were pushing and shoving, and everyone was trying to get around us—two gringos who barely understood the language and felt like they had just landed on the moon.

We waited for several minutes for our DEA *escolta*, or armed guard, to meet us as we exited the jetway, but we didn't see anyone who looked like they were searching for us, so we just followed the crowd to the immigration booths, manned by somber, officious men in khaki fatigues. As we stood in line, a DEA agent approached us, but there was no armed guard as per the protocol we were told to expect. He barely looked at us as he motioned for us to get into the special line reserved for diplomats. We could tell he was unhappy to be at the airport at such a late hour on a Sunday night, and based on the few snippets of conversation we managed to exchange that evening, we found out he had left a good party—maybe even a promising date—in order to attend to our needs. He was the duty agent, which required him to handle a variety of responsibilities that weren't already assigned to someone else.

And as we made our way through customs, it looked

like he might be with us for the whole night because the Colombian officials on duty refused to allow us to leave with our pet cat, Puff, even though we had filled out all the paperwork before we left Miami.

To this day, we don't know if the problems that emerged around Puff had something to do with our diplomatic passports or if everyone around us was just having a really bad day. Whatever their reasons, this was not an auspicious welcome, and the three of us—Connie and me and certainly Puff—were rattled by the experience.

By the time we cleared Puff's formalities, it was the middle of the night. The agent proceeded to be even more of a jerk and drove us to a ramshackle boardinghouse in an out-of-the-way neighborhood. He made it clear that no hotel in Bogotá would admit us with a cat. He simply dropped us off at the curb as if to say, "Good luck with that!"

Connie and I carried our own bags to our room on the second floor. Strangely, the door to our room did not reach to the ceiling. The opening was large enough for me or any other person to climb through. In fact, there was absolutely nothing secure about where we were staying, and our bags took up much of the floor space so that we had to try to maneuver around them whenever we crossed from one part of the room to the other.

When we were ready to go to sleep, I put my 9 mm pistol on my bedside table. When we each lay down on the worn, saggy mattress, we rolled toward the center and bumped into each other on my side of the bed. Puff must have sensed that something was up, and he jumped up in bed with us. Even he didn't feel comfortable that first night in Bogotá.

As tired as we were, neither of us could fall asleep. That's when we heard the gunshots outside the boarding-house. I immediately grabbed my pistol, but then the shots turned into machine-gun fire. I looked at my little weapon and thought, *What am I going to do with this?*

Although the machine-gun fire lasted only a few seconds, Connie and I looked at each other and began wondering what we'd gotten ourselves into this time. But we also told ourselves that we would learn to make the best of our new adventure.

Maybe the positive attitude helped, because the next day—our first at the embassy—one of my supervisors offered us his temporary apartment so that we could move out of the boardinghouse with Puff. Ruben Prieto and his wife, Frances, had been living in a hotel in the trendy Zona Rosa and were scheduled to move into temporary quarters, but when I told him our harrowing arrival story, he and his wife graciously gave up their temporary apartment and stayed put in their hotel. Like us, they were cat lovers. We stayed in their apartment for a few months until we found a permanent place to live.

That first week was more of an orientation than anything else, and I wasn't given any special assignment. I immediately developed a liking for Javier and Gary and was thrilled to be told that I would work with them on the Escobar operation. Of course, I already knew a lot about Escobar based on my own research in Miami, but I never thought I would be one of the lead case agents on the operation in Colombia. On top of everything, I was really fortunate because when it came to working with the CNP, Javier and Gary had already developed a trusted and respected relationship with them. While I knew I still had to earn the Colombians' trust and respect on my own, I was accepted much more quickly because Javier and Gary vouched for me right away. Eventually, Gary was promoted and relocated to Barranquilla as the resident agent in charge, which left Javier and me to work together as partners.

Bogotá appeared to be on high alert the week Connie and I arrived. There were army tanks in the streets and grim-faced soldiers wielding AK-47s everywhere you looked. There were military jeeps with .30-caliber machine guns mounted in the back being handled by some very young-looking soldiers.

The U.S. embassy itself was a mini fortress. Several sets of security personnel guarded the building. There were Colombian security teams who watched the perimeter. They wore ugly brown uniforms and carried .38-caliber revolvers or 12-gauge shotguns. The Colombian National Police had full-time officers patrolling the perimeter as well. They also carried revolvers and long guns—typically a Galil 7.62 mm rifle. In addition, there were plainclothes cops blending in with the visitors. There were cameras everywhere.

Once inside the compound, there were more brown-uniformed guards and members of the embassy's regional security office, a branch of the State Department that is responsible for the security of the embassy and its personnel.

The primary entrance to the embassy building was guarded by U.S. Marines with .45-caliber pistols, 12-gauge shotguns, and M16 and AR-15 rifles. They were located inside the front entrance doors in a bulletproof station where they had access to all cameras and patrolled all locked security doors. Part of their job was to check offices during the night to make sure that no one left sensitive documents lying around. If you did, you were given a pink slip. If you accumulated more than three of those little pieces of paper, you were deemed a security breach and sent back to the United States.

The private security guards were responsible for checking your car when you entered the embassy gates. They would open the hood and check under the car with a flashlight and a mirror, looking for explosive devices. The next security check came from the Marines at the main door.

Once we made it through all the security checks and got our badges, I began to work closely with Javier. I was impressed from the moment I met him. He had arrived in Colombia three years before. He spoke Spanish, and I would soon come to appreciate that he even had the Medellín and Bogotá accents down. He knew everyone—the cops, the small-time drug dealers that he had managed to turn into sources, and all the good bars.

At first, we worked from the basement offices, but even-

tually, we were all moved to the third floor of the embassy, which became an exclusive DEA wing, behind a
heavy security door. Javier and I shared an office, and our
windows looked out on the parking area adjacent to the
primary embassy compound entrance. The security people
demanded that we keep the curtains drawn at all times so
that no one on the outside could see into our offices. This
was true of the entire embassy. Javier and I each had a desk
and several file cabinets, and since I was the DEA primary
firearms instructor, we had lockable closets where I stored
all the DEA ammo and weapons.

I got an earful from my new boss, Joe Toft, almost as
soon as I arrived. He was nice enough, but he made it very
clear that he needed to have any intelligence that we gathered before anyone else. It was essentially his job to present our findings to the ambassador, and we had better
make sure it was accurate. Later, I learned that he was
under constant pressure from DEA HQ in Washington
as well as other agencies within the embassy. There was a
lot of competition between the DEA and the CIA, and
Toft wanted the DEA to be out in front, and that meant
that the information he provided to the ambassador had
to be accurate. If the information that we provided to him
was based solely on uncorroborated intelligence, he wanted
to know that up front, and then he wanted to know what
exactly we were doing to stand it up.

One of the major problems I would come to have
with Toft was that he tended to believe whoever got him

information first. He was very close to the heads of the CNP and DAS in Bogotá, and if they told him something before we could get to him, he always believed their version over ours. Then he would berate us for not getting the information to him quicker. This despite the fact that often the information wasn't complete or even accurate. The worst butt-chewings I ever received were from Toft, and they were a direct result of him receiving incomplete intelligence from somebody else. He chewed me out in the DEA hallway where everyone could see and hear. He was dead wrong, of course, but when it came time to apologize, he called me into his office and closed his door. Toft couldn't ever admit he was wrong in front of others.

Despite his temper, I knew that Toft had our backs and he desperately wanted to win, and that meant capturing Pablo Escobar. To do that, we pretty much had everything at our disposal—from weapons to helicopters and even our own armored vehicles. As DEA agents, we were issued armored Ford Broncos. We had priority over other embassy employees, and that engendered a lot of jealousy because most embassy personnel were picked up and dropped off by an armored embassy van that took forever to wind its way through the city's snarling morning traffic. Embassy staff were not allowed to take local taxis or public transportation.

Bogotá was a city of just over four million people where the roads had been built for a fraction of that population density. The embassy van often made many stops to pick up employees scattered throughout the city. Adding to the misery during those daily commutes was the fact that because of rationing, electricity was often shut down and there were no traffic signals. The result was mayhem, chaos, a disaster. Not sure you can really understand it unless you lived through it. Imagine traffic in New York City with no working traffic lights. To top it all off, Colombians drive like speed fiends, so we felt we took our lives into our hands whenever we hit the road.

Connie and I did experience a tragic event one evening after returning home from the embassy. It seemed to take us forever to get home that evening because of the power rationing and no traffic signals. When we finally arrived home, we found Puff collapsed on the floor, still breathing but obviously in distress. Because it was later in the evening, the veterinary office was closed for the day. But Connie was able to call the vet at home and describe Puff's condition. The vet agreed to meet us at her office, but again, we had to deal with the horrible traffic. We arrived at the vet's office about fifteen minutes before she did. Sadly, Puff passed away in Connie's lap.

Overwhelmed by the security measures and cultural peculiarities of life in Colombia, Connie and I endured some tense moments, but mostly we learned to laugh at ourselves. And did we laugh—everything was funny from the constant mispronunciation of my name as "Steek" or "Stick" to the overwhelming traffic in Bogotá and the tiny cups of sugary coffee, called *tintos*, that I was forced to drink at every meeting! I'm a Diet Coke guy, and before Colombia, I never even drank coffee!

Some customs we just never got used to. For instance, we'd be the only diners in restaurants at six in the evening; the rest of the country ate after nine. It became a joke between us and the hostess at one of our favorite restaurants. I forget the name of it now, but it was the only place you could get a decent Philly cheesesteak sandwich. Despite our preference for dining early, the hostess always seated us, and we mostly had the restaurant all to ourselves.

One night as we were waiting for our food, a couple of young, dirty street kids started staring at us through the front windows of the restaurant. Connie and I felt guilty and ordered a sandwich for them. When I took it outside, fifteen to twenty street kids appeared out of nowhere along with two adults. All were dirty and wearing ragged clothing and appeared to be homeless. Connie and I pulled out all the pesos we had, which wasn't much, and ordered sandwiches for all of them. The manager of the restaurant was hesitant and said that the homeless were not allowed into the restaurant. We said we understood, and we took the sandwiches out to the hungry crowd. They were really appreciative of the food, and each one insisted upon shaking our hands. Then they all sat down in a big circle. The adults unwrapped one sandwich at a time, and passed it around. When that sandwich was gone, they unwrapped the next one and passed it around the circle. This way, they all got a fair share and an equal amount. We were impressed with their discipline and concern for one another. This behavior was not at all what we'd been led to believe about the homeless in Colombia. We knew that they could be dangerous and would protect one another, but we also saw caring and we personally experienced their gratitude.

But we were living in a war zone, and we learned to take nothing for granted. Violence was a constant. Real-life scenes of carnage played out on our TV screen on most nights. Even though we often had no clue what the newscasters and reporters were saying, we couldn't escape those awful images. In Bogotá, ambulance and fire truck sirens seemed to envelop the city like the early-morning fog, hiding the spectacular mountains that surrounded us.

Connie and I knew that every parked car could potentially explode, and we were pretty much prohibited from driving out into the country on our own for fear of kidnappers. Bogotá was considered a hardship post; families with children were not allowed. Years after we left Colombia, I'm hard-pressed to recall the intense pressure that characterized our daily life in Bogotá. As an American and a DEA agent, I had a $300,000 price on my head—a nice bit of cash for some ambitious *sicario*.

I didn't have the heart or the courage to tell Connie about that until long after we were safely out of there. After all, she had enough to deal with.

Connie didn't speak Spanish, and she had to take on

clerical jobs at the embassy because DEA spouses were forbidden to work outside the embassy. It was simply too dangerous.

Still, I couldn't complain about our new lifestyle. We moved into a spectacular apartment in the tony northern part of Bogotá. It was a sprawling four-bedroom apartment with a marbled foyer and floor-to-ceiling windows with a tremendous view of the Andes to the north and an equestrian club to the east. Whenever I looked down at the cantering, beautifully groomed horses and their riders decked out in their polished black boots, I had the impression that I was spying on a different reality. It could have easily been a scene from the Palm Beach Polo and Country Club. But this was how the rich lived in Bogotá, in a bubble of opulence that was far removed from the decrepit shantytowns that surrounded the city—a place ruled by violence and corruption. Still, we were grateful to escape that reality from time to time and live in such a beautiful place, even if it was a walled compound with armed guards at the gates. We lived next door to the city's best shopping mall, and we had even brought our car, a gray 1989 Pontiac Grand Am. The problem was that there were almost no Pontiacs in Colombia, so when we took it for a spin, it always drew attention, people surrounding the car in parking lots to have a look.

On weekends, we liked to party. Often, we'd go to the Den, where the beers were ice-cold and you could help yourself to sliced roast beef and mustard at the bar. Javier and I would often stop by for a drink and quick sandwich after work when we worked very late, or if it was a Friday night, we'd hang out at Mr. Ribs. It wasn't unusual for fifteen to thirty DEA personnel and their spouses or girlfriends to show up for drinks. This was a huge breach of embassy security. The rules said no more than three embassy personnel could be in the same establishment at the same time. The theory was that if a location became known as a hangout for embassy staff, that location might become a target of the narcos and terrorist groups. The theory was also that if a place were attacked, the fewer Americans present the better. But DEA people didn't always follow the rules, nor did other embassy personnel who joined us at Mr. Ribs. The guys from the regional security office were regulars, and these guys were the rule enforcers at the embassy, and our friends!

But most of the time, we organized epic weekend parties that would take place at our homes, and many times we'd hire a Mariachi band. We always had a stereo blasting for dancing. Sometimes, we had servers working to bring out the food and drinks and do the cleanup. These parties always lasted until the early-morning hours. If it was a going-away party for an embassy staff member, we'd have a tradition called "the Circle of Gold." The gold in question was Jose Cuervo Gold tequila. We'd form a circle, open the first bottle, throw away the cap, and start taking shots directly from the bottle. We once went through five bottles in a single night. It was pretty ugly. The next day, a bunch of us met midafternoon at an outdoor restaurant to eat greasy food and nurse our hangovers together.

The Marines who worked at the embassy threw good parties at their shared home, which reminded me of a frat house. The bottom floor was the common area, where the parties were held. There was a bar area, a room with a pool table, and a kitchen. Past the kitchen was an indoor pool. The Marines always invited several young and beautiful Colombian girls, although we married guys usually went with our wives. The music was always loud and the beer cold.

During holidays and big sporting events in the States like the Super Bowl and college football bowls, we'd have dinner parties at each other's apartments. Everyone would bring food, drinks, ice, whatever we needed. Connie and I hosted the dinners for Thanksgiving and the Super Bowl. These events were like a taste of home for everyone. We ate well, enjoyed a variety of drinks, and made sure our guards had plenty to eat as well.

We needed those good times to let off steam. All of us braced ourselves for the worst every day, but somehow, we also managed to live pretty normal lives. I still don't know how we did it.

JAVIER

We watched it all on TV—the surrender of Pablo Escobar.

None of us saw it coming, and we all took it badly—a

crushing blow to our efforts to bring him to justice. It was June 19, 1991, and I was in Medellín, but Toft immediately called me back to Bogotá after the surrender was announced. We all watched the events live at the embassy in stunned silence: the yellow government chopper landing near the ranch-style prison that included a pool, jacuzzi, soccer field, and what we assumed were luxurious accommodations close to Escobar's hometown of Envigado in the mountains outside Medellín. The sprawling "jail" was housed in the former Rehabilitation Centre for Drug Addicts, renovated to Escobar's specifications, so spectacular that it was nicknamed La Catedral. It was also outfitted with serious security that was designed to keep Escobar from escaping but also to keep him safe from his enemies. Surrounding the refurbished facility was a double fence that was nearly ten feet high, with fifteen rows of 5,000-volt electrified barbed wire and seven watchtowers, in addition to two guardhouses at the compound's entrance. Escobar had agreed to pay for all his own expenses for running the prison and had also made the government promise there would be no visitations and no flyovers. In addition to taking a group of his most trusted hitmen with him for protection, he even distributed flyers after he was settled at La Catedral, asking the local campesinos to report any suspicious activity to him in exchange for cash.

Escobar, then forty-one, was the first to emerge from the chopper. He wore jeans and a white leather jacket and the beginnings of a beard that he had grown in hiding.

202 STEVE MURPHY and JAVIER F. PEÑA

Reporters breathlessly described how the world's most wanted man handed his loaded 9 mm pistol to the warden before being escorted to his five-star cell, complete with a customized bathroom—an Escobar obsession. Brand-new toilets and other bathroom fixtures were present in the hundreds of safe houses that he used while in hiding. He was followed by Father Rafael Garcia Herreros, the eighty-two-year-old "television priest" who had helped negotiate the surrender with the government. The charismatic, white-haired cleric was the host of *El Minuto de Dios* (*One Minute for God*), the country's longest-running television show, which featured the priest delivering a brief sermon right before the national evening news. On one of his programs in the days before Escobar was scheduled to give himself up, he had pronounced the murderous drug trafficker "a good man."

"Pablo, surrender to me as soon as possible," the priest said on one of his broadcasts. "I have a nice opening for you in Peace University."

Peace University was the name that the cleric had given to La Catedral. Garcia Herreros even promised his audience that Escobar would use his time in incarceration to study for a law degree. Escobar had already cast himself in the role of peacemaker, describing his surrender to a Medellín journalist who accompanied him on board the helicopter as "an act of peace."

"To these seven years of persecution, I wish to add all

the years of imprisonment necessary to contribute to the peace of my family and the peace of Colombia," he said.

The whole thing was pretty surreal—like something you might read in a short story by Gabriel García Márquez. In fact, the author and journalist wrote about the surrender, which was brokered by his friend, the diplomat and politician Luis Alberto Villamizar Cárdenas. Escobar called upon Villamizar, one of his sworn enemies and a loud proponent of extradition, to protect his rights when he turned himself in because he was said to be impressed with the way Villamizar, a political ally of Galán who had survived an Escobar-ordered assassination attempt, had negotiated the dramatic release of his wife and sister, who had been kidnapped by his own *sicarios* in 1990 and held for five months.

"For all these years, Escobar has been my family's cross, and mine," Villamizar told García Márquez, who wrote about his ordeal in *News of a Kidnapping* years later. "First he threatens me. Then he makes an attempt on my life, and it's a miracle I escape. He goes on threatening me. He assassinates Galán. He abducts my wife and sister, and now he wants me to defend his rights."

I told you the whole story was surreal. And it was made even more pathetic by the government's official response.

"I want to underline that the commitment of the government in the fight against drug trafficking remains unbending," Gaviria told the country with a straight face after the historic surrender. "No nation has paid a higher price in the war against drugs than Colombia, institutionally and with thousands of lives, and the international community must assume its responsibility in this conflict, which involves both consumers and producers."

None of us agents were privy to the high-level talks that went on between the U.S. ambassador and Gaviria, but the overall feeling was that the president had caved in to terrorism. At the embassy, the law enforcement crowd was angry, and so were the Colombian police. We all felt that we had lost and Escobar had challenged his country and won because Colombia let him surrender into his own prison and even allowed him to hire his own guards. And we all knew that he was going to continue to send loads of cocaine around the world, but this time they would all be protected by the Colombian government!

I knew that the guys at the Search Bloc were extremely disappointed because, in the year before the surrender, they were getting closer and closer to capturing Escobar, and they knew the drug lord was increasingly on the run and desperate. For our part, we had processed dozens of traffickers for extradition to the United States, and there were many more awaiting the procedure in Colombian jails.

"Even though the emperor has not fallen, the empire is crumbling," General Miguel Maza Márquez, the DAS director, famously declared in the summer of 1990 as elite security forces delivered blow after blow, chipping away at Escobar's hierarchy.

In June 1990, a Search Bloc team killed the Medellín Cartel's de facto military commander, Jhon Jairo Arias Tascón, nicknamed Pinina, when he resisted arrest in Medellín. Officials said Pinina organized Escobar's *sicarios* and the group's terrorist activities. A month later, Carlos Henao, Escobar's brother-in-law and an important security director for the cartel, was captured as was Edgar Escobar Taborda, the propaganda chief of the cartel and the author of the press releases signed by the Extraditables. Known as "the poet," he dutifully sent letters to the media, the federal human rights office, and the attorney general stating that the elite forces of the Search Bloc were behaving like barbarians, torturing and killing members of the cartel. Escobar was getting so desperate that he started to impose a "war tax" on shipments of cocaine, charging his fellow traffickers in the cartel an extra percentage on their loads so that he could finance his war against the government.

I'm pretty sure that Escobar was stunned by the succession of assaults against him when he secretly offered to negotiate a cease-fire with Gaviria in the summer of 1990. For a few days at least, there was a lull in the car bombs that had already killed thousands throughout the country. Then on August 11, 1990—four days after Gaviria was sworn into office—CNP cops delivered a debilitating blow to the Medellín Cartel when they gunned down Gustavo Gaviria, Escobar's cousin and right-hand man. Gaviria coordinated trafficking on important routes through Mexico, Panama, Haiti, and Puerto Rico. Gaviria was shot dead in a raid on a Medellín safe house. Gaviria, who had been inseparable from Escobar since childhood, handled the business affairs of the cocaine empire.

The blow was equal in importance only to the elimination of Rodríguez Gacha. Grief-stricken, Escobar raged against the police and the government, and the violence erupted anew.

Still, the government continued their secret negotiations with Escobar. We heard a few rumors, especially among the DIJIN guys, that the government was talking to Escobar, entertaining the idea of a surrender into a prison of his own design, with his own guards. But we didn't believe them at the time. It all just seemed too crazy.

Until it actually happened.

That's why the Colombian cops took it so personally. Escobar's men had corrupted the police, and one CNP lieutenant had even gone rogue. Pedro Fernando Chunza-Plazas had been in charge of training Escobar's *sicarios* on setting car bombs and killing cops in Medellín. Chunza was so important to the Medellín Cartel that Escobar put him in charge of protecting his own family.

When Escobar wasn't sending his hitmen on terrorist missions, he was paying off Colombian congressmen through his attorneys to vote no on extradition.

In the end, it was Escobar's campaign of terror and bribery that backed Gaviria into an impossible corner. We always said that you can't and shouldn't negotiate with a terrorist, but that's what Gaviria's government did. And while his government looked incredibly weak for catering to Escobar's demands, there was an important argument to be made for saving innocent people from getting blown up by random car bombs. Hours before the surrender, the Colombian congress had voted to ban extradition entirely, which provided Escobar with a certain level of insurance against Gaviria changing his mind.

Weeks following Escobar's negotiated surrender, a semblance of peace did return to Colombia. The car bombs stopped, and Colombians seemed to enjoy a return to a normal life. But the guys who had risked their lives in the search for Escobar felt incredibly betrayed, and the new government looked weak for catering to the drug lord's demands. Not only did the government allow Escobar to plead guilty to only one felony count, which carried a five-year sentence, the world's most wanted criminal would also be allowed to keep all his ill-gotten gains—his billions, his homes, his flashy cars. No one even mentioned seizing his assets.

Once safely inside his luxury cell, law enforcement knew that they would not be able to touch him. The Medellín Search Bloc was disbanded, and Martinez was awarded a diplomatic position in Spain. At the embassy, we went back to working drug cases.

I was stunned. The whole thing left a bad taste in my mouth. Everything had changed, but nothing had changed. Cocaine was still flowing out of the country. Pablo Escobar had taken on the Colombian government and won. And I couldn't shake the feeling that with Escobar directing his drug operations from his cushy jail, every dead Colombian cop had really died for nothing.

STEVE

One of my first jobs in Colombia had nothing to do with Pablo Escobar.

Of course, Escobar was still our focus, and we tried to collect any information and intelligence we could about Escobar's activities in "jail." We knew he wouldn't stop his criminal enterprise or his attempts to become richer and more powerful, but getting any intel on Escobar during this time was extremely difficult, largely because one of the stipulations of his surrender barred us from coming anywhere near La Catedral. We were not able to intercept any of his communications, which was very unusual. Intel from informants was almost nonexistent. And we couldn't get close enough to the perimeter of the prison to conduct any kind of surveillance.

With the investigation on Escobar hitting a wall shortly after I arrived in Colombia, I decided to devote myself to studying every file we had on the Medellín Cartel.

That's when I was assigned to Carlos Lehder. More accurately, my task was to organize a mini military-style operation to get his immediate family out of Colombia and relocated to an undisclosed location in the United States as quickly as possible. Lehder, a cofounder of the Medellín Cartel, was the only high-level member of the criminal enterprise ever to be prosecuted in the United States for smuggling drugs. After a seven-month trial in federal court in Jacksonville, Florida, he was sentenced to 135 years plus life in prison with no possibility of parole. To reduce his sentence and ensure the safety of his family in Colombia, he entered into a plea agreement with federal prosecutors to act as a key witness in the trial of Panamanian strongman Manuel Antonio Noriega, a former U.S. ally and CIA informant who was instrumental in fighting the spread of Communism in Central America and the Caribbean, an important part of the Iran-Contra affair, which involved running drugs and weapons to help undercover operatives arm the Contra guerrillas in their war against the Sandinistas in Nicaragua in the mid-1980s.

In the months before the beginning of the Noriega trial in September 1991, I rushed around Bogotá trying to find a safe place for Lehder's wife and daughter. Lehder rightly feared that his enemies in Colombia would target his family to prevent him from spilling the beans on Noriega's relationship with the cartel. We knew that Escobar had already sent his goons to the United States to bump off any witnesses.

In what was expected to be explosive testimony, Lehder would describe how Noriega did business with the Medellín Cartel and effectively sold them the use of his country as a transshipment point for a share in the drug profits. At the same time that he was helping the cartel, he was also providing intelligence to the DEA and the CIA. In 1982, when he was head of intelligence and narcotics enforcement in Panama, Noriega offered to "build a cocaine pipeline" for Escobar to the United States. He also offered to launder money for the cartel. After a clandestine visit to Escobar's ranch in Medellín, the drug lord promised Noriega $1,000 on every kilo of cocaine shipped through Panama. Lehder estimated that more than a ton of cocaine was shipped through the country en route to the United States every month. Noriega was also promised a 5 percent cut of the estimated $60 million that was deposited in Panamanian banks every week during the height of the drug trade. And this was all while the United States was paying him $200,000 a year to be an informant!

By 1988, the United States had pretty much tired of Noriega's duplicity, and he was indicted in a U.S. federal court on drug-trafficking charges. In December of 1989, following allegations that he had rigged national elections in Panama, President George H. W. Bush launched Operation Just Cause. During the U.S. military invasion of Panama, Noriega sought refuge at the Vatican embassy in Panama City. U.S. soldiers famously flushed him out by playing loud rock music by the Clash, Van Halen, and U2 on an endless loop for three days and nights. By January 3, 1990, Noriega surrendered and became a prisoner of the United States. He was flown to Miami to stand trial on drug-trafficking, racketeering, and money-laundering charges.

Lehder had been an eyewitness to the colonel's meetings with the cartel, and he had been in charge of flying drugs in and out of Panama. As he was preparing to take the stand, I was handed the classified mission to bring his family to safety.

Ensuring the safety of his family was such a sensitive undertaking that only a few very trusted and high-ranking members of the Colombian National Police were ever made aware of it, and the DEA hierarchy felt it would be safest for the family if we handled the transfer alone, without the Colombian authorities.

Toft gave me a stack of Colombian passports for the Lehder family. In addition to his wife and daughter, there were extended family members who had to leave Colombia as well. All the passports had already been stamped with U.S. visas. I called Lehder's wife and told her I had arranged for a safe place for them to stay while the final arrangements were being made. I then had one of our secretaries make reservations, in the name of one of our bodyguards, at a hotel in the stylish Zona Rosa section of Bogotá for a few days while the final arrangements to get her and the family out of the country were made. We used our local *escoltas* for most of the legwork. The DEA *escoltas* were mostly retired Colombian police officers who had been vetted by our office, and they were hired as full-time security and always armed. We gave one of our *escoltas* enough cash to secure the hotel rooms, and he returned with the room keys.

I then called Lehder's wife and advised her to meet me near the hotel. We didn't want the family to be seen at the hotel in the company of a bunch of Americans because it would draw too much attention to them. I met up with the small group, which included Lehder's beloved young daughter, Monica. They appeared very nervous and scared. I handed Lehder's wife the room keys and tried my best to reassure them, and I instructed them to stay inside their rooms and order room service for meals.

Unbeknownst to them, we had several DEA *escoltas* stationed in and around the hotel to protect them.

Later that day, we used a Colombian travel agency to book the airline tickets. DEA had a close working relationship with the owner of a local travel agency, and he agreed to purchase the tickets under false names. This, of course, was all prior to 9/11, so security measures were not very strict. We knew we could change the names on the tickets at the airline counter when everyone arrived at the airport.

The family remained in the hotel with no issues. We spoke with Lehder's wife several times on the phone, but the calls were very cryptic because we never knew who might be listening. We went to the hotel on their final evening in Bogotá, but we had an *escolta* speak with the wife so that no one saw her talking to a gringo.

Based on our instructions, the *escolta* told the family to be ready to move to the airport the following morning at 5:00. We'd booked their tickets on American Airlines, which had a single daily flight between Bogotá and Miami that departed Bogotá in the early morning.

The following morning, several other DEA agents and I, accompanied by several *escoltas*, arrived at the hotel and escorted the Lehder family into our SUVs. There were two SUVs for the family members accompanied by two agents and a driver, and a third SUV followed behind with extra security. All our agents were armed with handguns and had machine guns poised in readiness for an attack.

The Colombian government had authorized DEA agents to carry weapons in their country, and we all carried concealed weapons permits. Our *escoltas* carried revolvers, and a few of them carried Uzi submachine guns. Following a preplanned route that kept us off many of the main thoroughfares, we made it to El Dorado International Airport with no problems.

At the airport, we parked in the diplomatic parking lot, which was located near the main entrance to the international terminal. Two *escoltas* and two DEA agents conducted a quick reconnaissance of the airport to see if anything looked suspicious. Everything appeared to be normal, so we got the family out of our SUVs and got their luggage, and we all escorted them into the international terminal building. The DEA enjoyed a close working relationship with the personnel at American Airlines in Bogotá, and we'd already arranged to have the check-in process expedited so that the family could be moved to a less public and more secure location to await the flight. Once we entered the airport, we found our American Airlines contact person, moved the family and their luggage to a separate line, changed the names on the previously reserved airline tickets to the real names of the Lehder family, checked their luggage, and escorted them through the security checkpoints at the airport. We all moved to a private waiting room.

When the flight was ready to board, American Airlines allowed the family to embark first so they wouldn't have to stand in line. The family was very cooperative with us, and the wife thanked us for our assistance as they were getting on the plane. The flight departed with no issues, and the Lehder family arrived safely in Miami a few hours later. Once in Miami, the family was met by members of the U.S. Marshals Service, and I never heard anything about them again.

I didn't think much about the Lehder family until a year later, when a strange letter arrived at the U.S. embassy in Bogotá addressed to me. The return address label indicated that it had been sent from the U.S. Federal Bureau of Prisons, Inmate Monitoring Section, Washington, D.C.

And the address on the envelope was written in Spanish. This was very unusual. In fact, I'd never received or even seen anything like this. The envelope contained a single page of notebook paper with a handwritten message addressed to me. The letter read, "USA-92, DEA Special Agent Steve Murphy, Bogotá, Colombia—I most sincerely wish to thank you for helping my family and country. At your service, CL."

I've received letters from inmates before offering to assist with providing information about ongoing investigations, but these are usually taken with a grain of salt. But I've never received a thank-you note from an inmate.

I showed the letter to Javier. Of course, both of us knew instantly who it was from.

JAVIER

We nicknamed him Oscar.

I still can't reveal his true identity. Let's just say he was a source—a good source, who told his story to Colombia's attorney general and then to us. Oscar's information was so important that we decided to fly him to the United States to have him fully debriefed. Later, he testified in secret to Congress. We knew that Escobar would try to kill him, which was why we put him in witness protection in the United States.

We met him in Medellín, and he provided us with a harrowing picture of what was really going down at La Catedral a year after Escobar walked through the prison's gates in a grand show of peacefully turning himself into authorities.

Oscar told us what we had suspected all along—that Escobar was holding court with bad guys inside the jail, where he had access to safe radio transmitters, fax machines, and telephones. He was ordering the kidnapping and killing of his enemies, including any potential witnesses in the Noriega trial in Miami. One of his hitmen was even captured in the United States while carrying out Escobar's orders.

Oscar knew what he was talking about. He told us that he was the only survivor of a massacre of traffickers that had been ordered by Escobar from his jail cell.

The whole thing started over a bag of cash—rotting cash—after Escobar's *sicarios* found it in the ground, the bills deteriorating because they had not been properly buried. The hitmen took the money back to Escobar at the prison and told him that they had found it at a property owned by Gerardo Moncada, one of Escobar's traffickers, in Medellín. The *sicarios* told Escobar that Moncada and his partner, Fernando Galeano, had been holding out on him by not telling him about the cash. Oscar said the *sicarios* were jealous of Moncada and Galeano and went to Escobar to get them out of the way. The plan seemed to work as Escobar worked himself up into such a frenzy, yelling that he had been betrayed by two of his most trusted associates. He demanded that both men be brought to the prison for an "interview." Neither Moncada nor Galeano thought much of the request for a meeting with the boss. They even dispensed with their head of security, Diego Fernando Murillo Bejarano—better known as Don Berna.

But when Moncada walked in and saw the bag of deteriorating cash on the floor, he knew immediately what Escobar was thinking. Moncada tripped over his words as he started telling Escobar that they were not holding out on him. They had buried the cash some five years before and had forgotten all about it. Escobar kept silent, but everyone in the room could feel the tension. He accused them of cheating him out of $20 million in proceeds from the cocaine trade and reminded them that they were only able to do business because he had sacrificed his own freedom to fight against extradition. He told them that they would owe him $200,000 on every shipment of coke that they sent abroad. When the two men, who had been childhood friends and business associates for years, balked at the price, Escobar could barely contain his rage. According to Oscar, he picked up a large stick and started clubbing Moncada. The *sicarios* jumped in and killed Galeano. The bodies were burned and cut into small pieces. And then Escobar made it clear that he would take over all of Moncada's and Galeano's assets—ranches, businesses, and homes. He also ordered the hit on their families and business associates. In a grisly reminder of his dominance, he instructed his goons to send the two men's charred penises to their wives.

Escobar's savagery would end up spelling his own doom.

Oscar's intelligence proved so devastating that the Colombian government could no longer ignore what was going on at La Catedral. Gaviria ordered Escobar moved to a more secure prison—a converted army barracks on the outskirts of Medellín. Of course, the drug lord refused to go quietly and demanded a meeting with high-level federal officials to be conducted at La Catedral. That's when the deputy minister of justice, Eduardo Mendoza, and the country's director of prisons, Lieutenant Colonel Hernando Navas, were dispatched to La Catedral to negotiate the transfer. The government officials naïvely arrived without armed *escoltas* to tell Escobar that he was being moved to the barracks and would be returned to La Catedral once security there had been improved.

But when they arrived at the jail, Escobar was in no mood to talk. After being escorted to the drug lord's private prison suite, the two government officials were surrounded by his henchmen and told that they were going to leave there dead. Mendoza and Navas were held hostage, along with the prison warden. Mendoza would later describe how Escobar's most trusted *sicario*, Popeye, thrust the barrel of an Uzi against his head and promised to kill him. At about 4:00 a.m., as Escobar's goons continued their death threats, Mendoza heard two explosions followed by shouting and gunfire. Hundreds of government troops had swarmed the prison to rescue the hostages and to capture Escobar, who managed to escape with his brother, Roberto, and a handful of other inmates through a tunnel. Although the heavily armed troops and their tracking dogs surrounded the area around Envigado searching for Escobar and his henchmen, they were long gone, hidden away in one of the many safe houses that the cartel maintained in and around Medellín.

Mendoza, his clothes in tatters, later told a press conference that he was saved by a soldier and was forced to crawl through mud during the melee to avoid the barrage of bullets that ricocheted off the prison walls.

I heard about Escobar's escape when I turned on the news the following morning. When I got to the embassy, things were hectic with everyone asking questions. We didn't have much information that morning, but everyone kept coming into the office and asking us what was going on. The ambassador was talking with the Colombian president, Joe Toft was talking with the head of the CNP, and we were talking with our counterparts at the CNP. And I'm sure the CIA was talking with their counterparts in the Colombian military and intel sections. It wasn't long before Toft called Steve and me into his office and told us that the ambassador wanted us in Medellín right away; the DEA plane was already waiting at the Bogotá airport. The request had come from the CNP, who told Toft that everything was in a state of confusion. The media was going crazy with the escape; someone on a radio station claiming to be Escobar said the Colombian government had broken their contract and that he had done nothing wrong.

Both of us returned home to pack a bag of clothes and rushed to the airport. Toft said our government wanted an inventory of what was at the prison to see if there was any actionable intelligence.

Like everyone else at the DEA office, we were thrilled!

The escape meant that we were all free to go after our biggest target. The search was back on! This was our shot at finally seeing justice done to Escobar.

The Huey helicopter, mounted with two .30-caliber machine guns on each side, was waiting for us when we arrived at Rionegro Airport in Medellín. We couldn't fail to notice that the CNP helicopter had had repair work done on the windshield to cover an obvious bullet hole. In fact, for the next eighteen months of the search for Escobar, every CNP helicopter we flew in had at least one bullet hole in it. We exchanged a few nervous chuckles with the pilot as we lifted off and headed to the Carlos Holguín school, anxious to get the official permission from the CNP commander to enter La Catedral.

Even though Steve had already been in Colombia for a year, I was still a little skeptical about him. His Spanish was still rusty, but I could tell he was trying and took every opportunity to practice. We were not very close, and while Escobar was in jail, we sat together during DEA presentations and conducted a few operations, but nothing to equal the magnitude of the Escobar search.

I wasn't sure about him because, in so many ways, Steve and I were complete opposites. But while it may have seemed an odd match, our differences would later work to our advantage as a team. Steve was super organized, and I just hated paperwork. But I had built a large network of law enforcement contacts in Colombia whom we could call upon at a moment's notice.

This new search for Escobar would bring us together, and in many ways, Steve would become my most trusted partner and my best friend.

The Virgin Mary watched over me as I lay wide awake, tossing and turning, in Pablo Escobar's bed.

I never imagined that's how I would spend my first night at La Catedral, but then I never thought I would ever enter the lion's lair—the luxurious suite of rooms that passed for the billionaire drug dealer's prison cell.

It all started off on an official military footing. Toft had sent us to La Catedral to collect as much intelligence as we could possibly find at the prison the day after Escobar's daring escape. But once Steve and I landed at the Carlos Holguín academy in Medellín, we had to get official permission to visit the prison. We had to formally present ourselves to the commanding officer—a man we never really liked, who had taken over when Hugo Martinez was sent

222 STEVE MURPHY and JAVIER F. PEÑA

to Spain after Escobar's surrender. Colonel Lino Pinzon was tall and self-important—imposing in his perfectly starched CNP uniform. We always got the feeling that he never wanted us Americans around, and who could blame him? We just might have felt the same way if our roles were reversed. In any event, there was no cordial greeting, no sugary cups of *tinto* when we met with him in his office to discuss the logistics of entering La Catedral. Pinzon made it clear that he was in charge and would make the decisions on how to carry out the new manhunt. After a very short, mostly one-sided conversation, we were dismissed. As important as this new mission to track down Escobar was to us, neither Steve nor I ever got any sense of urgency from the colonel.

In the days after Escobar's escape, confusion reigned at the base, and I suppose that Pinzon had his own way of trying to control it. There was no infrastructure in place to capture Escobar and little consultation with law enforcement partners like us and the DIJIN guys. When a couple of plainclothes DIJIN officers did show up at the base to start their work, they were formally greeted by Pinzon, who was determined to rule with an iron fist. It was a bad idea from the start, and things just got worse as the days wore on. The Colombian intelligence operatives hated Pinzon, who forced them to get up at 6:00 a.m. with the other young CNP recruits to do push-ups. This was after they had been out all night chasing leads on Escobar. The DIJIN guys were used to answering to no one but their own boss back in Bogotá, but Pinzon insisted they answer to him. We saw the writing on the wall right away, and we knew the situation couldn't go on. One of the first requests we made of Toft was to urge his pal Octavio Vargas Silva, the architect of the original Bloque de Búsqueda, to bring back Martinez immediately and give him back his old job as the leader of the Search Bloc on the ground in Medellín. We practically begged him. We felt Martinez was the only one we could work with.

After the formalities at the academy, Steve and I got back in the Huey helicopter and flew the short distance to Envigado, about twenty minutes away. The chopper had to land on a grassy hill some two miles away from La Catedral because Escobar had installed poles around the property to prevent any kind of armed landings. There was also a cannon on the grounds to shoot down any planes that got too close. I have to hand it to him: He thought everything through like a military strategist. No doubt he was worried about potential attacks from his enemies in the government and the rival cartels.

We walked uphill on a bumpy, dirt road that had been partly washed away by rainstorms and was strewn with large rocks. We were met at the prison gates by a small group of DIJIN officers. They had already done a reconnaissance of the whole place and pointed out the firing range, where prisoners practiced shooting, and the warden's house, which was just outside the security barriers. At the back of the prison, there was a hole in the rear perimeter fence. This wasn't a gate; it was just a hole in the fence so people could walk in and out without going through any checkpoints. There was also a full-sized soccer field, complete with lights for night games. Later, we found trophies in a number of the cells that indicated that Escobar held his own tournaments at the prison.

Inside, the place was a mess after the gun battle between Colombian authorities and Escobar's men. Our shoes crunched on the broken glass from the shot-out windows, and the walls were pockmarked with myriad bullet holes.

In the main building, there were a few offices for the prison staff followed by two sets of steel bars painted green—the only ones we saw inside the entire prison, seemingly built for show, as if to somehow prove that the resort-like complex we were about to enter was indeed a prison. It was Escobar's little inside joke—a sop to the Colombian authorities that he was indeed in prison, even if it was one of his own design!

Past the bars, there was an infirmary, storage rooms, a kitchen, and more offices. Pool and Ping-Pong tables, and a large, garish oil painting of Escobar and Father Rafael Garcia Herreros dominated a large recreation room. Escobar had poured millions into the Catholic priest's charities, and had, of course, used him to help negotiate with the Colombian government when he made his big show of surrendering.

The prison was pretty much what we suspected—a

country club filled with luxury items, such as state-of-the-art televisions, refrigerators, and stereo equipment. Still, we marveled at its design and organization. Neither U.S. nor Colombian intelligence had any idea how Escobar's henchmen had managed to carry these huge items to the top of the hill. Nor did we have any intelligence that Escobar had contracted with architects and builders to construct chalets on a hillside behind the jail. Later, we learned from CNP officials that Escobar never slept in the same place for more than two consecutive nights. That included his own prison "cell." He used the nearby cottages for parties and alternated sleeping in each of them. The cottages were all beautifully appointed, with planters, hanging baskets, and luxurious upholstery and drapery. One of them had a bathroom built like a bunker, with reinforced cement walls that must have been more than three feet thick. One of the bedrooms in each of the chalets had a hidden door that led to a tunnel for a quick escape into the mountains. We heard that Escobar had plans to turn the prison into a resort once he had served his time.

Cash had been buried throughout the property, or so we were told. Shortly after the escape, we heard rumors that three low-ranking police officers guarding the prison had found a hidden *caleta* with millions of dollars and had kept their discovery secret. After they returned to Bogotá, they all retired. No one ever said how much they had found, but it was probably an enormous amount. We'd also heard that a *campesino* found a cache of money on a riverbank that had lodged out of a dirt hole near the jail. The *campesino* admitted to police that he had taken some of the cash, but when the cops asked him why he didn't take everything, he answered that he didn't have time because he had to rush home to milk his cows.

In those first intense and chaotic weeks at the prison, helicopters continuously took off and landed, transporting an army of experts to scour the buildings and the surrounding area. We brought in special ground radars and expert investigators to search for buried human remains, but we didn't find any on the prison grounds.

Escobar's own "cell" was a sprawling bedroom and office, which was surprisingly neat. The bed was made, and the bathroom was very clean. Escobar had a thing about clean and well-proportioned bathrooms, and each time we raided a safe house that Escobar used, we always found a curiously sparkling bathroom with brand-new fixtures.

The private apartment also housed a multitude of different weapons. He also had security armbands and a high-powered, state-of-the-art telescope mounted near the railing of his patio, just outside the doorway to his prison cell. A CNP officer told us that Escobar used it so he could see his wife and children when talking with them on the phone.

In his adjoining office, we found a film canister in the trash. When we had the film developed, we found pictures of Escobar, including the now infamous image of him in a blue sweater, which we turned into wanted posters, offering $2 million for information leading to his capture. The Colombian government separately offered more than $6 million. And speaking of wanted posters, he had every wanted poster that had ever been issued against him in Colombia and just about every article that had appeared about him in his files. There were also stacks of self-published hardcover books signed by Escobar and his *sicarios*. The leather-bound volumes, featuring satirical cartoons making fun of the United States, were each signed by Escobar and encased in gift boxes, which were also made of the finest, supple leather. No one ever found out who printed them. We had more important things to do.

We were fascinated by what we were finding, and we rushed to have everything photographed. In addition to the piles of satirical books, we found volumes on how to take care of homing pigeons. Several pigeon coops were located throughout the prison, including outside of Escobar's cell. The pigeons were used to deliver messages to various Escobar associates and members of the cartel.

Inside Escobar's office, we also found an empty safe. No doubt he had grabbed whatever cash he was keeping there for his escape. There were also lace negligees and sex toys, including vibrators, neatly arranged in a closet. In Escobar's correspondence files, which were surprisingly neat and methodically organized, he kept all the threatening notes from his enemies. We also found letters from mothers offering up their daughters for sex with the drug lord.

Despite his philandering, he was devoted to his children.

Outside his cell was a sitting area that overlooked a playground, complete with a playhouse that had electricity and running water.

We immediately joined the intelligence officers and Alonzo Arango Salazar—the second-in-command at DIJIN—who was running the show as they combed through Escobar's possessions. We had a good relationship with Arango, who pretty much welcomed us with open arms, and we joined him in the systematic search of the prison—a process that would take some three months to complete. Among the experts we brought in was ATF agent J. J. Ballesteros, who stayed at the prison for several weeks combing through the huge cache of weapons and doing traces on the guns that we seized. J. J. was stationed in Bogotá and was assigned to the DEA office at the embassy. He never told his bosses at ATF headquarters in Washington that he had joined us in Envigado for the search, and he stayed at the jail for several days before anyone knew he was missing. When the ATF hierarchy in D.C. found out, they immediately ordered him back to Bogotá, which was too bad for us. J. J. had earned a brilliant reputation with the CNP; he spoke fluent Spanish, and his work at La Catedral proved invaluable to us.

J. J.'s flight from the jail was one of the more lighthearted moments we experienced during the search. The other was Arango's dare. He had a twisted sense of humor, to be sure, and he dared me to sleep in Escobar's bed on that first night. By nightfall, Steve had already gone back to Bogotá to manage the search for Escobar from DEA headquarters, and I was alone with the Colombian cops and DIJIN officers assigned to the jail. The Colombian officers slept in the dorms adjacent to Escobar's apartment—no doubt the rooms once occupied by Escobar's small army of *sicarios*.

I only managed one night in Escobar's bed, and for the other nights that I slept in the prison, I joined the CNP guys in the dorms. There was nothing wrong with the bed. In fact, it was surprisingly comfortable—large and custom-made, with a base made out of cement and two firm mattresses stacked on top of each other. I made sure to change the sheets, and when it was time to hit the sack, I crawled under the colorful comforter. An eerie silence enveloped the bedroom, and I tossed and turned, wide awake. Sleep wouldn't come, even though I was exhausted from the flight from Bogotá and a hectic and exciting day spent combing through Escobar's stuff.

Outside, the mountain air was brisk and bracing. We were so far out in the country that there was only darkness—so palpable and deep that it made my skin crawl. I noticed the Virgin as soon as I walked into the room. Now, wide awake, I turned on the bedside lamp and got up to pace the room. There she was, illuminated in the glow from the lamp. She was made of ceramic—the very image of serenity as she clutched the infant Jesus in her arms. I couldn't help thinking how a guy who killed thousands of innocent people could pray to the Virgin Mary, could dare to seek her protection, her blessing.

I went back to bed but lay awake all night trying to make sense of Pablo Escobar, how it could be that his evil soul harbored any hint of goodness, any belief in God and the Virgin. The more I thought this through, the angrier I became. Images of the coffins of dead cops from all the funerals I had attended since arriving in Colombia, the twisted wreckage of the Avianca bombing, and the panic in the streets of Bogotá that accompanied the assassination of Galán all played out in my mind.

Sleep became impossible.

The clanging of pots from the nearby kitchen at 5:00 a.m. signaled a welcome end to my tortured night. The CNP guys were making breakfast, and the earthy, slightly nutty aroma of freshly brewed coffee wafted into the bedroom. I don't particularly like coffee, and I rarely, if ever, drink it, but smelling it brought me back to reality, ushering in a brand-new day and somehow renewing my strength for the enormous task that lay ahead of us—bringing the murderous drug lord to justice.

STEVE

It was the boiled chicken that got to me: gray and shriveled, with remnants of feathers still sticking out of the tough, goose-bumpy skin. I forced myself to eat it with the rice and potatoes that were served to us at practically every meal at the Holguín base, because we didn't always get a piece of chicken or any other protein. It was what the Colombian cops ate, and it was important that we demonstrated that we were with them for the long haul in the renewed search for Pablo Escobar.

So I ate the chicken. When we didn't get chicken, that left rice and potatoes. Because both were bland tasting, we put ketchup on the rice to give it some taste. To this day, I still enjoy eating rice.

In order to build their trust, we slept in bunk beds in the dorm rooms with as many as seven cops to a room. The mattresses were lumpy and damp, and we were each given nothing but a thin army-issue blanket against the mountain chill. In the mornings, only cold water came out of the showerheads in spurts. Toilet paper and soap were luxuries.

The Holguín base was the focal point of the search, and both Javier and I felt it was important to bunk with the local cops and endure the same hardships they did, which was why I ended up eating all that chicken, and in the early days, at least, taking orders from Pinzon, who was pretty much in over his head. Luckily, our lobbying to bring back Martinez eventually paid off, and Toft and the ambassador were able to persuade CNP director General Octavio Vargas Silva, who in turn convinced the Colombian president that Hugo Martinez was the only man for the job.

Two months after Escobar escaped, Martinez returned from Spain to the Holguín base to command the search.

That's when I met the colonel for the first time. He was tall and in great physical shape. He had a full head of dark hair and always wore green fatigues. He was friendly but had a professional air of authority about him. He never spent any time chitchatting and always looked you in the eye when he was talking to you. He listened to what you had to say and was unfailingly polite, but there was never any question that he was in charge. He didn't need to say he was the boss; you just knew he was.

By the time I met Martinez, I had been in Colombia for more than a year. It was because of Javier that I ended up having a good relationship with him. Javier vouched for me as his partner, which meant that Martinez welcomed me at the Search Bloc from the beginning. His office door was always open to me, and he was patient in dealing with my halting Spanish and my endless questions.

Javier and I weren't the only ones who were happy to see Martinez back in charge; the feeling of excitement and relief spread throughout the ranks. Suddenly, there was a collective sense of hope, and we all had the feeling that we were really going to get Escobar this time. Javier and I liked to joke that we had managed to put the band back together, and we were blasting off, full steam ahead.

In the weeks immediately after Escobar's escape, Toft wanted to make sure that at least one of us was always in Medellín and the other was at the embassy. Our jobs were to monitor the prison search, mining it for any scraps of intelligence, but our priority was to find Escobar. It was an intense time, with intelligence experts and other analysts coming and going, as well as the groups of curious government officials who behaved like morbid tourists, wanting a glimpse of the prison where the world's most famous outlaw resided for a year.

Neither of us were really given any time off, and we began to work really long hours. In Bogotá, we'd each try to get back to our apartments at least once a day to grab a few hours' sleep, shower, and change our clothes. It was pretty chaotic, but it grew into a controlled chaos. At Christmas, we were told that one of us had to stay in the country. Javier, who was single, graciously volunteered so that Connie and I could head back home to see our families. He took vacations at other times, but really in those intense eighteen months during the second search, we pretty much lived and breathed Pablo Escobar. None of us had much of a social life. I only saw Connie intermittently, and Javier pretty much worked nonstop.

I don't think either of us really minded working round the clock. We both desperately wanted to find Escobar, and we felt the only way that we would make any headway was to actively monitor the tip line that we had set up at the base and go on as many raids as Martinez would let us join. Technically, it was against U.S. policy for us to accompany Colombian law enforcement on raids, and Javier and I had some pretty long discussions about defying orders that required us to remain within the perimeter of the base in Medellín. We knew that order existed for our own safety, and all American personnel on the base had to obey the same rule. But we also knew we couldn't do our jobs properly if we stayed back and simply expected the CNP to do the life-threatening work—to pursue Escobar and his organization. So at the beginning of our time living in Medellín, Javier and I both agreed we needed to be out with the CNP, mostly with the elite DIJIN unit. We decided we would go outside of the base with the CNP when we felt it was for a good reason. And we agreed we would not tell the other Americans when we were going out. That way, we didn't put them in an awkward position of reporting our activities back to Bogotá. The U.S. military guys were very smart and probably knew what we were up to, but they never asked us, and we never told them.

This don't-ask-don't-tell existence carried over the long year and a half that we chased Escobar during the second manhunt. I can't say that Toft knew we were leaving the base and accompanying the CNP on operations and surveillance missions, but he was an intelligent guy, so he probably suspected something was going on. For instance, we were given certain orders that suggested he knew we were participating in raids. The orders included not carrying long guns—shotguns or rifles—or wearing any khaki-colored clothing that made us look like Colombian police or military. We didn't question those orders, and Toft pretty much left us alone.

We always made sure he knew about the information we were gathering in Medellín, the missions undertaken by the CNP, and the results of those missions. He knew we were disseminating intelligence that we'd obtained in Medellín to other DEA offices worldwide, and he made sure we had the resources we needed to do our jobs there. But he never asked us if we were going outside of the base, and we never mentioned it.

The Colombians also knew we were breaking the rules, and they were very careful trying to never put us in a situation in which our lives were at extreme risk. As a result, we always allowed the Colombians to take the lead. In turn, they strove to make sure we were out of harm's way, although that was kind of wishful thinking since we risked our lives every day that we spent in Medellín.

But our biggest problems had nothing to do with the danger that surrounded us, the lousy food, our relationship with the Colombian cops, or even the long hours we worked. It still pains me to admit that our biggest obstacles in the epic search to find Pablo Escobar were often our fellow Americans.

The relations between the DEA and U.S. intelligence agencies, such as the CIA and NSA, in Colombia were strained at best. There was an unhealthy competition between us and the CIA, largely because the CIA chief of station in Colombia seemed to have contempt for our work.

As the lead DEA agents in Colombia, Javier and I were focused on law enforcement and bringing Escobar to justice. In a general sense, we were always looking for evidence that could be used against any narcotics traffickers in a U.S. court. The CIA had a different mission, and their focus was on insurgent groups like the FARC and their connections to Communist regimes. The FARC had grown so powerful, killing dozens of Colombian security forces, that on November 9, 1992, Gaviria declared a state of emergency. He lashed out at "the terrorists, murderers, and kidnappers, against that handful of deranged fanatics who have not read in the newspapers the story of the end of Communist totalitarianism."

And, of course, Gaviria was aware that the FARC was no longer in the business of just spreading their Marxist ideology. As Gaviria noted so well, "They only seek the enrichment of their leaders and the growth of checkbooks based on kidnapping, extortion, hired assassins, and protection money."

Gaviria's state of emergency was a boon for the Escobar manhunt because it meant that any bad guy who provided us information that allowed us to get closer to Escobar's capture could see a major reduction in their jail sentences. Although the country's constitutional court—Colombia's highest judicial body—was to throw this provision out in May 1993, we benefited from the few months that it was in place, reaping a great deal of intelligence from captured hitmen and small-time crooks who gave us valuable leads on Escobar.

In the early days, we received a lot of information and

intelligence to corroborate the FARC's cozy relationship with the cocaine cartels. We knew that members of the FARC were providing security for the Medellín Cartel's jungle-based cocaine labs. We dutifully passed this information on to CIA personnel. But the CIA leadership either didn't want to admit there was a crossover between drugs and Communism, because it blurred the lines, or maybe there were other reasons that were never revealed to us. Regardless, it created a terrible working relationship between the DEA and the CIA—and the sad part was that both the drug cartels and the insurgent groups benefited from this infighting.

In Medellín, they even managed to drive a wedge between us and the army's Delta Force and the navy's SEAL Team Six, who were stationed at the Holguín base right after Escobar escaped. From the outset, it was clear that the spooks had access to highly classified data related to Escobar, but they refused to share it with us because we didn't have the "appropriate" security clearances. It took intervention from Joe Toft, who went to the American ambassador, Morris Busby, to get us the clearance, but the CIA still handed over their information reluctantly and in a piecemeal fashion. I can still remember the humiliation of going into their offices at the U.S. embassy in Bogotá. Whenever we walked in, they would activate a flashing blue light throughout their office space to let everyone know that there was an "outsider" in their midst. We were then required to sit at a child-sized desk located just outside the office of the chief of station and his assistant, where we were allowed to review the data. We always had two sets of eyes watching everything we did. Believe me, we never felt welcome.

In the end, we never found their information of much use to our mission. In many cases, we found that their cables contained the exact same intelligence that we had reported days before. Yet those reports never said that the information came from the DEA! Any intelligence on Escobar in the CIA reports was always attributed to a "reliable source of information." Obviously, this demonstrated that the CIA was given access to every report and cable we prepared, but we didn't enjoy that same professional courtesy.

Things got so bad that Javier and I believed that the CIA was intercepting our home phones to find out what additional information we were discussing between us. It's illegal for the CIA to investigate American citizens, so if this were true, they would have been committing a crime. We didn't have any proof, but we did encounter several instances in which the CIA knew the intimate details of our conversations. Also, when we hung up the phone after our conversations, we would pick up the receiver immediately afterward and find nothing but silence on the line; there was never a dial tone. As we waited on the line we heard several *clicks* before the dial tone would return.

Were we being overly paranoid? Maybe, but we were not about to take any chances as we continued on the most important mission of our careers. If it wasn't the CIA monitoring our phones, it could have been the Colombian government. On a trip back to the United States, I purchased a few fax machines. We installed one at Javier's apartment and another at my place in Bogotá, and we had another set up at the Carlos Holguín school. We already had one at our office in the embassy. At that time, fax-intercept technology was relatively new and not commonly used, so anytime Javier and I had something important to say, we wrote it out on a piece of paper and sent it through the fax machine.

When we did need to speak on the phone, we devised our own special code. We used different terms so that no one would know what we were referring to exactly. A lot of the conversations consisted of inferences, and if you didn't know what or who we were talking about, you most likely wouldn't be able to figure it out. For specific bad guys, we used nicknames or other words that only we were aware of. We might refer to the person that we talked about earlier without mentioning the name. For locations, we would refer to previous events that occurred in or near that location, rather than saying exactly where. For events, we would refer to a similar instance that had already taken place. For example, we would refer to a doper who had been previously killed during a firefight with the cops to talk about a current target. If we had information about a location outside Medellín, we would refer to that location by naming someone we both knew who lived there. For instance, if we talked about Barranquilla, we'd say, "Where Gary lives," or if it was Cali, we'd say, "Where Javier and Max work," or if it was Miami, we'd say, "Where I used to live." New York was "where Sam was."

In hindsight, maybe we were overly cautious, but we were on edge, living in a place where we ourselves had been targeted by the bad guys, both of us with bounties on our heads worth hundreds of thousands of dollars. Yes, we were paranoid. And as the search for Escobar intensified, we became even more so. Javier and I both knew we could trust no one.

And after the CIA threatened to haul Javier off to jail, we knew we were simply on our own.

JAVIER

There was no mistaking Pablo Escobar's voice, even over the static of the radio. It was deep and guttural. He spoke in rapid-fire sentence fragments and with a marked *paisa* accent. He seemed happy to greet his teenaged son, Juan Pablo, with whom he spoke every day at 5:00 p.m. But after his escape, our ability to trace those calls became intermittent, and Colombian intelligence officials at the CNP base had heard almost nothing from Escobar for nearly four months, largely because they were not working with the correct radio frequency.

I had obtained the frequency from a source who worked

for the attorney general's office. The source had spoken several times to Juan Pablo to broker a surrender. He had memorized the frequency and passed it on to me. Later, he was killed by Escobar's goons. I gave the frequency to the two CIA operatives stationed at the Holguín base.

We had our own data collection center at the base that was operated by CNP officers. The government of Colombia also established a tip line and offered a large reward for anyone who could provide information about Escobar's whereabouts. The Colombian government paid for cheery TV ads, encouraging its citizens to call the number with any tips. With all the excitement of winning a lottery, the ads breathlessly promised up to $6.2 million and a new life abroad to anyone giving information that would lead to Escobar's capture.

U.S. visas carried a lot of weight in Colombia, and Steve and I managed to get a lot of intelligence from the lower-ranking cops and intelligence officers we befriended on the base by promising them visas. Steve and I would buy their burgers and beers when they wanted to escape the meager rations at the base and head to the nearby Candilejas Bar. Majors Hugo Aguilar and Danilo Gonzalez became our good friends and would always share intelligence with us. They both worked day and night and were responsible for many successful raids against the Medellín Cartel. Once they found out we could facilitate U.S. visas for them under a special program at the embassy that expedited the paperwork in exchange for cooperation and intelligence on

Escobar, they practically lined up to help us! We'd fill out an official form stating they were helping us, and they would get a five-year entry visa, which was like gold to them. We were soon being inundated with passports from other officers. In the long run, this was great for us, as we built more personal relationships, which helped us do a better job.

At the base, we were also swamped with tip calls. Sometimes, callers would only want to speak to a gringo because they didn't trust Colombian law enforcement, so while I was at the base, I pretty much spent most of my time in the data collection center. Whenever Steve and I answered the tip line, we would meet the potential informants at the bus depot in Medellín. We did not want them to come to the Search Bloc. The tip line and the data center were monitored twenty-four hours a day.

The main purpose of the data center was to intercept conversations of Escobar and members of the cartel in an attempt to locate and capture as many bad guys as we could find. Access to the data center was through Martinez's office, where there was a bookcase recessed into the wall. Inside the bookcase was a hidden button. Pushing the button released the mechanism holding the bookcase in place. Once the mechanism was released, the bookcase swung out into the colonel's office so we could step through to the data center. The CIA was fully aware of the CNP data center, and months into the new search for Escobar, the agents approached Martinez about initiating their own competing room. Martinez agreed, provided that his men would have access to any information the CIA collected.

The CIA's data center at the Holguín base was tiny, and every bit of available floor space seemed to be piled with high stacks of documents, computers, and a small machine—like a ham radio—that intercepted radio frequencies. I pushed some documents off a chair and sat down, anticipating Escobar's late-afternoon call to his son. At precisely 5:00 p.m., the two CIA agents monitoring the radio motioned for me to get closer.

We had him!

I knew immediately it was Escobar, as I had heard his voice on intercepts over the last few years. He spoke quickly and with a heavy accent, a kind of southern drawl in Spanish punctuated with *pues* (well, then) after every few words. After years of studying his habits, we already knew the codes. For instance, *los tombos* was the expression for the CNP and referred to the three-cornered, slanted safari hats worn by the Colombian police. Locations were expressed with numbers. *Caleta 3* was a ranch hideout. We were all ecstatic as we listened to the brief conversation. Again, it was the first time in months that we had heard anything from him. The CIA agents recorded Escobar's call and then replayed it for me on a cassette tape. I asked if I could take the cassette to Colonel Martinez to listen to the conversation between the drug lord and his son. When they agreed, I went across the hall to grab Martinez and told him I had a surprise for him. He immediately knew that it was good news, and we took our places in the tiny room, getting as close to the table where the cassette tape recorder sat as we possibly could. When he heard Escobar and Juan Pablo speaking through the static, a look of what I can only describe as pure joy spread across Martinez's face. We all listened intently to the short conversation, which detailed how Juan Pablo needed to get in touch with Attorney General Gustavo de Greiff Restrepo to negotiate Escobar's surrender. Unbeknownst to the Colombian president, de Greiff had gone rogue and was secretly offering Escobar protection and a short-term prison sentence as long as he turned himself in. We figured that de Greiff wanted to be the next Colombian hero and ride the wave to the presidency of Colombia. De Greiff was brokering the surrender deal through one of his Medellín-based deputies, who had somehow managed to befriend Juan Pablo and ended up giving me the radio frequency. On the radio phone, Escobar urged his son to get him the best surrender deal possible from de Greiff's office. He was willing to go back to jail, he told his son, but it had to be La Catedral or another jail in Medellín.

"Dios te bendiga," Escobar said, uttering the familiar blessing with which he ended every conversation with Juan Pablo. He always told him he loved him and punctuated everything with *"agate pues!"*—"get moving already!" Then we heard a *click*, which meant he'd turned off his radio phone.

Martinez was very excited, and as we walked back to his office, he asked me for a copy of the cassette tape, which I agreed to provide. I figured it was no big deal when I walked back to the tiny office and asked the CIA guys for a copy. They told me to come back for it in about half an hour. I went to my dorm room to write a report about the conversation I'd heard on the tape, and five minutes later, someone knocked on my door. It was a CNP officer who said that the gringos—which was how the Colombian cops referred to all of us Americans, including the CIA—wanted to speak to me. When I returned to their tiny room, they handed me the phone with the CIA chief of station on the other line. He practically screamed down the receiver.

"Under no circumstances are you to give Martinez a copy of that tape!" he yelled. "Do I make myself clear, Peña?"

To be honest, it was about as clear as mud.

When I hesitated, the angry voice on the line threatened to arrest me and haul me up on treason charges.

Treason?

My blood ran cold, and my mind raced back to the humiliation of my final days of my college internship in Texas. I felt like the young recruit nervously sitting across from the commander of the Huntsville prison who was calling me a lazy Mexican and threatening to ruin my career in law enforcement before it had even started. All because I wanted to change my shift to attend a family wedding.

But as I listened to the CIA station chief's tirade, I knew something didn't sound quite right. Still, he repeated the threat, and I ended the conversation by reluctantly promising I would not share the recording with Martinez.

Shaken and angry, I returned to my room, and as I was trying to reach Joe Toft in Bogotá, another CNP officer knocked on my door. This time, it was Martinez who wanted to see me. I walked slowly to the colonel's officer, turning over in my mind how I was going to break the news to him. In the end, I decided to be up front with the man who was pretty much our only hope for capturing Escobar.

To this day, I have never forgotten the look of betrayal and sadness that I saw come over Martinez's face as I told him what had transpired with the tape. For my part, I was completely embarrassed in his presence. Here I was, in his office, at his base guarded by his troops. We Americans were there as his guests. I told him that if I were in his position, I would immediately kick out all the gringos, including the DEA.

There was nothing more to say, and it seemed almost undignified to try to articulate the petty jealousy and interoffice rivalry that seemed to be the root cause of the incident.

I gave the frequency to Martinez, which he wrote down on a piece of paper and gave to one of his radio room men. Then he took off to Bogotá to consult with his boss, Vargas. The needless uproar over the cassette tape nearly ended our cooperation with the most capable and hardworking law enforcement officials in Colombia. I'm sure there were panicked phone calls back and forth between Toft and Vargas to smooth over what threatened to turn into an international incident.

Disappointed, I returned to my bunk, restarted my clunky laptop, and continued to write out my report.

STEVE

The letter from Pablo Escobar was handwritten in block capital letters on unlined paper, and it was addressed to Colonel Martinez at the Carlos Holguín school. Copies were also sent to the attorney general of Colombia, the governor of Antioquía, and the mayor of Medellín. The signature included a thumbprint.

"I have been notified of the telephone threats that you ordered against my mother a day after 'personnel' under your command exploded a car bomb at a building where some of my relatives live. I want to let you know that your terrorist actions have not stopped my battle and that my positions have not changed."

The letter was dated January 28, 1993, and when we saw it, we knew what it meant: Pablo Escobar was desperate. We knew that his legions of loyal hitmen were being killed, his property was being blown up or seized, and his family was in danger.

But while the Search Bloc was tightening the noose,

the threats were coming from a different quarter. Escobar's own enemies had decided to take revenge, "to erase Pablo Escobar from the face of the earth."

The shadowy vigilante group called itself Perseguidos por Pablo Escobar (People Persecuted by Pablo Escobar) and referred to themselves as Los Pepes. Los Pepes were financed by rival members of the Cali Cartel and the remaining Moncada/Galeano families—the relatives of slain traffickers Fernando Galeano and Gerardo Moncada, whose brutal murders at La Catedral led to Escobar's escape from the prison.

"We want to make Pablo Escobar feel the effects in his own flesh of his brand of terrorism," the group said in its first press release in January 1993. "Every time that Pablo Escobar carries out an act of terrorism against defenseless people, we will respond with a similar act."

In the first few months of 1993, Los Pepes went on a murderous rampage—a scorched-earth policy that saw them killing more than twenty of Escobar's closest associates and detonating eleven car bombs in Medellín. In addition to killing many of Escobar's lawyers, accountants, and business associates, they went after the maids who cleaned his family's homes and the tutors who taught his children. They also went after the homes of Escobar's distant relatives, forcing many of them to leave the country. Some of them tried to take up residency in Chile, but authorities there were too afraid to allow them to stay.

Los Pepes had an almost theatrical sense of symbolic

revenge, targeting people and properties that were close to Escobar's heart. Take La Manuela, the twenty-acre ranch that was located near the drug dealer's birthplace, Rionegro. The ranch was one of Escobar's favorite homes, named for his young daughter. It had a soccer field, tennis courts, and even a disco in the sprawling ranch-style home that dominated the property. Los Pepes burned most of it to the ground. Later, looters descended on the charred remains of the mansion, digging through its walls in the hopes of finding hidden packages of cash.

Even Escobar's prized antique car collection became a target as Los Pepes torched a warehouse where the trafficker kept his vintage cars, including a 1933 Pontiac that Escobar claimed was once owned by Al Capone.

In his letter to Martinez, Escobar may not yet have been aware of the authors of the new attacks that were beginning to rain down on him and his family. He continued to blame the CNP and had the nerve to upbraid them for their use of torture and violence against his own goons. In his letter, he referred to "the hundreds of young people that you have killed in your torture center at the Carlos Holguín school."

If torture was going on at the police academy, we didn't know about it. In the eighteen months that Javier and I alternated living there, we were surrounded by representatives from different branches of law enforcement and human rights monitors appointed by the attorney general's office in Bogotá to keep an eye on us and the Colombian police. They were the watchdogs whose jobs were to make sure that no human rights violations were taking place at Carlos Holguín. In addition to the Colombians, our fellow Americans from the CIA and SEAL Team Six also reported on our activities to the embassy.

When the CNP interviewed a defendant at the base— or anywhere, for that matter—we were never present. The Colombian authorities would tell us verbally what they got out of the defendant or give us an intelligence report. If the CNP wanted us to pay the informant, we would sign them up through DEA paperwork and debrief them ourselves. We were willing to overlook certain unorthodox procedures to get the job done, but neither Javier nor I ever crossed any lines. After all, the DEA manual is crystal clear on our obligations. In addition to upholding the U.S. Constitution wherever we may find ourselves, we are prohibited from subjecting detainees to "any cruel or inhuman treatment," and "if such activity is observed by the DEA representative, he shall withdraw to indicate his disapproval."

What we could offer a defendant detainee if we felt his or her information was needed was money and sometimes a new life in the United States. In the brutal war zone that was Colombia during the second manhunt for Escobar, a defendant's most important concern was always safety. If Escobar knew that one of his former hitmen had cooperated with the police or with us, he was pretty much marked for death. We offered them safety and the chance to be relocated to an undisclosed location in the United States.

If we ever needed a reminder that Escobar was willing to strike, even in his cornered, desperate state, it was there in the letters that he sent Martinez with increasing frequency after Los Pepes arrived on the scene. Escobar had declared all-out war on Colombia in mid-January 1993, two weeks before he sent that first letter to Martinez.

"I will seek reprisals against family members of the government," he wrote in his tight block letters. "Don't forget that you also have a family."

Martinez was no stranger to threats. Escobar had paid off a cook to try to poison his food, co-opted a police cadet to shoot him, firebombed his home, and sent one of his former colleagues during the first manhunt in 1990 to offer him a $6 million bribe to call off the war against him during the first Bloque de Búsqueda. In exchange for the bribe, Escobar wanted the colonel to end the search or, better yet, to pretend to be conducting the search but not do any damage to Escobar himself. At one point, while Martinez was listening to Escobar speak on wiretap of his phone, the drug kingpin addressed him personally. "Colonel, I'm going to kill you," said Escobar. "I'm going to kill all of your family up to the third generation, and then I will dig up your grandparents and shoot them and bury them again. Do you hear me?"

But if he was frightened, Martinez tried not to let it show, especially around his men in the CNP. During the second search for Escobar, he took precautions to ensure the safety of his family. He moved them out of their home and installed them at the base, where he could keep an eye on them. They lived in a house at the police academy, which was probably the securest part of Medellín. Martinez had to clear the arrangements with Vargas because just about every officer who worked on the search for Escobar wanted to live there with their families.

The colonel's son, Lieutenant Hugo Martinez, also worked on the base. Like his father, he was tall and slim and clean-shaven with a professional demeanor—the kind of person you immediately liked as soon as you met him. He didn't come across as pretentious or snobby even though his father was the leader of the Bloque de Búsqueda. The lieutenant was technical-minded and learned how to use the radio direction finding (RDF) equipment. RDFing is the art of locating a particular radio frequency. Within the radio frequency spectrum, there are literally thousands of frequencies, and the challenge was to try to find the one that Escobar was using. Escobar basically used radio phones, which worked on radio frequencies, to communicate with his family. Because he knew that we were listening to his calls, he constantly changed frequencies to thwart our efforts.

The young lieutenant was always talking to us about what he'd learned about tracking the frequencies, and he would head out into the city to practice using his RDF equipment. On those practice runs, he was trying to triangulate telephone conversations using the RDF equipment. Afterward, he would go back to the base and meet with his father to discuss what he had found. They would also ask for advice from other technical experts. When he'd return from his various field exercises, the lieutenant would try to explain what he'd learned, what mistakes he'd made, and how he corrected them. Javier and I were of little help because this was an area we were not experienced or proficient in. Besides, I lacked the technical Spanish vocabulary to truly understand a lot of what he was saying, so his very detailed explanations were really above my head. Some of the other CNP guys were skeptical about the equipment the lieutenant was using, but maybe they were also a little jealous because he was the son of the colonel.

As for the colonel himself, Martinez was not really happy about having his son involved in the hunt for Escobar, largely because of the danger involved.

When it came to his family, Martinez was understandably protective. And Javier and I couldn't help noticing that he was particularly spooked by that first letter from Escobar. Who wouldn't be? In a moment of utter panic, Martinez threatened to leave the Search Bloc, and we hastily arranged U.S. visas for his entire family. But in the end, they stuck it out. Maybe it had something to do with the excitement over the second manhunt. We could all feel in our bones that something had changed; life on the run was finally getting to Escobar. His concern for the safety of his wife and children bordered on panic. He was scrambling to get them out of Colombia, and a month after sending his chastising and threatening letter to Martinez, Escobar told his wife, Maria Victoria, to take their eight-year-old daughter, Manuela, and sixteen-year-old son, Juan Pablo, and head to Miami. But when they tried to board their flight at Bogotá's international airport, Colombian authorities refused to allow the family onto the plane.

Escobar was so freaked out that he appealed to the U.S. government to help his family. In an interview with *The New York Times*, conducted by fax while he was in hiding, Escobar promised to turn himself in if the United States would guarantee the safety of his wife and children and provide them with residency visas.

Of course, we quickly rejected that offer. So the war continued.

Between Los Pepes and the CNP, we felt there was no way that Escobar would be able to escape. Less than two months after the letter arrived at the base, Escobar was dealt a near-fatal blow. Javier was in Medellín when a few members of the Search Bloc went out on a raid to capture Mario Castaño Molina, better known as El Chopo, Escobar's most important lieutenant. El Chopo was responsible for coordinating Escobar's terrorist activities and organizing the dwindling army of *sicarios* who were still loyal to their boss. He was also personally responsible for dozens of murders. The CNP learned of his whereabouts after their counterparts in the DIJIN raided a ranch outside Medellín where Escobar stored dynamite and weapons. In exchange for short prison terms, the two *sicarios* captured at the ranch told the authorities where to find El Chopo, who was staying at a hotel in Medellín. Martinez was really excited to have tracked down Escobar's number-two man and told the eight-man DIJIN task force to bring back El Chopo alive. He felt sure that El Chopo knew Escobar's whereabouts. In the meantime, DIJIN operatives had been bugging El Chopo's phone at the hotel, and they waited to pounce when they intercepted a call from the hitman ordering lunch. When the DIJIN guys arrived at the hotel, they knocked on his door.

"Your lunch is here, sir," said one of the officers as the other men brandished their weapons.

When El Chopo opened the door, one of the agents offered to make a deal with him: They would keep him alive in exchange for information about where Escobar was hiding. But the hitman wasn't listening. El Chopo drew his Browning 9 mm automatic pistol and started shooting wildly. But he was outnumbered and outgunned, and the DIJIN guys shot him dead. He died in an instant, his contorted body riddled with forty-eight bullets. While they had failed to secure any intelligence from El Chopo on Escobar, the Search Bloc had delivered the first in a series of major death blows to the drug lord. Vargas was so ecstatic that he flew all the way in from Bogotá to personally congratulate the members of the Search Bloc for their fine police work.

In a classified report that we prepared for Toft on what we called Operation Medellín in March 1993, we noted that "Escobar is worried and under extreme pressure due to the CNP's constant everyday operations aimed at arresting him. To date, the CNP has executed approximately three thousand search warrants, aimed at arresting him." They targeted his accountants, lawyers, and financiers as well as his *sicarios*. Authorities seized more than $14 million of the drug dealer's assets, including three ranches in the Medellín area. A total of twenty-five of Escobar's loyal hitmen had been killed, either by the CNP or Los Pepes. Ninety-five others were arrested, and twenty-two had voluntarily surrendered to authorities.

But the collateral damage was also severe. Between July 22, 1992, when Escobar escaped, and mid-March 1993, when we wrote our report to Toft, 136 police officers had been killed in the line of duty by Escobar's hitmen. The death tolls throughout the country had also increased. Colombia had seen its deadliest year, with nearly 29,000 homicides reported in 1992, compared to 25,110 for the previous year. In Medellín and Bogotá, 112 civilians had died from random car bomb attacks, and 427 had been injured.

About a month after El Chopo's death, Connie and I were both in Bogotá when we returned home to gray smoke clouds—the aftermath of a powerful car bomb. We had already seen the news at the embassy and gasped at the frenzy of twisted metal, smoke, and the blood-strewn faces of shocked witnesses to the bombing of the Centro 93 shopping mall in the posh northern part of the city, mere blocks from where we lived. Twenty people died in that bombing, including four children. The blast from a car packed with 440 pounds of explosives left the fashionable shopping center in a pile of rubble. Shops on an adjoining busy street were also destroyed, and more than two dozen cars parked in a nearby lot and on the street were completely pulped. The explosion left much of the northern part of the city enveloped in a thick cloud of smoke, even hours after the blast.

Connie and I had been to that mall several times; Connie had just been to the mall two days before the explosion. The front of the shopping area was all glass, so when the bomb exploded, you can imagine what happened; millions of shards of glass flew through the air, killing and maiming anyone they struck.

When we returned home that night, Connie and I watched footage on TV of firefighters carrying the lifeless bodies of small children. Apparently, many mothers were at the mall with their school-age children shopping for school supplies when the bomb went off. I still believe that the real target of the bomb was one of the drugstores owned by Cali Cartel leaders across the street from the shopping area, but the blast had accomplished what it was designed to do—sow panic throughout the country.

After seeing all that carnage, our first reaction was shock that anyone could be so heartless. Then we got mad about what had happened to so many innocent people, once again. And what made it even worse were the deaths and mutilations of the kids.

Years after it occurred, the images of desperation and devastation haunt me still. I remember the cries of a distraught woman as she stepped over debris and dead bodies frantically searching for her son, shouting into the camera, "You miserable . . . My God, why haven't they caught him?" Everyone knew she was referring to Pablo Escobar. As with every other brutal act of terror that he perpetrated on the Colombian people, Pablo Escobar never actually took credit for any of the shopping center bombings. But everyone knew he was responsible.

While Escobar set off a lot of bombs around Colombia, the bombings at our local shopping centers somehow cemented my resolve to do everything we could to catch him. We were already committed to our mission, but these incidents sealed it for me, and I decided to do whatever it took to get Escobar off the street. .

Los Pepes also knew it was Escobar who was behind the latest mall bombing, and the next day, they struck in a twisted act of revenge that pretty much resulted in turning every decent person against them. On Saturday April 17—a day after the Centro 93 bombing—fifteen gunmen working for Los Pepes killed Guido Parra Montoya, one of Escobar's longtime attorneys, and his sixteen-year-old son. Parra had been the main mediator between Escobar and the Colombian government, and later de Greiff, trying to broker a deal for his surrender. Los Pepes struck without mercy. They dragged the father and son from their Medellín condominium, shot them dead, and stuffed the corpses in the trunk of a stolen taxi.

"What do you think of the trade for the bombing in Bogotá?" read the handwritten sign that was wrapped around the head of one of the victims. Another sign read, "You were kidnapped because of your work for Pablo Escobar."

Los Pepes were fond of these dramatic flourishes and later left another placard attached to the mutilated body of another Escobar associate. Juan Guillermo Londono White, a currency dealer and cartel moneyman, was denounced as the "servile front man and initiator of kidnappings for Pablo Escobar" according to the hand-scrawled placard attached to his corpse and signed *Los Pepes*. All Los Pepes' calling cards were designed to hearken back to the days when Escobar's Extraditables would leave a note at the scene of their crimes—usually a card wrapped around the neck of a bloodied victim.

If we ever harbored any sympathy for Los Pepes or secretly cheered them on for going after Escobar and his associates, those sentiments quickly faded after the grisly murders of Parra and his innocent son.

Still, there was a tremendous amount of interest in their activities. Although we had no advance intelligence about who was part of the vigilante group, Toft demanded almost hourly updates of their activities, especially when prominent people were found dead. In true Toft fashion, he didn't want to read about the actions of Los Pepes in the next day's newspapers; he needed to know what they did as soon as it took place. The issues with Los Pepes became top priority for the U.S. embassy because, eventually, accusations were made that the CNP was providing information to Los Pepes and possibly even working with them.

During a meeting with a secret source—a high-ranking politician within the Colombian government—Toft, Javier, and I learned that Los Pepes had indeed infiltrated the Search Bloc.

"They had bandits working within the Bloque de Búsqueda and identified two of these individuals as 'Alberto' and 'Bernardo,'" we wrote after debriefing our source. The information that the source was imparting to us had come from Rodriguez-Orejuela of the Cali Cartel, who insisted that the CNP's General Vargas and Colonel Martinez knew about the arrangement and that the Cali Cartel was offering to pay "10 million USD immediately following Escobar's capture and/or death."

For the record, we were never able to verify any of this information, and we all strongly doubted that the general and colonel could be involved in such a shady set of affairs. But when some of the Washington weenies got wind of this, they wanted to withdraw the Special Ops Americans (Delta Force and SEAL Team Six) from Colombia and tried to prevent Javier and me from traveling and living in Medellín.

Who were the leaders of Los Pepes? We all had our suspicions, and at one point Pablo Escobar even accused Colonel Martinez of being their shadowy commander.

We stayed as far away from them as we could, but at one point, they got a little too close for comfort.

JAVIER

At just over five feet, with flowing auburn hair that grazed her shoulders, Dolly Moncada was petite and pretty. Dressed simply in neatly pressed jeans, a silk blouse, and no makeup or jewelry, she didn't look like one of Colombia's richest women.

In fact, when I met her, I was convinced she was in dire straits. She was the widow of Gerardo Moncada, the Escobar associate who had been killed at La Catedral. My meeting with her was brokered through Oscar, our informant who had first told us the news that Escobar had killed Moncada and Galeano inside the prison and then ordered the wholesale slaughter of their entire families in Medellín—the massacre that precipitated his flight from jail.

Dolly had somehow escaped the carnage, but just barely. The day I met her at her home high above the Medellín hills, she was clearly nervous and frightened. After her husband's death, she was pretty much a sitting duck—an enemy of Escobar.

I'm a sucker for a pretty woman, especially a vulnerable one, so I promised I would do whatever I could to help her.

Still, there was something about her that I didn't quite trust, something that betrayed the tough-as-nails character behind the soft, feminine demeanor she tried to project. She seemed fragile, but this was also a woman who was used to being in charge.

I met her a few days after Pablo Escobar's goons had ransacked her palatial home and turned it upside down. As we stood talking in her sprawling living room, with its breathtaking view of the city of Medellín and the huge backyard swimming pool, I looked around me at the broken dishes scattered on the floor, the overturned couches and chairs. She told me and the representative from the Colombian attorney general's office who accompanied me on that unusual visit that most of her possessions had been stolen by the intruders. The only item that appeared to be intact was a ceramic scotch bottle. I was a scotch drinker back then, so I noticed the bottle right away. It had an inlaid portrait of Princess Diana and Prince Charles, and it was numbered. I could tell that it was a collector's item. I wondered where they could have possibly gotten it and how much they paid for it.

When Dolly saw me eyeing the bottle, she nervously picked it up and handed it to me. I thanked her and set it back down. I had never accepted a bribe in my entire career in law enforcement, and I wasn't about to start.

When she spoke, her voice trembled, and she wrung her hands to keep them from shaking. She told me she had five young children to look after, and she was clearly at wits' end, so I did my best to reassure her. She was very afraid—and rightly so—that Escobar was going to kill her and her family. It was too dangerous to interview her in Medellín, so we made arrangements to have her fly to Washington with her family. I assured her that the United States would help, and after I left her mansion, I immediately set about getting residency visas for her and several of her family members. At the time, I thought she couldn't possibly be penniless. She must have had money—possibly millions of dollars—stashed away. Still, the DEA paid for all the plane tickets, and I even accompanied the family—there were ten people in total—to Washington and turned them all over to our agents before returning to Colombia. They were supposed to stay in a hotel where they would be fully debriefed by our DEA colleagues, but when the agents arrived to interview Dolly, she and the rest of her family had simply disappeared. They never fulfilled their obligations to tell us about Escobar or Los Pepes.

In addition to Dolly Moncada, I also met Don Berna, although again I had no idea he was tied to Los Pepes. I knew very little about him, only that Attorney General de Greiff had allowed him to visit the Search Bloc and authorized him to be used as an informant. Somehow, he had convinced de Greiff that he could provide valuable information in the search for Escobar. So with the AG's backing, Berna was allowed to come onto the base. Still, Steve and I were very cautious around Berna because we didn't fully understand what his role was. He visited the Search Bloc on a few occasions. It was hard to miss him. He was a big man with a bushy mustache, fond of untucked short-sleeved shirts and blue jeans. He arrived in a convoy of all-wheel-drive vehicles—usually shiny, black Toyota Land Cruisers—and always seemed surrounded by a dozen gun-toting bodyguards. I often saw him speaking to the DIJIN guys. One time, Martinez, who refused to meet with him, confided in me that he was skeptical about the information that Don Berna was sharing with his men. But everyone humored him because of de Greiff's directive.

It was one of the elite members of the Search Bloc—Danilo—who introduced me to Don Berna. I remember that the most striking thing about him, besides his girth, was his massive watch. He caught me staring at it, and I told him that it was a nice watch. Then he took it off his wrist and handed it to me. I was shocked and began to protest that I couldn't accept such a valuable gift. It was a gold Rado and probably worth tens of thousands of dollars. I panicked, but Danilo urged me to accept it. He said that Don Berna would be offended if I declined.

"He may even have you killed if you refuse it." Danilo laughed.

It wasn't funny.

I took the watch but immediately wrote a report to Toft and sent the watch to DEA headquarters in Bogotá. As with Dolly Moncada's bottle of scotch, there was no way I wanted even the appearance of graft.

On several occasions, when members of the Search Bloc advance teams were out on various missions and we had to go and meet first-time informants outside the base, Don Berna would send his goons, and they would do a military-style sweep to make sure that the coast was clear. When they arrived at the bus station where we usually met informants, people immediately moved away from him and his men and gave them a wide berth. We always met people who called on the tip line at the bus depot, because it was so large and allowed for easy anonymity. Medellín's bus station is the busiest in Colombia, with hundreds of buses arriving and leaving daily as well as myriad restaurants and businesses. It was a great place to get lost and an even better place to interview a would-be informant because we could just blend into the crowd.

We met many informants at the bus station, setting up our rendezvous at places with names like Kokorico or Pollos Frisby, which was a Colombian version of KFC but so much better. I have to admit that it was always a treat for us to leave the base and eat something besides the rice, beans, and tiny piece of chicken that we had at most of our meals. We never minded too much about the drive to the bus depot, even though about 70 percent of the tipsters had nothing to tell us and their information never panned out. But 30 percent of the interviews we did produced actionable intelligence. I remember one of the informants gave us financial intelligence, and we raided a shopping center owned by Luis Carlos Molina, a huge financier who was giving millions to Escobar. He had also arranged the murder of Guillermo Cano Isaza, the editor of *El Espectador*, who was gunned down on Escobar's orders in 1986. When we did the raid, I remember hitting the main offices, and we seized about half a million dollars in cash. Molina was not there, but the representative who accompanied us from the attorney general's office seized the cash. The informant was later killed by Escobar's people.

In those final months of the search for Escobar, there was a great deal of activity at the Holguín base. In addition to frequent visits from Don Berna, another "source" turned out to be a red-haired, bearded guy whom everyone called Chaplin. Later, we found out he was a plant from the leaders of the Cali Cartel who was sent to keep tabs on the CNP's work.

I also began to notice a CNP colonel who had just been released by the FARC after five years in captivity in the jungle and had moved into one of the base houses with his family. The colonel had suffered a lot of mental and physical abuse and just seemed lost. He had nothing to do with the Search Bloc but was allowed to stay because there was nowhere else for him to go. The colonel, whose name I never learned, was a stark reminder—if one were ever needed—of the human cost of the various wars that were tearing the country apart.

One of the bright spots were our interactions with Major Jesús Gómez Padilla, the second in charge of the uniformed division. He was one of the great unsung heroes of the search. He spoke in broken English and always tried to take care of Steve and me. Gomez had been trained by U.S. forces, and he was a master at field operations, especially in the jungles surrounding Medellín. We went with him on a lot of operations, especially in the jungle and mountains, chasing Escobar. In one instance, he led us on an operation to an Escobar-owned finca, or ranch, following intelligence we had gathered from one of Escobar's relatives who reached out to us at the base. She called us at the tip line and told us that Escobar was hiding out at the finca. We left immediately but had just missed him. One of the problems turned out to be that she had no telephone and had to walk to a nearby store to call us on the tip line, which was why it took us a few hours to mount the operation. After we did an inventory of the finca, we found various posters and photographs showing Escobar dressed as Mexican revolutionary Pancho Villa and in full old-style gangster garb.

On another occasion, we got a tip from a woman who would only speak to a gringo, so I got on the phone. She told me that one of Escobar's *sicarios* was dating a friend of hers and would be meeting her at a Medellín discothèque that night.

I knew we had to act right away, but it was late on a Saturday night, and the base was practically empty, so I contacted one of the captains, who went by the nickname *Galletas* (Cookies). He immediately put together an advance team of four other DIJIN guys, and we went off to the disco to meet our source. She told me she would be wearing a red dress and sitting at the bar of what turned out to be a rustic-style dance hall frequented by working-class people who danced all night to salsa and meringue tunes.

The disco was dark and loud, with about eighty people crowding the sawdust-covered dance floor and others standing against the rough-hewn wooden bar nursing bottles of beer and downing shots of aguardiente. I saw the informant right away—a long-haired brunette wearing high heels and a short, tight red dress. I was dressed in my usual blue jeans and polo shirt to blend into the crowd, but as I approached the bar, the pretty informant knew immediately who I was and began to walk in my direction, pulling me onto the dance floor as the Colombian officers—my backup—stayed by the door. She had said on the phone that she didn't want to deal with the Colombian cops because she didn't trust them. I never asked her why, but had told the two CNP officers who had accompanied me to hang back. The dance floor was crowded with sweating couples, and the music was loud and pulsating. I could barely hear what she was telling me as she brushed up close to me and spoke in my ear. As we approached a couple on the dance floor, she gestured with her eyes in the direction of a short, skinny teenager with a dark complexion who was slow dancing with a young girl. He was in such a tight embrace with his partner that he never noticed as I approached him from the side. I took out my gun and placed it against his stomach and told him he was under arrest. There was a minor skirmish as he tried to fight me and take off. The dancing stopped when someone noticed my gun. I heard screams and was aware of people trying to run out of the bar, but I kept my focus and held on to my weapon with one hand and the shoulder of the teenager with the other. The music came to a sudden stop. When he tried to escape, the CNP guys moved in quickly to subdue him, brushing past frightened revelers, crashing beer bottles and shattering glasses of aguardiente as they dragged the bad guy out of the bar and pushed him into the back seat of a waiting police car that was parked outside the club. Despite the panic, no one was hurt. After we made our way out of the club, dragging our captive, the salsa music came back on, and couples headed back to the dance floor. They continued to dance as if nothing had happened.

We conducted the interview at the base in the presence of Juan, a representative from de Greiff's office who asked the questions and then allowed me to ask my own. Juan was pretty serious most of the time, but he was also a lot of fun and became a good friend and close ally for us at the base.

Juan was tall, well-built, and unafraid of anyone or anything. He was well-respected by the CNP. It was Juan who had befriended Juan Pablo and gotten us Escobar's radio frequency. He trusted us completely and would let us have any information he gathered from the CNP raids in Medellín. Steve and I would make sure to take him for coffee and burgers, and we bunked with him when we were at the base.

It was Juan who did most of the talking when we sat down to debrief our teenage captive. The *sicario* was just seventeen years old but a veteran of the drug wars in Medellín. He told us in a very cocky tone of voice that he had already killed ten police officers. In that same tone of voice, which really grated on me, he said that he loved Pablo Escobar and was happy to kill and die for him. He made a hundred dollars for every dead cop and gave most of his earnings to his mother. Escobar had given him a new life in the shantytown where he grew up, he said, and had allowed him to rescue his mother from a life of abject poverty. She now had a brand-new refrigerator, food, and a roof over her head, and those were the only things he really cared about. Whatever cash from his misdeeds that was left over was used to buy new tennis shoes, blue jeans, and beer for himself. He knew that life expectancy among Escobar's hitmen was just twenty-two and that his life of crime would probably be cut short by a policeman's bullet or he would die in an attack by vigilantes. In addition to Escobar's wealthy associates in the cartel, Los Pepes—along with some corrupt members of the police department—had targeted the young hitmen who worked for Escobar. Human rights groups had chronicled several massacres of young people in the dirt-poor *comunas* surrounding the city. In the meantime, he knew that he would never leave the impoverished barrio where he spent his whole life, but it didn't matter. He repeated that he would die for Escobar, whom he considered a saint. When I heard that, I knew that it was one of the main reasons that Escobar was still at large and why our task to hunt him down had proven so fruitless over the years. It was this warped code of honor and loyalty that allowed Escobar to hide in plain sight, protected by his own people, willing to sacrifice their own lives for him.

Following his arrest, the informant called me back, and I arranged to have the DEA pay her $5,000 for her tip. I never found out what happened to the cocky, tough-talking teenage hitman. But I won't soon forget what he told me when I asked him to tell us his name.

"Angelito," he said. Little Angel.

STEVE

I tried to call Connie once a day when I was in Medellín. If I couldn't reach her, I would relay messages through

Javier, whom I called early every morning at the embassy to fill him in on what had taken place the night before in Medellín.

If I had time, and if Connie had arrived at the embassy for work, he'd find her so we could talk for a few minutes. But many times, I simply had no time to talk because we would head out on an operation or surveillance. When this happened, Javier always made a point of letting Connie know I was okay and would speak to her later in the day. I think Connie just wanted to know that I was okay so she could get on with her day.

Connie was already accustomed to me being away from home. It started when we were in Miami and I was working long hours. During our time in South Florida, I was frequently away from home for days at a time while following suspects, conducting controlled deliveries, and traveling to whatever part of the world we needed to visit. But when Escobar escaped and Javier and I started alternating living at the base in Medellín, "being away from home" was taken to a whole new level.

Connie never let her rudimentary Spanish or fear of random car bombs stand in the way of living her life in Bogotá. When she went out, Connie used what little Spanish she knew, accompanied by a lot of hand gestures and smiles. I think it was her ability to laugh at herself that made Colombians accept her with open arms. When Connie wasn't working or had a day off, and I wasn't home, she spent her free time with friends, both American and Colombian. She also enjoyed reading, went shopping, and spent time outside walking in the fresh air and getting some exercise. Despite all the State Department warnings about constantly being on alert in Bogotá, Connie tried to do the same things we did back in the United States. During the eighteen-month manhunt for Escobar, Connie was alone a lot, but she rarely ever complained. She knew what Javier and I were doing and that it was top priority for the embassy and Colombia, so she did everything she could to support me.

Sure, there were inconveniences: She had to ride in the secure embassy van to and from work—a drive that often took more than an hour at rush hour—and she had to carry a walkie-talkie tuned to the Marines' frequency at the embassy in case she found herself in a dangerous situation and needed help. Connie is very savvy and learned quickly to be aware of her surroundings. Whenever she went out alone in Bogotá, she paid close attention to what others around her were doing and whether she was being followed or if someone was paying her undue attention.

To pass the time and rein in her anxiety, Connie did a series of jobs at the U.S. embassy. Unable to work as a registered nurse in Colombia, she plunged into taking care of the community of American expatriates who worked for the embassy. Due to the violence in Colombia at that time, embassy spouses were not authorized to work anywhere but the embassy, so Connie worked with another DEA wife, Mary Lou Rinehart, as a community liaison officer (CLO).

Their primary responsibility was to prepare welcome packages for new U.S. citizens working in the embassy and help them get settled in Bogotá. They also planned many of the social functions involving embassy personnel, coordinated and oversaw the annual Salvation Army Christmas party for underprivileged Colombian children, and did a great deal of volunteer work with Catholic churches that were helping the homeless in Bogotá. She also handled pretty much anything else that needed to be done.

Among the many important duties of the CLOs was maintaining the tennis court schedule at the ambassador's residence. While this may sound trivial, it was anything but. Embassy staffers would wait in line outside the CLO office on Monday mornings to get the time slots they wanted at the tennis courts. Connie always made sure to take care of Toft, a competitive tennis player, to ensure he got the day and time he wanted each week.

After Escobar's escape, Connie also did a stint at the DEA office as our file clerk. When I was in Bogotá, having Connie working in the same office gave us the opportunity to see each other throughout the day, but we also gave each other space to do our respective jobs. Connie would go with her friends to lunch and I'd go with mine, although most days I ate at my desk or in the embassy cafeteria because of the workload we dealt with in the Escobar search.

When Connie started working for the U.S. post office in the embassy, our lives changed forever.

Among her duties was accompanying the U.S. mail to the international airport to make sure it got safely onto the plane, and sorting through letters and parcels that arrived from the States. One day, she noticed a copy of *Time* magazine that featured a cover story on international adoptions. According to the newsweekly, Colombia was the leading country in the world for American adoptions. Connie read the article with great excitement and almost immediately made contact with the government agency that was facilitating adoptions in Bogotá.

Somehow, Connie became very close with the woman who was in charge of the Instituto Colombiano de Bienestar Familiar, the federal agency that oversaw adoptions for the whole country. Before we knew it, we were in line to adopt a child in Colombia! And with the help of Connie's new friend—a woman we will call Alissa (not her real name)—many bureaucratic obstacles were suddenly made manageable if not removed altogether. Although we went through the normal process, Bienestar had us approved as foster parents in record time after doing a home study. I have to say that it also helped that we were diplomats. When Alissa told us that she had a potential child for us to adopt, we raced to her office. She said she couldn't show us the file of the child that was on her desk, but when she walked out of her office to head to a meeting, Connie and I hung behind and snuck a look.

I fell in love with the infant girl swaddled in blankets in the photo right away. Her name was Monica, and we repeated the name, both of us dreaming about how we would lavish all our love on this precious little girl, taking her through the trauma of her first tooth, to the first day of kindergarten, and to her high school prom! We were really getting ahead of ourselves, and I don't think either of us slept the night before we were scheduled to pick up the tiny bundle that would become our daughter. The next day, we traveled to Zipaquirá, a small city north of Bogotá, with a DEA driver. We drove down a steep, narrow road to Bienestar, which wasn't exactly an orphanage but more like a local facility for foster families. The neat white concrete building had a red tile roof and was located on a slight incline near the bottom of the hill. Connie and I held hands as we walked through the sunny, open-air entryway to the receptionist at the front desk. Although it was a warm October day, the Bienestar offices with their red tile floors, simple wooden furniture, and cavernous rooms felt cold and drafty to us.

Alissa met us at the Zipaquirá Bienestar facility and was warmly greeted by the receptionist and the other officials. She led us down the main hallway into a large room to await the arrival of the foster mother and the baby. The foster mother was in her forties, well-dressed and attractive. She was holding Monica, and as she gave the Bienestar staff explicit instructions on Monica's feeding schedule, both Connie and I detected a sad note of reluctance to give up the baby who had been her charge for the last few months. Finally, the foster mother handed Monica to Alissa and tearfully left the room.

With her big black eyes, perfect olive complexion, and wisps of dark brown hair, Monica was a beautiful, healthy baby. She stared at us uncomprehending at first, and we had been warned that it might take her a while to smile, to accept us. She might experience some kind of separation anxiety, so we braced ourselves for disappointment. But she seemed content and allowed us to cradle her without fussing in the drafty offices. It didn't take long for Monica to warm up to us. She smiled in the car after leaving Zipaquirá, and our hearts just melted. We were officially her foster parents and were warned that the full adoption formalities would take a few more weeks to complete. Monica's diaper leaked onto Connie on the way to the embassy, where we immediately took her to introduce her to everyone in the DEA office—her new American family!

Back then, during the Escobar manhunt, Bogotá was considered a no-kids zone, and if you had a child while posted there, you had to transfer after six months. But because we were in the midst of the Escobar manhunt, I petitioned the DEA to stay longer. So Monica—the only embassy child—was absolutely spoiled by everyone, including the eternal bachelor Javier.

Once Monica came into our lives, Connie became a stay-at-home mom, which involved a lot more work than she had ever done at the embassy.

As we were settling down with our new little girl, Pablo Escobar was growing incredibly anxious about his own family. By late November 1993, the family was on the move—this time to Frankfurt, where they owned property.

We found out through de Greiff's office that Escobar's wife, nine-year-old daughter, and Juan Pablo along with his twenty-one-year-old girlfriend would be flying to Frankfurt on Lufthansa—a day before the flight was scheduled to leave. We didn't have a lot of time before the scheduled commercial flight, so we scrambled to come up with a plan—one that would quickly reach the highest levels of both the American and German governments.

When we consulted the flight manifests, we saw that everyone was booked in first class, and we rushed to get an agent on the plane. We dispatched an agent named Ken Magee and outfitted him with state-of-the-art spy cameras. One of them was a covert, tiny 35 mm camera nestled in a small photo equipment bag. The lens was discreetly pointing out of a small hole in the bag. The camera switch was hidden in the handle of the bag so that he could point the bag in the direction of where he wanted to take the picture and snap the photo without having to remove the camera. It was important for us to document who the family was traveling with and who they talked to on their journey.

The CNP, under orders from General Vargas, sent Colonel Leonardo Gallego to go on the flight. We knew and

trusted Gallego, who was a very smart, capable, and trust-
worthy officer. Our DEA office in Frankfurt got involved
along with the Colombian government and, of course,
DEA headquarters in Washington and the Bogotá
embassy. Our position was very clear: Under no circumstances were the Escobars allowed to seek asylum in
Germany, and they must be returned to Colombia as
quickly as possible. The family never found out we had an
agent and CNP officer on the flight.

Hours before the flight was scheduled to take off, I
grabbed my own camera equipment, and Javier and I
rushed to El Dorado International Airport. In the first
place, we wanted to confirm that the people listed on the
flight manifests were indeed Escobar's family. And although this was a very long shot, we wanted to look
around to see if maybe Pablo Escobar himself would show
up. We knew that wasn't going to happen, but shame on
us if he did and we weren't prepared.

The scene at the airport was a zoo. Someone had leaked
the story to the Colombian press, and there were crowds
of people taking photos, so I didn't look out of place when
I started snapping pictures with my own tiny 35 mm Pen-
tax that I always carried in my pocket. Again, we wanted
to know if anyone else would be traveling with the family.
Javier and I stayed back and watched the scene unfold. We
saw several armed guards from de Greiff's office escorting
the family. The guards wore plain clothes and carried ba-
tons and rifles, which they used to beat back photographers

who tried to film the Escobars as they walked through the airport. De Greiff had ordered the guards to protect the family, and they were given access to a private room in the international section of the airport where they were hidden from the general public to wait for their flight. On the one hand, it was a good idea for security reasons, especially since Los Pepes were trying to kill them. But on the other hand, no other Colombians were receiving specialized treatment like that, and I am sure that de Greiff saw this as an opportunity to show Escobar that the AG's office was trying to help him out. In hindsight, I think that was very naïve on de Greiff's part. I'll never believe that Escobar had any intentions of surrendering a second time as de Greiff believed. I think Escobar just wanted to get his family to a location where he wouldn't have to worry about their safety, and then he would restart his bombing and killing campaign at a level greater than anything we'd seen before. We also felt that de Greiff wanted to get all the credit if Escobar did surrender a second time to help him with his campaign to run for president of Colombia. The whole thing was extremely self-serving and politically charged.

Once the plane took off, Javier and I returned to the embassy, and the work started. Toft went into a meeting with Ambassador Busby, who understood the gravity of the situation. If the family was allowed to stay in Germany under the country's rather loose asylum standards, we would lose an important edge in bringing Escobar to justice. I felt sure that we were closing in on him and that he was making more and more mistakes in contacting his son and allowing us to pinpoint his hiding places with increasing precision in Colombia.

The ambassador didn't waste time while the Lufthansa flight was in the air. He wanted to exert as much pressure as he could on Germany to return the family, and he went straight to "Washington," as Toft told us. By that, he meant Secretary of State Warren Christopher and even President Bill Clinton, who was urged to contact the German chancellor, Helmut Kohl, to make sure the Germans were aware of the situation. Obviously, the whole thing was a pretty sensitive issue, and it was all playing out under the spotlight of the global media. For their part, the Colombian government was squarely behind the U.S. position and was applying their own pressure on the Germans.

When the flight arrived in Frankfurt, Toft told us that negotiations were still ongoing with the German government. The plane taxied to a special section of the runway, and the Escobar family was taken in a private bus to be placed in a special "quarantine" room at Frankfurt Airport until a final decision could be made. Colonel Gallego later told us that the Germans had no idea what to do and were in panic mode. Many of the authorities wanted them to stay, while others wanted them to leave. At some point, the decision was made to allow them to stay the night in Germany while negotiations were going on with the Colombian president, the German chancellor, and American authorities. Magee, our agent on the flight, called us to confirm this was being done and that DEA Frankfurt agents were at the airport with their German counterparts monitoring the situation. It was a tense standoff. Magee told us that the German authorities still had not made up their minds about the Escobars and were leaning toward giving them asylum. Later, we found out that heated arguments among the representatives of the three governments went to the very last minute. The Escobars had applied to stay for three months and were planning to seek asylum when the Germans finally decided to send them back to Colombia.

"All of them applied to enter Germany, where they wanted to stay for three months as tourists," a German police statement said. "After conclusion of questioning by the border police, the German interior ministry decided to turn them back."

They returned on the next flight to Bogotá, where Magee sat two rows ahead of them, accompanied by four German immigration officers. Magee managed to photograph the family's passports on the flight, and when he inspected their seats after they left the plane, he found several envelopes marked with large amounts of money that totaled $80,000. Later, we found out that in addition to the cash, Maria Victoria, Escobar's wife, had also been carrying large amounts of gold and jewelry. Magee also found a crumpled-up letter that was written in English and said, in part, "We have a friend in Frankfurt. He says he will be looking for us so he can help us. Tell him to call Gustavo de Greiff." Whoever the note was destined for never received it, as the Escobars were under constant surveillance once they reached Frankfurt and were never able to deliver it.

Once they landed in Bogotá, the Colombian government ordered de Greiff's office to stand down. De Greiff's office would no longer be in charge of their protection, and the family was escorted by CNP officers to the Tequendama, a towering five-star hotel in central Bogotá. The sprawling high-rise complex features more than five hundred guest suites, several restaurants, swimming pools, shops, and a spa. It was partly designed by Le Corbusier in the 1950s and was at one time considered the height of chic and elegance by Colombia's upper classes. The Tequendama regularly hosted international events and conferences and was the hotel of choice for visiting dignitaries.

But during the bloody reign of Escobar, it was also a target, and Javier and I narrowly escaped one of the drug lord's car bombs in late January 1993—two weeks after Escobar had pronounced his new all-out war against Colombian authorities in the midst of the second manhunt. Javier and I were scheduled to meet an informant at the hotel, and I was in my truck waiting outside Javier's apartment when I heard on the car radio that two powerful bombs had exploded in the center of town—one at a parking lot that destroyed dozens of parked cars and another at the Tequendama. Both bombs packed more than one hundred pounds of explosives. We drove in the direction of the hotel, but because of the explosions, traffic was at a standstill. We decided to return home and contacted our informant, who had not been at the hotel when the bombs exploded.

To this day, we still don't know if we were the targets.

Nearly a year later when the Escobars moved into their sprawling suite at the Tequendama, there was still plywood on some of the hotel's windows that had been shattered during the blast. Several military officers stood at the entrance in SWAT gear and wielding AK-47s, fierce-looking German shepherds straining on their leashes by their sides. And when news spread that the Escobar family was about to take up residence in the hotel, many of the other guests and the residents of the nearby residential tower bolted.

The Colombian National Police's intelligence division had arranged for Escobar's suite to be wired before they settled in. Officers were then positioned a floor above so they could listen in on their phone calls to Escobar, who was increasingly worried about the fate of his family. We were all hoping, now that the family was in Colombia, that Escobar would call them with greater frequency and maybe even linger on the line so that we could finally trap him.

Los Pepes, who claimed that they had largely ceased their terror campaign against Escobar's associates, issued a release to Colombian media on the day of the family's return to Colombia, noting that they were ready to resume their war against the drug dealer.

Escobar called almost right after the bleary-eyed family, exhausted and on edge, arrived at the hotel. He urged Juan Pablo to make contact with human rights groups and the United Nations. On November 30, 1993, Escobar issued his own press release complete with his signature and thumbprint. It was addressed to those he suspected of making up the vigilante group, including Colonel Martinez, the Castaño brothers, and members of the Cali Cartel.

"Mr. Pepes," began the letter. "You say in your lying communiqué that you have never attacked my family and I ask you: Why did you bomb the building where my mother lived? Why did you kidnap my nephew Nicolas? Why did you torture and strangle my brother-in-law Carlos Henao? Why did you try to kidnap my sister Gloria? You have always characterized yourselves by being hypocrites and liars."

Escobar went on to accuse the group of strong ties to the Colombian authorities: "The prosecutor's office has a lot of evidence against you. The government knows that is Los Pepes' military branch, the same one that massacres innocent young men at street corners. I have been raided 10,000 times. You haven't been at all. Everything is confiscated from me. Nothing is taken away from you. The government will never offer a warrant for you. The government will never apply faceless justice to criminal and terrorist policemen."

Whatever Escobar said in his note, which was delivered to national media in Colombia, the reality was that his family was caught in a trap, hostages of the brutal war that he had started. After returning to Colombia, Maria Victoria had begged authorities to allow her to leave the country, to go anywhere so that she could live in peace with her children.

For the Escobars, surrounded by Colombian military and police, the Tequendama was a virtual prison and for them would prove to be cursed. But maybe it was cursed for all of us. After all, *tequendama* means "he who precipitates downward" in the Chibcha language of Colombia's Muisca tribe. In many ways, it would prove the most appropriate site for their imminent downfall.

PART FOUR

PART FOUR

JAVIER

I knew it was a wild-goose chase even before I boarded the plane to Miami. I didn't want to go because I knew that Lieutenant Martinez's radio frequency intercepts were bringing us closer and closer to Pablo Escobar's hiding place. We were certain that he was still in Medellín. We were also certain that he was increasingly desperate.

Escobar's top associates were dropping like flies. A few days after Escobar's family tried to flee to Germany in late November, Juan Camilo Zapata, a major trafficker and money launderer for the Medellín Cartel, was gunned down by members of the Search Bloc at his ranch on the outskirts of Medellín. On November 26, 1993, the day he died, I sent the following cable: "The Bogotá Country Office (BCO) received information from the Colombian National Police/Medellín Task Force regarding the death of Juan Camilo Zapata-Vasquez . . . This occurred earlier the same day in Medellín, Colombia, while trying to serve an outstanding warrant charging Zapata with murder."

Zapata bred horses and was the owner of the Castillo Marroquín, a Moorish-style castle in the northern part of

Bogotá, where he threw lavish parties and had a disco-thèque. During the first search for Escobar, we raided the castle, but he was long gone. In those early years of hunting Escobar, Zapata managed to fly under the radar and wasn't very well known, even to Colombian law enforcement, although we tried really hard to convince them that he was a major player. Zapata, known by his underworld nickname, El Caballista, was also responsible for organizing kidnappings for the cartel. He also headed the drug gangs in Bogotá.

"According to the CNP, they were able to pinpoint Zapata's location through the use of electronic tracking equipment," the cable went on to say. "At approximately 5:30 p.m., the CNP/Medellín task force arrived at the Finca La Florida, located in the Antioquían community of Copacabana. When approached by the CNP, Zapata fired several rounds from a 9 mm pistol. The CNP returned fire, killing Zapata."

With Zapata and others out of the picture, we all knew we were getting closer to the target himself.

December 1, 1993, was Escobar's forty-fourth birthday, and he got careless; he celebrated by staying longer on the radio phone with his family. Later, we found out he even had a small celebration in hiding, complete with a birthday cake and a joint, accompanied by a lone bodyguard.

About a week before his birthday, you could feel the anticipation and excitement at the base. The atmosphere was positively electric. Escobar was speaking on the phone with greater frequency, and we knew that he was completely hard up for cash, as all his money launderers and *sicarios* were being rounded up by law enforcement or killed. We were also flooded with calls on the tip line, and tips poured in from Colombians with sightings of Escobar in Medellín. In addition, Steve and I were sending out about ten teletypes a day to our agents all over the world with tips on other members of the Medellín Cartel who had left Colombia. The leads, which led to dozens of arrests in the United States, were based on our intensive telephone intercepts, debriefings, and informants. We were also picking up a lot of leads from our colleagues in the States that we were passing on to the Search Bloc.

In Colombia, the calls between Escobar and Juan Pablo were getting longer and more frequent as de Greiff continued to put pressure on the drug lord to surrender to him. With his father on the run, the seventeen-year-old Juan Pablo had taken over the leadership of the organization. "Juan Pablo is the main person coordinating Escobar's daily activities (i.e., security, mail, strategies)," we wrote in a classified DEA cable on September 21, 1993. "Juan Pablo has been overheard threatening people on behalf of Pablo . . . Juan Pablo Escobar's lead in the Pablo Escobar organization is another indication that Pablo Escobar is at an all-time low as he is having to rely on his son . . . to manage his activities."

In the last two weeks of his life, we intercepted Escobar pleading with his son to try to find him cash, as all his purveyors had either died or gone underground to escape Los Pepes and the police. It was those calls that ultimately led to his demise because they allowed Lieutenant Martinez to track him with greater precision. We all knew that the Search Bloc was getting closer, and there was a great sense of excitement as we went out on raids. In many cases, we knew that we had just narrowly missed him, and during one of the last raids on a ranch outside Medellín, Escobar had abandoned the house but had gone into the nearby forests to get better reception on his phone. When he realized that the ranch had been raided, he somehow managed to escape. But while we may have narrowly missed catching him in those last days, we were absolutely sure that Escobar was where he had always been—in his hometown of Medellín, hiding in plain sight.

But the order to go to Miami came directly from Ambassador Busby, who had been briefed by federal agents there that Escobar was on his way to Haiti and that our old source Navegante, who had assisted us with the hunt for Rodríguez Gacha, would give me the information, but he wanted to do so in person. Navegante was then living at an undisclosed location in South Florida. And he insisted upon giving me—and only me—the tip about Escobar.

I didn't want to go. I argued with Toft; I argued with Busby. But in the end, I couldn't really argue with the U.S. ambassador, and so a day after Escobar's birthday— December 2, 1993—I made my way to El Dorado International Airport and got on the first flight to Miami.

When I arrived in Miami in the afternoon, I was met at the airport by one of the local DEA agents, who drove me to the prearranged meeting place—a cavernous warehouse next to the international airport.

Navegante was on the phone when I walked in. As soon as I saw him, I could tell something big was going down. He had a startled expression on his face, and his eyes were wide open as he watched me enter the warehouse with the other agent. As I got closer, he cradled the phone on his shoulder and looked right at me.

"Acaban de matar a Escobar," he said.

They just killed Escobar.

STEVE

December 2, 1993, was a Thursday. I was in Medellín at the Carlos Holguín base while Javier was being sent to Miami to follow up on a potential lead. We knew it would be a waste of time, but it wasn't much different from the thousands of false starts and fruitless raids that had characterized the second manhunt for Pablo Escobar.

To tell you the truth, Colombia was getting to me, and I was counting the days before Christmas and our trip back to the States for a two-week vacation. This would be Monica's first Christmas with the whole family, and absolutely everyone was excited to meet her. I also couldn't wait to see my two sons, Josh and Zach.

I woke up early that morning, mostly because my room was located directly over the kitchen area. Even with the windows closed in our barracks, we could still hear the kitchen staff clanging pots and pans at the usual time— about 3:30 in the morning—as they prepared breakfast for the troops. I got up between 5:00 and 6:00 a.m., got dressed, and went to find out what was being planned by the CNP commanders that day.

Because of the activities of Los Pepes, it seemed that more reliable intelligence was coming in. More and more daily operations were being conducted. For days, the atmosphere at the base was simply on fire, as if we knew we were getting very close to capturing Escobar. We hadn't seen this type of excitement for many months.

First, I checked in with the other gringos to see what they had going and to learn what new intelligence they were working on. Curiously, I found one of the CIA guys packing up their data collection equipment and carrying it onto a truck he rented. I can't say I was that sorry to see them go.

Next, I checked in with the guys who were manning the tip line, and then with the data collection guys. After that, I knocked on Colonel Martinez's office door, but it was too early and he had not yet arrived. He sometimes attended other meetings and was known to work in his bunk room in the mornings. I also called the DEA head office at the embassy to let them know I was still alive and kicking and to see if they had anything new.

A short time later, the DIJIN unit we worked closely with left the base to accompany Lieutenant Hugo Martinez and the units operating the direction finding equipment. The equipment used triangulation to locate where radio frequencies were coming from. At that time, mobile telephones worked on radio frequencies, and Lieutenant Martinez had spent months figuring out the frequency used by Escobar to talk with his family, who were then the only residents of the Tequendama Hotel in Bogotá.

We knew what frequency Escobar was talking on when he contacted his son to issue instructions and get updates. Every time Lieutenant Martinez got close with his RDFing equipment, the DIJIN guys would stage themselves in the general area of the signal.

After lunch, I was standing in the doorway of the room used by the Delta Force and Navy SEALs (the other gringos on the base), and I saw the CIA agent drive out of the base with the agency's monitoring equipment, totally oblivious to the excitement around him. At the same time, I saw Colonel Martinez's executive staff hurrying to the colonel's office. I followed them to see what was happening. When I got to the door, Colonel Martinez motioned for me to come into his office with the others. He was talking and listening to a handheld portable police radio. The other Colombian police officers were obviously excited and were making arrangements to mount the entire Search Bloc for an operation. Obviously, it takes more than a few minutes to get six hundred police officers geared up and ready, to get the transport vehicles started and lined up, to brief the various levels of command as to what is taking place, and then mount up all the troops to go out.

I wasn't sure who Colonel Martinez was talking to on the radio, but I had a good idea that it was the DIJIN advance group. They believed they'd located Escobar.

And then everything seemed to happen at once. Martinez's executive staff began discussing different tactics and options, but it was obvious Colonel Martinez was in total control of the situation. He told his people in the field that we were getting everyone together and would be heading their way as quickly as possible. It sounded like he wanted the frontline troops to wait until help arrived, but he also told them to go ahead with their mission if they had no other choice.

Then the radio was quiet for several minutes, and I worried that this could be another false alarm. In the eighteen months since Escobar escaped from jail, we had lived through fifteen thousand raids and hundreds of sightings of Escobar. In every case, he eluded us.

Still, something was different. Everyone was talking quietly with the colonel, and there was a very distinct sense of excitement in the air. I stood stock-still, straining to listen to the police radio.

After what seemed like an eternity, a triumphant voice came over the static of the radio.

"Viva Colombia!"

Everyone in the room gave a loud cheer.

We all knew Escobar was dead.

JAVIER

I'm not sure I said anything to Navegante when I heard the news. I simply turned around and had the DEA agent drive me back to the airport, where I managed to catch a flight back to Bogotá. Steve also called me to tell me the great news, and by the time I boarded my flight, the whole world knew that Pablo Escobar was dead.

The flight back to Bogotá was full of press people on their way to cover the story. I recognized many of them from Telemundo and Univision, but I did not say anything to anyone.

A lot of different emotions were racing through my mind as I took my seat on the plane. I was thrilled about Escobar's death and was eager to get back to Colombia as quickly as possible. But I was also angry. After six long years of tracking Escobar in Colombia, I had been called out of the country on a tip I instinctively knew to be false. I'm not sure how Haiti came into the picture. We had also received intelligence that Escobar was hiding in a church in Bogotá. But nothing fit the pattern. Escobar was a creature of Medellín. His strongest support as well as his greatest enemies were in his hometown, and he never strayed very far. He had poured millions into community development in the shantytowns and was still beloved by thousands of impoverished residents of the city. Medellín was his comfort zone. On top of that, we knew he was worried sick about his family's safety. It was unlikely he would ever leave Medellín, let alone Colombia.

After I got back to Bogotá, I headed straight for the embassy. Toft came out of his office when he heard that I had arrived and congratulated me on Escobar's death. We never spoke about Miami again. It was as if it had never happened.

STEVE

After congratulating Colonel Martinez and the others, I ran to the room where the tip line was located to report these events to the DEA office in Bogotá. I called the front office at the embassy but couldn't get through. After several attempts, I called the DEA administrative office. One of the administrative assistants finally answered. I asked her to get Toft on the phone as soon as possible. I told her it was urgent. It seemed to take several long minutes before I heard his gruff voice on the line.

"The Colombian police just killed Escobar," he said before I even had the chance to say hello.

He had already been contacted by his friend, CNP head Vargas. So much for being the first to tell Toft about a major event like this. His own contacts had beat me to it.

I told him I was heading out to the site in the Los Olivos neighborhood near the Atanasio Girardot Sports Complex that Escobar had built during his heyday in the early 1980s when he was still acting like Robin Hood. I told him I would report back later.

"Make sure you get a good look at the body," ordered Toft. "Make sure Escobar's really dead."

I ran to the barracks to get my gear and camera, but when I came back out to the quad area, the entire Search Bloc had already vanished. The only people left were the guards and civilian personnel. I started going through myriad options in my mind on how I was going to get myself to the site where the gun battle had just taken place. At that point, a lone Jeep returned to the compound. It was Colonel Martinez, his driver, and a bodyguard. He'd come back to retrieve his video camera, and at his invitation, I jumped into the jeep and rode to the scene.

It was a quiet, residential district of two- and three-story row houses. Across the way was a small drainage waterway that ran down the street with a few small footbridges across the water. The telephone conversation between Juan Pablo and Escobar that resulted in pinpointing Escobar's location had first led Lieutenant Martinez to the wrong place. Then he realized that there was water nearby that had negatively affected his readings. It was only after he compensated for the water and recalibrated his equipment that he was able to pinpoint Escobar's exact hiding place in Los Olivos.

When I arrived with the colonel's entourage, people

were already streaming over the footpaths and gathering outside the house to find out what all the gunfire was about. As more and more police officers arrived, more and more people came out to watch. The word spread quickly that Escobar had been killed.

I accompanied Colonel Martinez into the three-story residence and saw several of the plainclothes DIJIN officers we worked with. All were excited and quick to tell me that Escobar had been killed. There was a lot of handshaking and backslapping. I learned that when Lieutenant Martinez located Escobar using the direction finding equipment, the DIJIN quickly stationed officers in the front and the rear of the house. Concerned that Escobar might have an alternate escape route that no one knew about or that he might call in reinforcements to help him escape, the DIJIN officers decided to bust through the door and capture him right away. The officers blasted the front door of the house open and rushed inside. Lieutenant Martinez had already seen Escobar through a window on the second floor of the house, but the officers took no chances. They searched and cleared the first floor. They made their way to the second floor, where Escobar had been seen, and that's when Escobar began shooting at the police, who returned fire. Escobar made his way to the third floor with the police in hot pursuit. A window on that floor was next to the terra-cotta roof of the adjacent house, and Escobar's bodyguard jumped out onto the roof and started firing his gun to cover Escobar's escape. The police ordered him to stop and drop his weapon. When he continued to fire, Colombian National Police officers shot him, and he fell off the roof. Alvaro de Jesús Agudelo, known as El Limón (the Lemon), fell ten feet, landing on a grassy area next to the house. He was dead even before he hit the ground.

Escobar clambered barefoot out the same window and onto the roof of the adjoining house to escape. He stayed close to the wall of another house that was to the right side of the window. This wall gave him some protection from the officers on the ground but not from the officers who were pursuing him. Escobar carried two handguns, and he fired at the officers behind him as he started to move across the roof. These officers and the officers on the ground returned fire, striking Escobar several times. Escobar fell, his body sprawled on the roof, his white belly spilling out of an ill-fitting navy polo shirt.

The *pop-pop* of bullets that ended the life of the world's first narcoterrorist happened so quickly that no one could quite believe he was really dead.

But dead he was.

After years of disappointments in the search for the world's most brutal drug trafficker, it was a very good day for the Colombian National Police. They were thrilled with their accomplishment, and I was very happy for them.

And even though Escobar and his lone bodyguard had engaged the police in a firefight, none of the officers had been injured. One of the DIJIN officers did have a close call. As he came around a corner on the second floor to go up the stairs in pursuit of Escobar, he tripped and fell flat. At that exact moment, Escobar fired a shot at him. If the officer hadn't tripped and fallen, he would have been struck by Escobar's bullet. That fall ended up saving his life.

Colonel Martinez and I, along with several other CNP officers, went to the third-floor window where Escobar and his bodyguard had jumped out onto the roof of the neighboring two-story house. I saw almost all the DIJIN officers standing on the roof, some still holding their long guns, along with a body lying on the roof tiles. I glanced at the remains of the world's most wanted man: He looked almost nothing like the stocky, mustachioed, smirking villain in the wanted posters. Escobar had put on a huge amount of weight in hiding. He had a scruffy beard. His blood-splattered blue jeans looked new and were neatly rolled up at the ankles, obviously too long for him. The soles of his feet were cut and grimy from his desperate run through the house and the broken, uneven tiles on the roof.

When the officers saw me, they shouted to let me know they'd gotten Escobar. I waved back and then took several photos.

Next, I accompanied Colonel Martinez and his entourage back downstairs, and we walked around the block to the back street. When we reached the home where Escobar was lying on the roof, I saw a body sprawled on the grass—the remains of El Limón, the last *sicario*.

I took photos for later examination and evaluation. Next, we climbed a ladder to the roof where Escobar was located.

I took numerous photos of Escobar's body, as well as of his double shoulder holster rig and the two handguns he'd used to shoot at the police. I also took photos of the DIJIN officers standing near Escobar's body. Many of the officers, including some uniformed officers, wanted their photo taken with Escobar, so I took those. The DIJIN officers wanted me to join them for a photo with Escobar, which I did. That photo of me on the roof, crouched behind Escobar's body and clutching at one of his shirtsleeves, has become rather well-known, but it also created some challenges for me, especially in Washington and Bogotá in the immediate aftermath of Escobar's death. The photo made it seem that an American had killed Escobar when all the work had actually been done by Colombian law enforcement.

But I wasn't thinking about diplomatic expediency. Like everyone else around me, I was caught up in the euphoria of the moment. After so many years of terror, of hundreds of dead cops, the kidnappings and the bombs that killed innocent people, Pablo Escobar was dead. Let me underline that: He was dead. If I got caught up in that moment, well, okay, I admit it: I was overjoyed.

As I took photographs, I continued to examine the body. I saw a total of three wounds—one in the back of one leg, one in the buttocks, and one in the right ear. It was obvious that the wound that had killed him was the gunshot through his ear. As a young cop, I'd been trained in murder and suicide investigations, and I'd worked both before. As I looked at the area around the entry wound in Escobar's ear,

I didn't see any signs of gunpowder burns, which are indicative of a suicide by firearm or of a gunshot being fired at very close range. This was clearly not a suicide. Determining the cause of death was important because years later, his son, Juan Pablo, for one, would try to manipulate the truth and claim that his father committed suicide on the roof. Somehow, this was supposed to make him seem brave.

But suicide was out of the question. The double shoulder holster rig was lying next to Escobar's body along with two 9 mm handguns. The slide was locked back on one weapon, which indicated there were no bullets in that handgun. I'd already seen signs of a gun battle in the house, and there were obvious signs of another gun battle on the roof. After examining the scene and the evidence, I had no reason not to believe the Colombian police and their version of what had taken place. After all, Javier and I had entrusted our lives to these officers for the last year and a half, and not once did we suspect that we weren't being told the truth.

While we were on the roof, I could see the crowds swelling on the sidewalk below. They were coming out to see if Escobar really was dead. I saw Escobar's frantic mother and sister arrive. I watched as they argued with the police. Then the sister walked over to see the body of Escobar's bodyguard and began yelling at the police that they had killed the wrong person. This was not her brother, she said. They managed to calm her down and then told her that the body of her brother was lying dead on the roof.

The Colombian military arrived and set up a perimeter

to keep people away from the house while the investigation continued. The local media also began to arrive at the site, along with people from the medical examiner's office. I spoke with Lieutenant Colonel Norberto Peláez, one of the military commanders, and we both agreed it was better that I not be seen by the media. I didn't want to take any credit away from the Colombian National Police, nor did any of us want to create the appearance that the Americans had led and conducted this final operation. I climbed down off the roof and returned to the interior of the house where Escobar was killed. I took numerous photos of every room and the contents of the home. There was a yellow taxicab parked in the home's garage area, which confirmed our suspicions that Escobar was freely moving around Medellín while speaking to his son on his mobile phone. In the last conversation they had, Juan Pablo was going through a list of questions that were part of an interview request from a Colombian media outlet.

By the early evening, I had shot four rolls of film, and I was ready to go back to the base. Peláez went with me and provided a few other officers for protection. They were very concerned about my safety and insisted upon taking me back, which I appreciated. We were all still ecstatic about the day's events. I met with the other Americans at the base and relayed what I'd seen. I called Connie to let her know I was okay and then explained everything to Toft. I assured him I had no doubts whatsoever that Pablo Escobar was really dead.

Later that night, Escobar's mother, Hermilda, and two sisters would identify the body at the city morgue—the same morgue where the bodies of more than four hundred policemen had passed over the last sixteen months—all of them murdered by Escobar's henchmen during the second manhunt.

"Murderers!" shouted a grief-stricken Hermilda at the police who were guarding the morgue.

Toft congratulated all of us and advised that plans would be made to get me back to Bogotá.

As the police began to return to the base, security was dramatically increased. Everyone braced themselves for reprisals. We all felt there was a high probability of attacks against us at the base that night. The perimeter guards were increased, and everyone kept their weapons very close.

But that evening proved to be one of the quietest nights I'd ever spend in Medellín. Because of the efforts of the Colombian police and government fighting against Escobar, as well as the vicious attacks by Los Pepes, almost the entire Escobar organization had been killed or imprisoned, so the reality was that no one was left to launch an attack against us. Still, I can't say I slept soundly. Everyone was hyped up by the day's activities, and even though we all felt like the weight of the world had been lifted off our shoulders, we were still suspended in a haze of disbelief.

Did we really do this? Was it really all over? It all felt like a dream.

In Bogotá, Gaviria took to national television to break

the happy news, and in Washington, President Clinton got on the phone to the Colombian president: "Hundreds of Colombians—brave police officers and innocent people—lost their lives as a result of Escobar's terrorism. Your work honors the memory of all these victims."

After everyone returned to the base, I was approached by Peláez, who informed me that no one else's cameras had worked that day, and the photos I'd taken were the only ones showing the scene shortly after the firefight.

I had always liked Peláez. He was personable and very intelligent and spoke excellent English. He was also a graduate of the FBI's national academy, an international training program for executive-level leaders, and very much admired by his junior officers. At just over six feet tall, he was slender with dark hair and eyes and in excellent physical condition. He was a member of Colonel Martinez's executive staff and inner circle. While I lived at the base, Peláez often invited me to walk around the compound, and sometimes, we went into the surrounding neighborhood to grab a burger and a beer. We even went for ice cream together and talked about our families and where we grew up. I even told Peláez about Connie and me, and how happy we were to adopt Monica and how we were counting the days before we could show her off to our families back home. This may sound a little corny, but those walks to get ice cream really gave me a sense of normalcy and allowed me to forget for a few minutes the tension and state of high alert that characterized our daily lives at the base.

I trusted Peláez, so when he asked for my film, I agreed to hand it over without hesitation. I'd taken four rolls of 35 mm film, and Peláez handed it to a major who had the photos processed. The major agreed to return the negatives to me along with copies of the prints that I wanted. Later that evening, I learned that the film had been processed but the major was refusing to return my negatives or the prints. When I asked Peláez to intervene, I received the negatives and photos, but not all of them. The major had extracted several negatives, which I never saw again. Most of these were of the DIJIN officers standing on the roof with Escobar's body—the ones I took from the third-floor window.

The following morning, I received a call from the embassy informing me that Javier would be arriving at the police base in Medellín later that day, and both of us would return to Bogotá that evening. I made arrangements for a police helicopter to meet Javier at the Medellín airport and transport him to the base. I packed my bags and started saying my goodbyes to the other Americans and our police friends. When Javier arrived, there was more celebrating because he had been part of the manhunt since 1988. My biggest regret was that he had not been around when Escobar was killed.

I would have preferred that he'd been there to share in the jubilation when this investigation ended. On the other hand, Javier never carried a camera while in Medellín, so we wouldn't have captured the historic events that day if he'd been there instead of me.

Reporters from around the world descended on Medellín to cover the death of the world's most wanted man and the tumultuous funeral the next day. Thousands of Escobar's admirers from the shantytowns of Medellín crowded into the small chapel where his family had arranged to have a viewing with an open casket. The crowds fought to get close to his silver coffin and to touch his body as it was carried into the church in the pouring rain. Shouting "Viva Pablo!" the mourners seized the casket even before the religious ceremony could begin. The crowds got so out of control that Escobar's family was forced to flee for their own safety before the burial at the hilltop Montesacro Cemetery.

But we weren't sticking around for any of it. We just didn't care; we were happy he was dead. When Javier arrived, we took another look through the house in Los Olivos, combing through Escobar's wallet searching for numbers and names and any other things that could lead us to other Medellín Cartel members. But there was nothing.

Also, I learned from our bosses at the embassy of an incident the previous evening, the same day that Escobar was killed, that represented a potential threat against Connie and me. My immediate supervisor and his wife lived on the same street as Connie and me, but about twenty-seven blocks south of us. That evening, my supervisor's wife was walking her dog on the sidewalk near their apartment. She noticed a car with four men inside driving slowly up and down the street as if looking for an address. Eventually, the car slowed and asked her if she knew where señor Murphy lived. All of our spouses were very aware of potentially dangerous situations and how to handle themselves. She told the men she didn't know a señor Murphy, and she quickly made her way back to her apartment where an armed guard was posted. We never found out any further information on those men or why they were asking where I lived. But the DEA and the embassy took this as a serious threat and assigned a three-man security detail to our apartment building. The detail was stationed at the entrance gate of our three-building complex. After I returned home to Bogotá, I went to the embassy to work each day, but Connie stayed home taking care of Monica. We always found it ironic that these guards were stationed there to protect Connie and I, but they didn't know what we looked like. Connie would take Monica on walks in her stroller. They walked right past this security detail and they had no idea who she was.

That afternoon, Javier and I were transported to the Medellín airport via a Colombian National Police helicopter gunship. At the Rionegro airport, we boarded a plane for the ride back to Bogotá. At El Dorado International Airport, we took a taxi back to the embassy where people were waiting for us at the DEA office, eager to see the pictures I had taken after Escobar's death. I also knew that some of the people we worked closely with wanted to congratulate Javier and me. Both of us knew that it was their victory as well as ours.

There was heavy traffic as we arrived right at rush hour

on a rainy Friday, and the taxi driver was pretty good about
avoiding a lot of congestion. It felt strange sitting in the cab,
and I couldn't remember the last time I had done so. For all
our rides to and from the airport, we had always driven in a
DEA armored car with a military escort. Our plane was
late arriving from Medellín, which explained why no one
was there to meet us. Riding in a taxi in our blue jeans, polo
shirts, and sneakers in Colombia felt oddly liberating, a
true sign that maybe things were going back to normal in a
country that had been a battlefield for so many years.

We arrived at the embassy at around dinnertime—
American dinnertime. We checked in through the main
entrance and rode the elevator to the third floor, using our
swipe cards to access the DEA office space from the elevator lobby. As we walked down the hall, I found it strange
that there were a lot of people milling about after work
hours, speaking in loud voices about how proud they were
as Javier and I walked out of the elevator. Friday nights at
the embassy were usually deserted, as everyone was eager
to get a head start on their weekends. When Javier and I
finally walked into the office and saw the streamers and
balloons, we suddenly knew what was going on.

"PEG IS DEAD—YES!" was written in bold capital
letters on a streamer that hung in our office, and we walked
in to spontaneous applause from everyone we worked
with. One by one, they greeted us with hugs and hand-
shakes. I was surprised to see Connie so late on a Friday
without our baby daughter, but later I learned that she had

organized the whole thing and secured Rosa, our trusted babysitter, for Monica so that we could celebrate our great victory over Escobar. When I finally made it to the back of the room where she was waiting, she gave me a long hug and showered me with kisses. I felt the mixture of both relief and euphoria in her embrace. Our gamble to leave Miami had finally paid off. It had been a great adventure, but a difficult one. And now that it was over, we would soon be going back home with our little girl.

Javier and I finally made it to our own desks, where we dropped our bags and prepared to join the party, but we could hardly move as more and more people followed us to ask questions, give us their congratulations, or just offer us a cold beer. Connie and some of the other people in the office had arranged for several cases of beer and lots of pizza to celebrate.

When I pulled out the photos I'd taken in Medellín the day before, everyone crowded around me, and for a few hours, Javier and I retold the story of how the CNP had found and killed Escobar. Everyone wanted copies of our photos because they realized that they were part of history—they had all been involved in helping to end the reign of Pablo Escobar, the world's most wanted man. I think all of us in the DEA, as well as the other agencies we worked with, felt our own profound sense of relief after Escobar was killed.

After all, bringing Escobar to justice had been a team effort; it wasn't just Javier and me and our pals in Colombian law enforcement. Other DEA personnel had contributed significantly to this manhunt but didn't get the same recognition. Their work was very important, and it all contributed to the goal of putting so much pressure on Escobar that he finally made the fatal mistake of staying on his phone too long that day. The Escobar case had top priority at the embassy, which caused other investigations to slow down somewhat. Resources were directed to us and the Escobar operation. Now that Escobar was gone, it meant we could all get back to work addressing other threats against the Colombians and our own country.

The Colombian National Police deserve and earned the lion's share of the credit for their hard work, commitment, and sacrifices. They were true allies and friends, and they went out of their way to protect Javier and me. And all U.S. personnel who contributed to this investigation also deserve recognition for their efforts—not just the people within the embassy in Bogotá but all over the world. We sent countless leads to DEA offices worldwide, as well as other U.S. law enforcement agencies, and every office followed up on these leads immediately and professionally. After all these years, the massive manhunt for Pablo Escobar is still recognized as one of the best examples of what can be accomplished when agencies and countries put aside their egos and differences to work together for the betterment of mankind.

Eventually, we ran out of beer and pizza, and we headed out to find a club. Connie had arranged for our friend to spend the night at our apartment so she could look after Monica. And out we went to continue our party! I don't remember any of the restaurants, clubs, or bars we visited that night, even though it was one of the best nights of my life.

We all knew that at the very moment Escobar was shot dead—barefoot and frantic on that terra-cotta roof—every citizen in Colombia was safer. Weeks later, when we examined the murder rate in Medellín, we weren't so surprised to see that it had dropped by almost 80 percent.

We celebrated all night and into the next morning.

As the sun rose over Bogotá, I held on tightly to Connie's hand as we left the bar and headed out into the street. Everything felt lighter that morning, and even the smog that seemed to constantly envelop the city appeared to lift as Colombians woke to a brave new day.

As we approached our apartment, the sun was rising.

A newspaper vendor was already out selling the morning papers. I had seen some of the Colombian papers that had come out on the day Javier and I returned to Bogotá. We even posed with a copy of *El Tiempo* that declared, "AL FIN, CAYO!" ("At last, he fell!") plastered across its front page.

But it was the headline in *La Prensa* that stayed with me on that glorious early morning: "IMMORTAL JOY!—COLOMBIA BETWEEN DELIRIUM AND RELIEF," proclaimed the bold headline that dominated the entire front page.

I couldn't have said it better myself.

CONCLUSION

JAVIER

After Escobar's death, it took less than two weeks for the cocaine cartels to start up again.

Of course, the Cali Cartel had benefited greatly from the destruction of the Medellín Cartel. When you look at the history of the war on drugs, when the main group of traffickers gets dismantled, there is always another one ready to take its place. More importantly, the leaders of the Cali Cartel—the Orejuela brothers—watched and learned from all of Pablo Escobar's mistakes while he was still alive. The leaders of the Cali Cartel learned the importance of keeping a low profile and focusing on improving their distribution networks. I've always made the point that the Medellín Cartel functioned like a bunch of cowboys in the

Wild West, while the Cali traffickers were more business-like, more sophisticated—like Wall Street businessmen.

I'm not saying that the war on drugs had been a complete failure. The Escobar search had been a huge success, but maybe it was successful because it was a personal war for so many of us involved. We had all lost friends and attended police funerals. We lived through kidnappings, car bombs, and the Avianca bombing—all of it caused by one man. It took nearly a decade to get rid of Escobar, but we helped the Colombians take back their country, and I'm proud of that. I'm also proud to say that this was the first time in history that an entire cartel had been dismantled.

But despite the death of the most murderous drug trafficker, little had changed in Colombia, where the new cartels still controlled the political process. By way of proof, an informant gave us a copy of an intercept that featured Miguel Ángel Rodríguez Orejuela, the head of the Cali Cartel, telling an associate that he had arranged to deposit more than $3.5 million to the presidential campaign of Ernesto Samper. The elections were days away, and Samper was neck and neck with the other leading candidate, Andrés Pastrana Arango.

Ambassador Busby listened to the tapes in stunned silence and passed them on to Joe Toft, who flew off the handle. The tapes had also been delivered to President Gaviria, who sent them off to the prosecutor general. But Toft was livid and knew that the authorities would probably do nothing before the vote, so he asked Washington for permission to leak the tapes to the press. It was denied, and we all sat back and watched as Samper squeaked to victory.

But Toft, a thirty-year veteran of the drug wars in the United States and Latin America, had clearly had enough. He leaked the tapes to Colombian and U.S. reporters, and then he personally went on Colombian TV to denounce the "narco democracy" that the country had become. After that, he resigned from the DEA.

None of us could blame him. We had all fought long and hard, and it seemed in that moment of Samper's victory, the sacrifice of hundreds of brave police officers, jurists, and journalists who had fought against Escobar was pretty much in vain.

As I prepared to leave Colombia after Samper's victory, I thought back on that distant summer night when my old partner Gary Sheridan and I were suddenly locked into a restaurant when Escobar's thugs assassinated presidential candidate Luis Carlos Galán during a campaign stop on the outskirts of Bogotá.

Escobar's handpicked *sicario* Jhon Jairo Velásquez Vásquez, known to most of us as Popeye, was one of the goons who had pulled the trigger. Popeye, who bragged about killing nearly three hundred people while working for Escobar but is suspected of murdering exponentially more, was eventually convicted of Galán's murder and went to prison in Colombia. But by 2014, he was out of jail after serving twenty-two years of a thirty-year sentence.

The last I heard, he was leading grim tours in Medellín, showing visitors the sites of some of the worst massacres in the city and taking them to the cemetery to point out all the people he had killed.

You'd go crazy trying to make sense of things that happen in Colombia.

And it just got crazier. A few years ago, General Miguel Maza Márquez, who was a good friend of the DEA while we were hunting Escobar and in charge of the now defunct DAS—the Colombian equivalent of the FBI—was found guilty of Galán's murder. I was devastated when I heard he had been arrested for reducing the security detail around Galán just before he was assassinated. I don't know why he changed the security around Galán, but I am pretty sure it wasn't to have him killed. No one was more committed to the fight against Escobar than Maza, who had survived seven different attempts on his life by the Medellín Cartel, including a car bomb that had exploded outside his Bogotá office.

Shortly after he left government in the summer of 1994, Gustavo de Greiff went on an international speaking tour urging the end of the worldwide war on drugs. The man responsible for prosecuting Colombia's cocaine cartels now wanted to legalize drugs! I told you that we could never make sense of Colombia! We certainly could never make sense of de Greiff, whose decision to negotiate with a murderer like Escobar prolonged the war against him and led to the deaths of thousands of innocent victims.

But he has a point on the war on drugs. Despite the billions that have been earmarked for law enforcement and crop substitution to help poor farmers move away from lucrative coca cultivation, a lot of this war has been a failure. I recently saw statistics compiled by the United Nations that showed that Colombia had a record level of coca cultivation in 2017. Enough coca was produced to manufacture more than 1,300 tons of cocaine, up more than 30 percent from the previous year's harvest, according to the UN Office on Drugs and Crime in Colombia.

The consumption of illegal drugs is a global problem. There are traffickers who are waiting for the chance to step up and make money, not caring who will die due to consumption or get killed because they stood in the way of doing business. We need better enforcement around the world to arrest those who are responsible for sending these deadly goods. The worst threat you can make to a foreign drug trafficker is extradition to the United States.

But we also need to be mindful of social education priorities, and we need to be better at helping people to understand the dangers of consuming drugs.

I will always remember that Pablo Escobar used to have signs at his jungle cocaine laboratories that read: "If you get caught using the product, I will kill you."

Granted, it was over the top, but Escobar's edict was a great message. As a society, we need to be tougher on drugs. We need to improve education on the dangers of addiction. We need to strengthen programs like Drug

Abuse Resistance Education (DARE), which teaches schoolkids about the danger of drug abuse and belonging to gangs. But we can't just leave this to the school systems; drug awareness needs to be all-encompassing. It needs to happen in faith groups and in the home. It's everyone's issue and everyone's problem.

If there is anything I have learned in the DEA, it's that fighting the war on drugs requires a total commitment from everyone on your team. If the good guys are going to win, they need everyone's support.

When I arrived in Colombia in March 1988, I had trouble with neckties. It's not that I didn't like wearing a suit and tie, it's just that my fingers were awkward when it came to that elaborate knot. They weren't nimble or practiced enough around such niceties, largely because I had spent most of my career chasing bad guys all over Texas and Mexico.

I could pull a trigger on any firearm, but I was hopeless with a necktie. Take it from me, there was never a need for a suit and tie when you were swilling stale beer in the grimy border towns where I cut my teeth as a young cop and then as an undercover agent for the Drug Enforcement Administration.

But Colombia was suddenly different. Even before I arrived, I knew it would be a milestone in my law enforcement career. As a special agent for the DEA assigned to

Bogotá, I was now a diplomat of sorts. My office was located in the U.S. embassy in Colombia's capital city, and I was expected to dress the part every day when I went into work.

Suit-and-tie. Suit-and-tie. Every day. I told myself it would be okay, as long as I could still wear my cowboy boots.

But I couldn't master the knot before I was scheduled to take up my new position. At home in Texas, every time I got in front of a mirror determined to conquer the knot, it always confronted me as if it were mocking my inability to deal with such a simple task. When I looked at my reflection after grappling with the tie, I focused on the thin piece of silk around my neck. Why couldn't I get it right? It was always lopsided and messy.

At first, my new girlfriend helped me out. We started dating shortly after I arrived in Bogotá, after she came out of a relationship with her State Department boyfriend. She was a tall, slim brunette with hazel eyes, and she was a veteran of DEA administrative posts in Europe. She was an incredibly hard worker, heading into the embassy on weekends to keep up with the cable traffic and working late most weeknights. We kept our relationship a secret, but everyone eventually found out. Before joining the DEA, she worked in the men's department at Saks Fifth Avenue, and she professionally knotted my small collection of ties and then ingeniously mounted each of them on Velcro. In my closet in Bogotá, I had several

Velcro-mounted ties with immaculate knots. All I needed to do was wind one end of the knotted tie around my shirt collar and fasten the Velcro strips together.

But I never imagined that my posting would last as long as it did. Halfway through my six years in the country, those Velcro ties started to look tired. The knots were dangerously close to unraveling, and the colors had started to fade. So I went back to the mirror, and I practiced with a new set of ties. I was determined more than ever to master the elusive knot.

Strangely, my necktie skills came together right after we tracked down and killed Pablo Emilio Escobar Gaviria. It was our colleagues from the Colombian National Police who actually pulled the trigger, but after spending every waking minute going after that scumbag for six years, it was our victory as well.

The CNP officers were so excited and relieved by the death of the notorious cocaine kingpin that it seemed they couldn't wait to honor every officer who had been part of the search, including the American DEA agents who had labored for so long by their side.

Those Americans were my partner Steve Murphy and me, both of us longtime cops who had somehow ended up far from home, chasing the world's most notorious criminal.

And so back to the tie. On the proudest day of my career, I took extra time in the mirror with the patterned red tie I had picked out the night before. I laid out a starched white shirt and made sure that my light gray suit was pressed. I combed and gelled my hair, and when I was done, I thought maybe I did look okay. Actually, I can admit it now as I look back on the photographs taken all those years ago: I looked better than okay. I looked great!

I glanced in the mirror again and adjusted my glasses. The Colombian government was about to proclaim me a hero, and I wanted to look my best at the awards ceremony organized by the director of the CNP and attended by the men I most admired in Colombia, who had been our local partners in the search for Escobar.

Sorry, I should really reverse that: We were their partners; they were always in charge, and they were among the bravest men I had ever met, willing to go out day and night knowing that there was a big chance they would never return. To me, the elite members of the CNP were the best of the best. And I knew that what made them so good was the knowledge that the fight against Escobar wasn't about dope or money.

It was revenge, pure and simple. Revenge for all the innocent people and hundreds of police officers and special agents Escobar had killed. The fight against Escobar was personal for them, and after I had lost trusted colleagues in Colombia and lived through the worst of Escobar's terror, the hunt for the world's most wanted drug trafficker became personal for me too.

Weeks before the CNP presented us with our awards, Escobar had been gunned down in Medellín, his body splayed among the broken terra-cotta roof tiles of the home that proved his final hideout. His shooting ended years of dangerous investigative work on the part of both Colombian and U.S. authorities—all of us working together to quite simply rid the world of evil.

For Escobar was pure evil. He was no hero. He may have spent a small fraction of some of the billions he made selling cocaine to fix up Medellín shantytowns and build a soccer stadium, but his brutality had brought Colombia to its knees for years.

The ceremony was very formal, and I was surprised to see all the men I had worked with in the upper echelons of the Colombian police in suits and formal police attire. During the two manhunts for Escobar, we had spent a great deal of time together living at the Carlos Holguín CNP base in Medellín, many of us in the plainclothes uniform of the undercover cop—in faded blue jeans and polo shirts.

Contrary to U.S. policy, which prohibits federal agents from accompanying local law enforcement on raids, Steve and I had accompanied these courageous officers on thousands of failed operations and ambushes in and around Medellín to bring Escobar to justice.

Now, here we were in our Sunday best, mingling and chatting over tumblers of whiskey like dignitaries at a cocktail reception. It was hard not to relive the events of December 2, 1993, the day that Escobar was killed and the Medellín Cartel ceased to be a force in cocaine trafficking or a terrorist menace. It was hard to put an exact number on the tens of thousands of innocent civilians Escobar and his army of *sicarios* had killed during a reign of terror that began when he ordered the fatal hit on a federal attorney general in 1984. It continued with the assassinations of judges, a presidential candidate, journalists, and hundreds of law enforcement officers.

Standing in the grand nineteenth-century hall where the awards ceremony was taking place, I flashed back to many of the police funerals I had attended in Medellín in the days that Escobar was offering his teenage assassins one hundred dollars per dead cop.

I knew I was accepting my award for those earnest young officers who had died in the line of duty. And I was proud to be standing next to their fearless commander, Colonel Hugo Martinez, the upstanding military man who had risked his own life as head of the Bloque de Búsqueda—the Search Bloc that had brought together six hundred elite law enforcement officers in the hunt for the world's first narcoterrorist. Whiskey in hand, I offered an informal toast to Martinez and his son, the lieutenant who had been named after his father, and made the older man beam with pride. Hugo Martinez Jr. was as fearless as his old man, possessed of an unshakeable resolve.

Silence descended on the ornate, high-ceilinged room with its oil paintings of Colombia's greatest heroes of independence. We knew that the death of Escobar was a milestone in Colombia's history, as important as its historic wars with Spain. With Simón Bolívar and the soldier and statesman Francisco José de Paula Santander Omaña staring down at us in their own elaborate military uniforms, we came to stiff attention as the awards presentation was about to begin. CNP general Octavio Vargas Silva, himself formally dressed in a khaki ceremonial uniform, the myriad and colorful medals arranged with military precision over the left breast pocket of his woolen suit, cleared his throat. Then he read a proclamation from the Colombian government before conferring the country's most prestigious law enforcement awards. Vargas was the original architect of the Bloque de Búsqueda and hand-picked every officer who was part of that incredible team, although he didn't get much credit for it in the end. For me, he was a great leader and an upstanding citizen. After he received his bonus from the Colombian government for leading the successful search against Escobar, he donated the cash to a fund for the families of officers who had been killed by Escobar's henchmen in the line of duty.

A woman police officer, also dressed in full regalia, solemnly followed Vargas holding a leather-bound box. Each medal was tied to a ribbon in the red, blue, and yellow silk colors of the Colombian flag and rested on a velvet pillow inside the boxes. When it came to my turn, I stood at attention as the general carefully removed the medal from the box and pinned it to the left side of my suit, just above my heart. We shook hands.

"Colombia thanks you for your bravery, Javier," said Vargas, a stocky military man with graying black hair and thick, bushy eyebrows. "You are a hero."

"*Soy un gran amigo de la Policía Nacional,*" I said, overwhelmed.

I had always felt very close to Vargas, partly because we both started at the same time chasing Escobar. He always called me by my first name, and he always listened to my advice on search strategies, even though I was just an agent and he was the head of Colombia's national police.

After he pinned the ribbon on my jacket, Vargas continued down the line to confer the other awards.

I was then, and remain today, deeply humbled by the whole ceremony. I still have the medal hanging in my man cave at home. The Colombians honored the DEA alongside their own brave law enforcement heroes, even though it was the Colombians who had made the ultimate sacrifice, losing so many police officers in the hunt for Escobar.

During the years I spent hunting Escobar, I had wanted to give up many times, outraged by the deaths of so many Colombians whom I counted as among my best friends. There was Captain Pedro Rojas, whom my old partner Gary Sheridan and I had convinced to go after cartel members in Montería. He and his driver ended up tortured and killed, their bodies cut into small pieces. I was devastated at that time. But somehow, the sacrifice of officers like Rojas who valiantly and unquestioningly gave their lives in the battle against evil renewed my spirit and gave me the strength to stay on and fight.

And I learned a great deal from them. The number-one thing I learned is that you cannot ever back down, especially as the rest of humanity is looking to you to see what you are going to do.

We are the good guys, and we will always win.

Weeks after the awards ceremony, I replayed every moment over and over in my mind, basking in the honor—the pride and sense of accomplishment of having had a role in history.

The Colombian government had recognized our valor and determination.

I held on to that precious thought for a long time, largely because in my own country, our work tracking down the world's most sought-after fugitive went pretty much unnoticed.

STEVE

I didn't get into police work to win awards, and we don't do our jobs to get special recognition.

Like Javier, I was deeply honored to be recognized in Colombia with the National Police's Distinguished Service Cross, but I was pretty dismayed when the death of the world's most wanted man didn't even make the front page of *DEA World*, our bimonthly, in-house publication, which is edited in Washington.

We got a small write-up in the magazine, and our boss Joe Toft promised he would put us up for the Attorney General's Distinguished Service Award, one of the most prestigious prizes in U.S. law enforcement. With our input, he wrote up the recommendations while Javier and I were still in Colombia, but the paperwork was submitted late, and the AG's office in Washington wouldn't accept it. By then, Javier and I had transferred back to the United States, and Toft had already retired. Our first- and second-level supervisors, who were still in Bogotá, promised us that they would do the follow-up and resubmit the recommendation the following year, in 1995. The write-up was finally submitted to the AG, but the names had been changed to our first- and second-level supervisors. It was hard for us not to feel that we had just been written out of history.

In June 1995, then attorney general Janet Reno presented the second-highest form of recognition bestowed on an employee of the Department of Justice to our first- and second-level supervisors at DEA. "For their dedicated, energetic efforts under dangerous and hostile conditions, in the eighteen-month investigation and recapture of Pablo Escobar Gaviria. Their emotionally and physically exhausting day-to-day supervision of the case eventually led to the demise of Escobar and his murderous associates within the Medellín Cartel, ending the Medellín Cartel and their reign of terror over Colombia," Reno said.

The two men were stand-up law enforcement guys with a ton of experience. One of them had helped put together the U.S. government's case against Carlos Lehder, the only member of the Medellín Cartel to be extradited and convicted in the United States.

But they had barely been to Medellín. They didn't live day in and day out at the mosquito-infested CNP barracks, where the Bloque de Búsqueda was based. They did good work at the embassy in Bogotá, but it was Javier and me who were the frontline soldiers in America's war on drugs. We were the gringos with the $300,000 price on our heads—the secret targets that Escobar's army of young hitmen would have loved to have killed.

After we returned to the States, a lot of people asked us how we survived those years in Colombia under so much pressure and fear. I think that we managed to survive in the face of so much horror because we were determined to rid the world of the evil Escobar. And I have to say that it was our belief in God that sustained us in our battle. Like some knights of yore, we were part of God's army, and we believed on some level that he had a plan for us. And that plan didn't include dying in Colombia.

We also knew that the DEA had our backs, especially after the torture and murder of our former DEA colleague Enrique "Kiki" Camarena Salazar in Mexico in 1985. The U.S. government responded to his death at the hands of Mexican drug kingpin Miguel Ángel Félix Gallardo's goons with swift and brutal force, going after the men who had brutally kidnapped Kiki, injecting him with amphetamines so that he remained conscious during more than thirty hours of torture before they killed him. On some level, Escobar must have realized that if he directly and deliberately came after Javier and me, the U.S. government would impose sanctions and restrictions that might actually halt or dramatically hinder his drug-trafficking operation and the flow of billions of dollars in proceeds. In this case, profits were probably much more important to Escobar than the murder of two DEA agents.

Javier and I also knew that the elite members of Colombian law enforcement—the CNP and DIJIN men we came to know so well—who worked on the search for Escobar always had our backs. These are the people we shared information with, who we lived with, ate with, shared some of the same dangerous situations with. We trusted them with our lives. When the bullets started flying, we knew these guys would stand and fight, not run away to safety. But because of the mutual respect we developed for each other, they knew we would stand beside them and fight as well.

After Escobar died, Javier and I went our separate ways. Javier spent some time in Puerto Rico chasing another group of narcos and eventually returned to Colombia to target the Cali Cartel, which had grown in importance after Escobar was out of the picture. In the summer of

1994, I left Colombia with my young family and took up postings in Greensboro, North Carolina, Atlanta, and Washington, D.C.

For years, we were silent about our roles in one of the world's greatest manhunts. We made no comment, even as a flurry of press reports and books erroneously credited others with Escobar's demise. One author even accused us of cooperating with Los Pepes, the murderous Colombian vigilantes who went after Escobar during the tail end of the second manhunt. Even though it was simply untrue, we remained silent. That kind of restraint is something you learn when you spend a lot of your working life undercover. You don't engage; you just do your job.

For years, we just did our jobs, which was dedicated to ridding the world of the scourge of drug traffickers.

And then six years ago, we suddenly found ourselves in the international spotlight when Netflix asked us for our help in putting together *Narcos*. Our work on the Escobar case was finally revealed to the world, albeit with poetic license on the part of the writers and producers of what has become a wildly popular series.

Both of us still look back at the Escobar hunt and pinch ourselves. We were really just two small-town guys who got the opportunity to work the case of a lifetime—to be frontline soldiers in the greatest manhunt in history.

EPILOGUE

STEVE

I never thought I would go back to Medellín after Escobar was killed, but a few months later, I found myself in a familiar routine, sitting in the back seat of a CNP jeep for the stomach-churning ride through the winding roads into the city. This time, Connie sat next to me. We were on our way to adopt our baby daughter, Mandy, from an orphanage in the city. We were full of anticipation and excitement as we left our Bogotá apartment in a predawn mist, even though it meant traveling to a place to which I had no desire to ever return. We left Monica asleep with a babysitter and happily set out on our journey.

Connie didn't say anything after we landed in Medellín, her first time in the city. I could tell she was nervous, probably reliving all the times that I had traveled to the city under much worse circumstances. We never spoke about it, but the full horror of what my job had entailed in the hunt for Pablo Escobar must have hit her all at once, and she had already turned visibly pale as we disembarked from our Avianca flight and were met on the tarmac of the Rionegro Airport by a full security detail of heavily armed CNP officers to escort us into the city. They were all members of the Search Bloc, and for me, it was a happy reunion. For Connie, it was more of a horror show.

They had wanted us to board the Huey helicopter gunship that was waiting for us on the runway, but Connie stopped in her tracks. She took one look at the helicopter and squeezed my hand, and then in a barely audible whisper, she leaned over and said, "There's absolutely no way I'm getting into that thing."

Maybe the security did seem over the top, but I barely noticed. I had gotten used to being a gringo target, and for all I knew, I was still a target in Colombia even after Escobar was dead and the Medellín Cartel was in tatters. For the past year and a half, I had become accustomed to looking over my shoulder and being escorted at all times by square-jawed Colombian police officers armed to the teeth. And while Connie had lived in Bogotá during Escobar's reign of terror, Medellín was different. For years, it had been ground zero for the drug wars—a city constantly on edge, where every parked car could still hold a bomb.

In fact, I had to get special permission from the embassy

to return to Medellín to adopt Mandy. After Escobar's death, Connie and I knew that we had very limited time in Colombia, which remained a nondependent post for DEA agents. We needed to leave with our daughter Monica, but we desperately wanted a sister for our baby. Alissa, who had served us so well during our first adoption, was leaving her job at the federal agency in Bogotá and could no longer help us. This time, I was the one who took the initiative after I met the deputy director of a Medellín adoption agency. She was visiting the embassy with a group of Americans who had just adopted children through the Medellín agency, Casa de María y el Niño. Connie gave the information to Alissa, who made the initial contact for us before she left her post in Bogotá. Weeks after Escobar was killed, we had several conversations by phone with the director, an enthusiastic woman named Maria who spoke excellent English. She promised to find us an infant, and by April 1994, she sent us a picture of Mandy in the mail. Of course, she was beautiful, with almost a full head of dark hair and deep dimples. We held out the small picture to Monica, who seemed nonplussed by the prospect of meeting her new little sister, but we were ecstatic and couldn't wait to hold Mandy in our arms.

Ambassador Busby himself signed off on our trip to Medellín to finalize Mandy's adoption, and I had warned Connie ahead of time that we would need armed escorts the whole time we were there. Moreover, we would only be allowed to be in the city during daytime hours. Staying overnight was considered too risky. While Escobar was no longer a threat, the situation was still tense with the remnants of gangs of *sicarios* roaming the hillside shantytowns.

When Connie pulled me aside at the Medellín airport, I approached the lieutenant who had come to meet us, and as graciously as I could, I told him that the helicopter would not work for us, as we had numerous appointments in the city. The lieutenant radioed the CNP colonel in charge in Bogotá who had set up our security detail, and he explained the situation. The colonel instructed the lieutenant to do whatever we needed done and to stay with us as long as we were in Medellín.

I'm not sure Connie was happy with the alternative as we were escorted throughout the city in a caravan of CNP jeeps in the company of heavily armed plainclothes police officers.

Once out of the airport, they drove through the winding highway into the city at breakneck speed.

Of course, Connie had heard me tell stories about this harrowing drive before, but she really didn't appreciate the circumstances until she lived it for herself. Although we no longer carried our pistols, our fingers hovering over the trigger, the driving was every bit as fast and dangerous. Connie was white-knuckled the entire trip, holding on to anything she could get her hands on. As we rattled over the treacherous mountain roads, I reached over to her, but she sat stock-still, visibly horrified by this crazy operation.

Casa de María y el Niño was the only home on a quiet street on the outskirts of the city. A long dirt driveway led to a gated fence that surrounded the property. When we passed the gate, we saw young children running and playing in the fields that surrounded the orphanage. They were excited by the arrival of the two gringos who descended from the police caravan, and some of the kids ran to greet us as we got out of our jeep. Others followed us and grabbed on to our hands as we made our way through the front lawn to the main building. Later, we found out that they were all hoping we had come to adopt them.

The building where the adoption agency was located was clean but spare. There were lots of pictures of children on the walls, and everyone we met there was polite and professional. As we walked through the halls, we could hear children singing, playing, and laughing. This was very impressive to us. We didn't hear any kids screaming or crying.

Maria, the director whom we had spoken to numerous times on the phone, was there to greet us when we entered. She was middle-aged, well-dressed, and extremely polite. Her English was fluent, and she told us that she had traveled many times to the United States. She carried a sheaf of documents that would allow us to become temporary foster parents until the adoption could be completed. We would need to return to Medellín another time to finalize everything, but we would be allowed to take Mandy with us once we saw her.

We signed all the paperwork in Maria's office, quickly noting Mandy's birth date, her weight at birth, and her mother's name. After the bureaucratic formalities, we were then shown to a larger room where Mandy was brought to us by an employee. She had been dropped off that morning by her foster mother, who had received another baby that same day.

Mandy, all of five months old, smiled at us as soon as we saw her, the little dimples forming on her soft cheeks. She had the most beautiful eyes and the longest eyelashes we'd ever seen on a child. She never once cried or fussed when people held her. Maria allowed us to hold her, and we fell in love right away.

We worried about Monica, who was now fourteen months old. We didn't know how she would handle a younger sister. On the night we arrived, Monica met us at the front door with Susan Jaquez, our closest friend in Colombia and the wife of a fellow DEA agent. Susan had been taking care of Monica while we were in Medellín and had helped to prepare her for Mandy's arrival, although we had been doing this for weeks, explaining to Monica that she would soon have another little girl to play with. When we walked into the apartment, she was very excited and immediately started acting like the big sister.

We arranged blankets on the floor and got down to

introduce all the girls, including Susan. Connie introduced Monica to Mandy and explained that this was her new sister. Immediately, Monica got next to Mandy and started babbling, offering Mandy a baby bottle, bringing her tissues and a little doll to play with. We kept a very close watch on the two of them because Monica didn't fully understand how delicate a baby can be. Monica tried to hand bigger toys and dolls to Mandy, who was too little to physically handle most of those items, so Monica would simply drop them. Most landed next to Mandy, but one or two landed on Mandy, so we had to be alert to that. But all in all, Monica and Mandy immediately became sisters and have had that special sister bond since that first day.

A few weeks later, we returned to the orphanage to finalize Mandy's adoption. Members of the CNP picked us up at Rionegro Airport, and this time there was no talk of getting into the helicopter gunship; we simply got into the waiting jeeps and were whisked into the city, where we would sign the legal paperwork officially making Mandy a member of our family.

We signed the papers in the spare office and prepared to go, eager to return to our two little girls in Bogotá.

Once the formalities were finished, Maria asked us if she could speak to us privately before we returned to Bogotá. We sat in straight-backed chairs in her office, worried that maybe something had gone wrong with the adoption. But Maria assured us that Mandy was legally ours and that no one could take her away from us.

"I want to know who you really are," said Maria, fixing me with a steady gaze.

When I asked her why she would ask us that, Maria apologized for the directness of the question, but by way of explanation, she said that her agency had finalized adoptions with many Americans but that she had never seen anyone like us—with so much attendant security.

"I work for the Department of Justice," I said, maybe too curtly. Anyway, I was hoping to leave it at that.

But she knew that there was something more to our story—something beyond what we had included in our official paperwork, where we had identified ourselves as U.S. government employees.

"Please, tell me what you do for the Department of Justice," she said. "It won't go beyond this room, but I need to know."

That's when I asked her if she knew what *DEA* stood for. Maria raised her eyebrows and then broke into a big smile.

"I thought that might be the case," she said. Then she pointed out the large window in her office to an eight-story condo that was located on a hill above the orphanage. She asked me if I knew who had once lived there.

I told her that it was the Monaco building, now abandoned, where Pablo Escobar once lived with his family—the same building that Los Pepes had attacked during the final months of their own murderous campaign against the Medellín Cartel.

I was still hesitant about this line of questioning and asked if this was a problem. Maria immediately answered that there was no problem and that she and all her employees at the orphanage had immense respect for the Colombian National Police and for what the Americans had done to try to sort out the problems with drug trafficking and violence in her country.

And then, with tears in her eyes, she told us the story of her teenage son who had been finishing high school and working hard to get into college. One day, he happened to be in the wrong place at the wrong time, passing a group of drug traffickers who were in the midst of a heated argument. Before her son and his friends could leave the area, the narcos started shooting at each other, and her son was stuck in the cross fire, killed instantly by a stray bullet.

I can't imagine how awful this was for Maria and her family, but I knew that it was the story of all of Colombia under the evil that was Pablo Escobar. There were thousands of similar stories of innocent people—children—who had paid the ultimate price.

At that point, I felt I owed Maria the truth, and I explained to her that my partner Javier and I were the two gringos who had spent nearly two years living at the nearby Holguín base, working with the Bloque de Búsqueda to get Escobar.

Maria was overwhelmed, and the tears flowed freely. She came around her desk and hugged both Connie and me.

"Thank you," she said through her tears as she held me in a tight embrace. "Thank you for adopting this sweet little girl. And thank you for all you have done for Colombia."

Then Maria escorted us to the police convoy that was waiting for us in front of the building and waved us goodbye.

ACKNOWLEDGMENTS

There's an old saying: "Find a job you love and you'll never work a day in your life."

Javier and I were blessed to find that job, working as DEA special agents.

We'd like to thank the DEA for giving us the resources and the backup in the search for Pablo Escobar. In particular, our boss Joe Toft stands out for his tenacious leadership and courage.

While Javier and I were the "boots on the ground" in Medellín, we recognize the men and women of the DEA who made sacrifices every day during the Escobar operation but never received the recognition they deserve. Fellow agents, analysts, investigators, and support staff were all involved, and each person played a special role directly and indirectly to help us achieve a successful conclusion to this case.

The Colombian National Police deserve special recognition and the lion's share of the credit in the search for

Escobar. Javier and I were honored to be invited to participate in the investigation led by them. Thousands of CNP officers were killed or wounded in the hunt for the world's first narcoterrorist, but that never shook the CNP's conviction to fight against evil. Their leadership won the day because they had the courage to take their country back from the brink.

Our families also deserve our heartfelt thanks. My wife, Connie, repeatedly gave up her career as a registered nurse to follow me to new posts and assignments. She spent many, many nights alone while I was out traveling, not knowing if I was safe, injured, or dead. It takes a special kind of person to be able to live with that kind of stress. Connie kept me focused on my mission, and she also kept me grounded.

Being a DEA agent is not just a job, it's a lifestyle. The demands of this lifestyle forced me and Javier to miss many family functions. In my case, it meant missing important school events and special days with my children. We thank everyone in our families for their patience and understanding during our prolonged absences.

Coming into this book project, we knew nothing about the writing and publishing world, but fortunately we were introduced to a group of professionals who had the knowledge and expertise to make *Manhunters* a reality, a group that have now become our friends. Our heartfelt thanks to our writer, Isabel Vincent, who took our crazy, fragmented stories and turned them into a work of art; to our literary agent, Luke Janklow, and Claire Dippel of Janklow &

Nesbit, who took the time to hold our hands through this entire process, and are still doing so today; to the creator and executive producer of *Narcos*, Eric Newman, who took interest in our story and introduced us to his long-time friend, Luke Janklow; and to Marc Resnick, Hannah O'Grady, Michelle Cashman, and the entire team at St. Martin's Press, who took a chance on two old guys to bring the truth to light and set the record straight. Thank you all for your support and wisdom!!!

Finally, we want to thank God for his divine protection and direction. When people ask us how we survived, we come up with a lot of different reasons, but we always give God the praise and glory first for keeping us alive under the most trying circumstances we ever experienced. We believe God has a plan for each one of us, and for us his plan included not being killed during what was often a harrowing and deadly search for the world's most brutal criminal.